Education in the Soviet Union

Education in the Soviet Union

Policies and Institutions since Stalin

MERVYN MATTHEWS
University of Surrey

London
GEORGE ALLEN & UNWIN
Boston   Sydney

© Mervyn Matthews, 1982.

George Allen & Unwin (Publishers) Ltd,
40 Museum Street, London WC1A 1LU, UK

George Allen & Unwin (Publishers) Ltd,
Park Lane, Hemel Hempstead, Herts HP2 4TE, UK

Allen & Unwin, Inc.,
9 Winchester Terrace, Winchester, Mass. 01890, USA

George Allen & Unwin Australia Pty Ltd,
8 Napier Street, North Sydney, NSW 2060, Australia

First published in 1982

British Library Cataloguing in Publication Data

Matthews, Mervyn
    Education in the Soviet Union: policies and institutions since Stalin.
    1. Education and state – History – 1953–
    I. Title
    379.47   LA832
    ISBN 0–04–370114–0

Library of Congress Cataloging in Publication Data

Matthews, Mervyn
    Education in the Soviet Union
    Bibliography: P.
    Includes Index.
1. Education – Soviet Union – History – 20th Century.
2. Communism and Education.   I. Title.
LA831.82.M33   370′.947   82–6656
ISBN 0–04–370114–0   AACR2

Set in 10 on 11 point Plantin by Phoenix Photosetting, Chatham
and printed in Great Britain
by Mackays of Chatham Ltd

Contents

To Mila, Owen and Emily

Preface

Many books have been written about education in the Soviet Union, and anyone opening these pages is justified in asking why I have added another. There are in my view two rather convincing answers to this question. The first is that the Soviet educational system is large and important: by 1980 about 100 million Soviet citizens were said to be learning in one kind of institution or another. A colossus of that size well justifies continuing examination. Secondly, I believe that a real need has arisen for a reasonably comprehensive, if brief, overview of how it has changed since the death of Stalin in 1953. To provide this, and to illustrate both success and failure, is the intention of this study.

The framework within which the material is presented should be fairly clear from the table of contents. The first two chapters are devoted to the 'general' school under the Khrushchev and Brezhnev leaderships, this being an obvious starting-point for any study of Soviet education. The two levels of technical training – elementary and middle-grade – are drawn together in Chapter 3, so as to make the material a little more manageable and avoid overlap with the more detailed discussion of higher education. I have tried to simplify this intricate topic by treating certain student matters separately; students have attracted immense interest in their own right, anyway. The final chapter, on what I have termed 'supplementary' services, describes institutions, courses and practices which, though important, could not be easily fitted into the body of the book. They have been brought in mainly to broaden the reader's perspective of the central institutions.

My main interests, in each educational sector, are the degree to which a facility is available; the manner in which it is administered, with particular reference to central control; day-to-day practice in educational establishments; the content of courses (in general, rather than specific, terms); and the problem of leavers' passage to a place of employment, since this has long been regarded by the authorities almost as an integral part of the educational process. Finally, when information is available, some matters of more direct social import are treated, particularly the relationship between educational institutions and certain social groups.

The principal actors in this unending play – the pupils, students and teachers – enjoy some attention. Others, like the parents and administrative personnel, get less than I would wish, but a full exploration of their roles would have made the book virtually unfinishable.

Most writers on Soviet education have relied primarily on Soviet specialist journals and newspapers, major items of legislation, official statistics and observations made during personal visits. While well aware of the advantages of this mix, I have changed it somewhat. First,

I have leaned more heavily on detailed legal provisions, as published in collections of laws and decrees, since they must, I believe, form the skeleton of any serious analysis. Secondly, I have tried to squeeze a little more than usual out of the statistics, partly by representing them diagrammatically. Thirdly, I have found it possible to clarify some situations by interviewing Soviet educational personnel who emigrated not too long ago and who seemed capable of discussing their experience in a reasonably unbiased way. (Many, I might add, retained a professional pride in their careers and showed no tendency to destructive criticism.) Finally, I have on occasion given prominence to the findings of Soviet sociological surveys, which, it seems to me, have been a little neglected by educationalists.

My exposition of each topic has varied according to the facts available, in line with the late Miss Marilyn Monroe's dictum that you must do the best you can with what you've got. Generally, if something has a recognisable history of change over the years, be it an institution or a practice, I explore the chronology first and then endeavour to use this as a means of explaining the present. If, on the other hand, there has been relatively little movement, I tend to begin with a description bearing on the late 1970s, adding only minimal comment on such dynamics as can be perceived.

My intention, as I have said, is to provide an overview of the whole field. Yet the reader should have no illusions about the limits of a study which cannot be in any sense encyclopaedic. Some themes, like educational theory, research, planning, finance, standing facilities and the minutiae of day-to-day administration, are dealt with somewhat cursorily, or omitted. International comparisons, which form a dimension on their own, have also been eschewed, except at one or two points. Education in the Russian Federated Republic has been explored at the expense of the minority areas; and since sex discrimination does not seem to be much of an issue in this sphere I have not (perhaps to the chagrin of lady-liberationists) gone out of my way to explore it. At the same time I have treated the matters I consider to be of major concern in relative detail, and hope most readers will find my balance of interests acceptable. A relatively free use of Soviet administrative terms and abbreviations has made it desirable to append a glossary (page 209).

The years that I am mainly concerned with are 1953 to the beginning of 1979. I have, however, included some brief introductory accounts of historical antecedents, and a rather fuller description of the early years of the so-called 'state labour reserve' schools. This last is drawn, in revised form, from a doctoral thesis which I toiled on many years ago. Together with some soporific passages, it contained unique material which I reckoned to be worthy of inclusion here. I make, incidentally, no apology for a 'leadership-based' approach. In a country with such pervasive centralist characteristics as the USSR, the policies of successive 'leaderships', if not individual leaders, are often rather distinct. I would argue that the Khrushchev–Brezhnev dichotomies in education by and large justify the divisions in the text, though I have not, of course, allowed them to dominate the whole study. Very many policies ran unchanged through both secretaryships.

Writing about Soviet education would obviously be much easier were it not for the existence of the Soviet censorship. The information available on any educational system, even in a liberal society, may be highly unsatisfactory. But *Glavlit*, as the Soviet organ is called, does us two particularly great disfavours. The first is to ban certain kinds of statistics, including (to mention but two) figures for annual age groups and 'flow' data for pupils and students at all levels. The second is to limit severely reports illustrating malfunction. So outside observers must devote much time and effort to estimating magnitudes long since registered in ministerial offices and to piecing together puzzles which would be common knowledge in other lands.

The best possible book on Soviet education would, I feel, be written by a large group of indigenous specialists who had worked for long periods in all branches of the system (from the Central Committee offices down to kindergartens), and who were aware of the broader problems involved, yet able to interpret their experience in a free and unrestrained manner. It seems unlikely that such a company will be assembled in the near future: so the majority of non-Soviet works on Soviet education must be produced by outsiders, concerned, like myself, to satisfy public interest abroad. My own experience consists of attendance at the Economics Faculty of Moscow University as a postgraduate for two years, in 1959–60 and 1963–4; conducting interviews in Moscow for the above-mentioned thesis; and more general observations during the periods I have lived in or visited Russia. My use of the testimonies of *émigré* Russians who were knowledgeable in specific aspects of education is a way of supplementing this.

As may be seen from the bibliography, I have already published certain items on Soviet education. When I have found it expedient to use this work, I have done so with due revision, updating and reference. My understanding of the large corpus of laws, reports and statistics may contain occasional flaws despite careful verification, so I must ask the indulgence of readers who light upon any.

My thanks are due to scholars whose advice has helped me in the writing of this book, or who have themselves produced relevant volumes on Soviet education. The projections of Soviet population provided by Dr Murray Feshbach were essential for the estimates of educational coverage, while Professor Harry Rigby was the source of much useful political information. Mr J. J. Tomiak made many useful suggestions for improvements in the presentation. I frequently had occasion to refer to the well-known work of Professors N. De Witt and A. Korol for basic information on the 1950s.

xiv *Preface*

Certain institutions have also helped me a great deal. I am grateful to the Research Committee at the University of Surrey for timely financial assistance with my interviewing programme, and to the library staff for their efficiency. The Australian National University granted me a Visiting Fellowship which enabled me to advance the text considerably. The Rockefeller Foundation provided a month in surroundings well suited to ease the painful processes of editing and revision. I wish to add a word of particular gratitude to Mrs Joan Prain and Mrs Judy Bridgeman for typing with great patience and care a large number of drafts.

May I, in conclusion, draw the reader's attention to a few technical points. The overwhelming majority of the items in the bibliography are mentioned in the text, and are traceable therefrom by author, editor or title (the last being mostly abbreviated or initialled, with a cross-reference). The listing of collections of laws, handbooks, etc., by editor rather than title does not correspond with the preferred Soviet usage. However, the publisher has asked me (in the interests of economy) to dispense where possible with numbered notes, and since many such titles are almost, or totally, identical, they could not easily be handled in that form by bracketed reference. I hope the solution chosen is adequate.

Locations are usually provided only for laws dealt with at some length, and for those which might be exceptionally difficult to find. I assume that anyone interested in the remainder will be sufficiently cognisant of Soviet scholarship to find them without too much trouble. This again frees the text from source detail which is of little interest to most readers.

Those who read cyrillic will notice that the transliteration used here has been slightly simplified: this is mainly for visual convenience and will not, I hope, greatly offend cognoscenti in these matters. The main departures from usual procedure are the omission of a character for the soft sign, the rendering of the Russian 'e' as 'e' (and not 'ie' or 'ye') and of ИЯ simply as 'ia'. When using Russian terms in the plural I have retained the Russian forms, mostly 'y' or 'i' (thus '*VUZ*' and '*VUZy*'). Russian titles are usually written with small letters, except for the first word. I have followed this practice.

1
General Education under Khrushchev

The principal element in the Soviet educational structure is the 'general' school. It was established in roughly its present form in the early 1930s, and grew rapidly in size. During the later Stalin years, however, it underwent comparatively little change of structure or function. It was in a sense natural that Khrushchev, on coming to power in 1953, should have viewed it as being in need of urgent reform. His tenure of office as First Secretary of the CPSU, from 1953 to 1964, marked a very agitated period in its history.

Khrushchev was keenly interested in education, and his main policies consisted not only in promoting further expansion but also in restructuring the school and redefining some of its aims so that it could better prepare pupils for worthwhile employment. In the mid-1950s he made some initial attempts at change, mainly of a curricular nature, which ended in failure. At the end of the decade the number of children in the senior classes of the general school began to fall as the contingents born during the war, what we shall term the 'war dent', began to pass through. Khrushchev then apparently decided that this was a good time for more radical reorganisation, and in December 1958 he introduced a reform designed to affect all branches of the educational system, the general school included. The years which followed saw efforts at its implementation and, even before his dismissal, clear signs of retreat.

These matters, which are the main concern of this chapter, can be better understood in the context of the Soviet school's basic aims and history, so I shall start with a short account of them. After considering Khrushchev's policies and their educational impact in some detail, I shall show how their relative failure promoted the establishment of a youth employment service, and comment on the lot of the teachers during these years. General school policies under Brezhnev were, as we have noted, distinct enough to warrant treatment in a separate chapter.

AIMS AND HISTORY – AN OVERVIEW

At the outbreak of the First World War Russia had a modest but growing educational system. The network of primary schools, run by the central government, local authorities and the church, contained about 8 million children aged between 8 and 11. This was said to be rather more than half of the number in the corresponding age-groups. More advanced schooling, up to university level, was provided by a great variety of state and private institutions – gymnasia, technical colleges (*realschulen*), commercial, technical, teachers' and military schools. There was said to be over half a million students in the state sector alone at this level. The political circumstances of the day did not, of course, greatly favour educational expansion; but it is noteworthy that the Provisional Government, which held office for a few months before the Bolsheviks came to power, had a vigorous programme in view.[1]

When they came to power, the Bolsheviks showed a clear understanding of the importance of education for their cause. Not only did the existing system, with its 'capitalist', 'exploitative' orientation have to be dismantled, but a new school, designed to suit Bolshevik ideas, had to be set up. These ideas, which were to form the basis of Soviet educational theory, were simple in essence if not in application. Though Marxist in character, they were tailored to fit the practical needs of a new, 'socialist' order.

The fact that man was a product of his social environment gave the educational system (it was thought) immense possibilities for moulding his personality, and through him society as a whole. 'Communist man' would be devoted to the ideals of the Revolution, completely socialistic in his outlook and firmly integrated in the socialist collective, of which he was a disciplined member. His abilities would be fully developed by active participation in collective activities, for 'individualism' and 'passivity' were regarded as barren and pointless. He would not only be free of the religious beliefs propounded by the bourgeois school, but would be a convinced atheist. Old chauvinistic attitudes would be replaced by a sympathy for the proletariats of all lands (a requirement later supplemented by 'Soviet patriotism'). Communist morality, the phrase used to sum up this mixture, also included eager participation in the political life of the country, suitable aesthetic, and maximum physical, development.

Bourgeois education was held to be scholastic and formal in nature. The Soviet school, by contrast, was to be thoroughly integrated in the social process. The Leninist precept of the 'unity of theory and practice' excluded any split between theoretical and practical disciplines or any division of the children on this basis. Streaming was socially divisive; the school was to be a cohesive whole, so that the children would all learn and act together, without distinction. And since a deeply materialistic outlook had to be inculcated into them, study was to be centred on the natural world (though not to the exclusion of cultural values). Man's ability to influence and ultimately control natural forces was in this way to be made clear.

In order to fulfil these tasks adequately the new school had to involve its charges in socially useful labour. Apart from its obvious relevance to other school work, this would accustom the children to group participation and direct their efforts to the nitty-gritty of communist construction. The principle of 'polytechnical' education was therefore deeply embedded in Soviet educational theory.

These aims undoubtedly contained much that was admirable. But they also included propositions which ran quite counter to liberal Western ideals. They left the individual no independence from the system; he was required to show unswerving allegiance to the Soviet state and all that it stood for, and mistrust any other 'non-socialist' orders. No provision was made for any values apart from Marxist ones (as interpreted by current Soviet leaderships), for critical thought in cultural and other matters or for creative growth in a non-collectivist direction.

The more central of these aims were expressed at the time of the Revolution itself: others took a few years of argument or official intervention to formulate. Some, as we shall see, were subject to varying interpretations or to neglect. Yet on the whole they continued to serve as the bedrock of Soviet educational theory and were broadly restated in the Fundamental Law on Soviet Education, promulgated by the Supreme Soviet on 19 July 1973.

As far as the practical reorganisation of the educational system was concerned, Lenin wasted no time whatever. On the day after the Bolshevik coup, his associate A. V. Lunacharski was nominated People's Commissar for Enlightenment.* On 9 November a State Commission for Enlightenment was set up to replace the former ministry: and although this commission was granted only general supervisory powers (for the local soviets were supposed to administer the schools themselves), it established the *principle* of centralised control. In January 1918 the church was formally deprived of its educational functions, and decrees passed in February and June 1918 gave the People's Commissariat for Enlightenment (*Narkompros*), which replaced the commission, ultimate control of the management, physical assets and finances of all educational institutions, regardless of their former standing. The content of teaching materials was soon brought under comprehensive censorship regulations. Party organisations throughout the land were required, under the terms of an often-reprinted circular letter of 4 November 1921, to ensure that the administration of education and culture was in the hands of approved communists and regularly supervised by local party officials. Within three or four years the overwhelming majority of teachers at all levels of the system had been persuaded to join a single, Bolshevik-controlled, trades union.

* I use this term to translate *prosveshchenie*, which signifies, in Soviet usage, general rather than vocational or higher education.

The new school, or 'unified labour school' as it was called, was established by a statute of 16 October 1918. It was obligatory for all, free, mixed (for boys and girls), strictly secular and polytechnic. It had a two-part structure: the primary one comprised a five-year course and was for children aged 8 to 13; the second, lasting four years, was for 13- to 17-year-olds. All the existing institutions below university level were fitted into this scheme, and those which straddled the age-groups were split up. The unified labour school was to be preceded by a system of pre-school institutions, and followed by another of vocational (or to use the Soviet term, 'professional') character. All the pupils' material requirements, together with buildings and equipment, were to be provided by the state. Education for non-Russians was to be provided in local languages. The new teachers trained were to be 'imbued with the ideas of communism'.

The establishment of a new system based on Bolshevik principles did not, of course, mean that all aspects of school life had been determined once and for all. In fact, it is generally accepted that, until the time of Khrushchev's intervention, the Soviet school went through three distinct phases of development.

The first coincided with the years of War Communism and the Civil War. Schools at this time enjoyed what would later be considered an undesirable degree of independence. The new statute placed the administration of each establishment in the hands of a school council, composed of the teachers, local citizens and pupils over the age of 12, with a single official representing the local soviet. The council was to be virtually free of outside control, providing only that it observed the requirements of state legislation. The total of school hours and the school week of five and a half days were fixed by law; but class organisation was not, and classes were to be replaced, where possible, by freely formed groups or circles. Exams were abolished, homework was declared illegal and no physical punishment was allowed for misdemeanours. Instruction was to be effected through observation and through labour which was socially useful in its own right. There was much argument about the form and content of teaching, the problems of supervision and how far the school should replace the family as a formative influence.

Such voluntarism, however, could not but evoke qualms in official circles, once the heady aspirations of War Communism had been jettisoned, and about 1921 the Soviet school moved into a second stage of development. Under the terms of another statute, approved in December 1923, it was to be run by a manager (the term 'director' was avoided) who was nominated by the local soviet and empowered to overrule the school council. Formal assessment of children's progress was permitted for purposes of passing up. But teachers were still left with much freedom in the matter of instruction, provided it was based on 'productive activity', was closely tied in with 'local production', and bore a 'class, proletarian' character. The children were encouraged to take part in running school affairs.

The Soviet school of the 1920s has been described both as 'experimental' and (by ardent pedagogues) 'romantic'. Within the framework of communist principles there was a great deal of pedagogical discussion. Such well-known figures as Nadezhda Krupskaya, Anton Makarenko and P. P. Blonski deliberated on the best methods of teaching, the development of the child's individual personality and the role of the collective. There was a keen interest in bourgeois educational practice. The so-called 'complex' method, which involved grouping the children into 'brigades' and having them work on active 'projects', continued to be widespread. It entailed much freedom of choice in the classroom, together with the downgrading of textbooks, rote learning and teacher–pupil formalities. The absence of specific restrictions permitted the growth of the 'pedology' movement, which involved testing children's aptitudes and intelligence so as to cater more sympathetically for individual needs.

In quantitative terms the coverage of the unified labour school increased steadily: enrolments, which had fallen (as a result of civil disruption and famine) to a low of 7·3 million in 1922, reached 18 million by the end of the decade. However, the geographical distribution of the population meant that the Soviet school was still overwhelmingly rural. The expansion of education facilities for juveniles was backed after December 1919 by a campaign against illiteracy, which was still, at the time of the 1926 population census, over 40 per cent among persons aged between 9 and 49. In addition, many part-time schools were started for those at work, and by 1930 enrolments topped a quarter of a million.

The qualitative successes of these years are measured less easily than the growth in numbers. Such successes may have been noteworthy, but the rapid stalinisation of Soviet life which took place after 1928 meant that the school could not enjoy so much freedom for experiment. In September 1929 Lunacharski resigned from the People's Commissariat of Enlightenment in protest against intensified government interference. This, in a sense, marked the transition to the third stage of educational policy.

A series of enactments brought about a shift in general school procedures. A decree of September 1931 stipulated that the traditional 'abstract' sciences, language, history and geography should predominate in school work and form the core of a controlled Marxist–Leninist curriculum. As a result manual activities gradually disappeared, and the polytechnical element was reduced to little more than a practical slant in science lessons. The use of the project method was condemned. A further decree of August 1932 called for a strict schedule of regulated study. As for school administration, the hand of the director was strengthened, while pupils' efforts were diverted from managing school affairs to improving the quality of learning and strengthening discipline. Officially approved textbooks were made the basic learning tool after February 1933, and a rigorous system of marks, examinations, incentives and awards was introduced in December 1935. Thus was the Stalinist general school brought into being. Though unheralded by a new statute, it differed markedly from what had gone before. A very specific reinterpretation of the Marxist–Leninist educational precepts had taken place.

Meanwhile, enrolments grew apace. After 1929 the standard course was lengthened to ten years and divided into three, instead of two, parts. The number of full-time pupils rose at an incredible speed, reaching 35·5 million in 1940; part-time enrolments were over a million more.

The Second World War inevitably caused immense damage to the school network, and full-time enrolments fell back to 27 million. The postwar years were devoted primarily to re-establishing the earlier coverage, improving it and replacing damaged facilities. Stalinism in its later forms weighed no less heavily on the Soviet people; and the few changes made in school practice (which we shall consider as preliminaries to Khrushchev's policies below) were most conservative in character. The death of Stalin in March 1953 allowed the school to enter what might justifiably be called its 'Khrushchevian' phase. We now pass on to a more detailed examination of what this entailed.

THE GROWTH OF NUMBERS AND FACILITIES

When Khrushchev grasped the reins of power, the full-time general school contained some 30 million pupils (see Figure 1.1).* Official data on the coverage of children by age-group are not available, but there is little doubt that more or less all of the 7- to 11-year-olds were attending the first four classes, which formed the primary stage. About two-thirds of the 12- to 14-year-olds were staying for seven classes, or 'incomplete secondary' school, 'secondary', in Soviet parlance, meaning intermediate between primary and higher. Perhaps a fifth of the remaining age-groups (the 15- to 17-year-olds) were completing the whole 'secondary general' school course of ten classes. Given the turbulence of Soviet history, this was a very respectable achievement, and the fact that the expansion of facilities often lagged behind plan should not be allowed to overshadow it.

By the time Khrushchev was dismissed in October 1964, the number of full-time pupils had reached 42 million. This growth was by no means steady, mainly because of the 'war dent', which affected the first

* A diagrammatic representation of the Soviet school system is to be found in Appendix B, and a set of figures for enrolments between 1950 and 1978 in Appendix A (pages 207 and 206, respectively).

class of the general school about 1950 and cleared the tenth only towards the mid-1960s. At its nadir age-groups fell by more than half, but it did at least ease the pressure on facilities. By the time of the December 1958 reform perhaps three-quarters of all eligible children

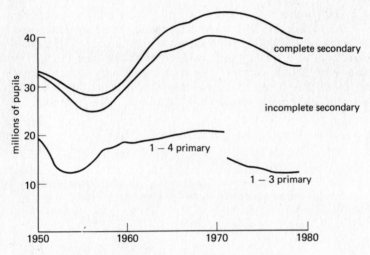

Figure 1.1 Full-time general school enrolments, 1950–78.

Sources: NONK, 1971, p. 68; *Narodnoe khozyaistvo SSSR* (henceforth *Nar. khoz.*), 1978, p. 467.

Notes: As of September for each year. The groups of classes are vertically (cumulatively) superimposed, so that each band shows enrolment of a certain type and the top line of the graph shows the total enrolment. The primary school, in official statistics, comprised classes 1–4 until 1970, and afterwards classes 1–3. The changeover from seven- to eight-year incomplete school after 1959 was gradual and not marked by a break in the statistical series. The top band therefore contains three classes in 1960, but only two in 1978.

were completing seven classes, and a third (1·3 million) were finishing the whole full-time course. There may have been further improvement in coverage afterwards, but the pattern was complicated by the passage of the 'dent' and by government preferences for part-time, as opposed to full-time, schooling.

The spread of general education cannot, in fact, be considered without reference to part-time facilities. The schools for young people and adults which had been set up in the early and mid-1920s were substantially reorganised as Schools for Working Youth and Schools for Rural Youth in July 1943 and July 1944 respectively. Their curricula and teaching practices were closely similar to those of the full-time general school, but their courses were necessarily longer. The number of pupils in them stood at just under 2 million in 1953, and remained remarkably stable until the 1958 reform. Then, with active official encouragement, numbers rose quickly, reaching over 4½ million by 1964. There was, understandably, a change in the balance of classes: while the numbers of pupils at the primary level fell off, those in the senior classes rose to over 2½ million (as against 8 million pupils in the full-time senior classes).*

The overall number of schools, as units, remained comparatively stable – there were 198,000 when Khrushchev came to power and 192,000 when he fell. Urban and rural schools continued to differ quite considerably in size, quality and provision of classes, and formed, in fact, two very distinct sectors. The countryside had a much larger number of small schools, the great majority of which offered only primary and incomplete education (Table 1.1). The provision of

Table 1.1   *Full-Time General School Network, USSR*

		Town			*Country*		
		Primary	*Incomplete secondary*	*Complete secondary*	*Primary*	*Incomplete secondary*	*Complete secondary*
1955	Schools	7·2	6·2	11·9	101·6	52·5	15·0
	Pupils	(115)	(355)	(758)	(27)	(137)	(407)
1969	Schools	6·1	11·9	14·3	88·3	50·6	17·6
	Pupils	(138)	(565)	(981)	(34)	(195)	(493)
1975	Schools	2·2	6·8	22·0	45·7	41·0	29·5
	Pupils	(72)	(372)	(879)	(19)	(151)	(443)

Source: NONK, 1977, pp. 28–31, adapted.
School numbers in thousands; average numbers of pupils per school absolute, bracketed for visual convenience.

educational facilities had always been exceptionally difficult outside the towns, as a result of such factors location, bad roads and lack of services. Teaching staff were unwilling to bear the deprivations of Soviet rural reality, while rural school buildings and equipment were of poorer quality. Some noteworthy changes did, however, occur in the network. Under Khrushchev there was some fall in the number of rural primary schools and an increase in the number of (more desirable) ten-year institutions. Even so, the vast majority of rural schools remained too small to be in any organisational sense efficient. The main shift in the towns was the doubling of the number of seven-year schools and an increase in their size.

There was a marked advance in terms of the numbers and

* *Narodnoe obrazovanie, nauka, i kultura v. SSSR. Statisticheski sbornik* (henceforth *NONK*), 1971, pp. 19, 121. For a note on title abbreviations in this text, see Bibliography, pp. 214–22.

qualifications of Soviet teachers. The total employed in the full-time general school rose from 1·5 million in 1953 to 2·2 million in 1964, so despite the rise in the number of pupils, the teacher–pupil ratio in this broad sense was kept at about 1:19. The proportion of teachers with higher education rose from nineteen to forty per hundred over the same period (*NONK*, 1977, pp. 6, 97).

As for administration, when Khrushchev came to power the formal control of the general school system lay with the relatively low-grade republican ministries of enlightenment, which acted through departments of education from the *oblast* down to the town soviets. These departments administered the schools through their directors, deputy directors and staffs. The departments were responsible, at one level or another, for the appointment of all school personnel and of the school inspectors (Danev, p. 164; *SDSh*, pp. 219 ff.). Naturally enough, current finance came through state and, for some things, collective farm channels, but schools were allowed to have their own bank accounts for minor expenses. Official funding (which was sometimes sufficient only for bare necessities) could occasionally be supplemented by material help from local organisations, factories or farms where the children's parents worked.

The Soviet school system was not, therefore, controlled by a single centralised ministry; but in practical matters the Ministry of Enlightenment of the RSFSR called the tune, and other republican bodies followed suit. Major pieces of educational legislation were supposed to originate in the various supreme soviets, or councils of ministers, which had law-making functions. Given the growth of the sector and Khrushchev's passion for organisational change, it is perhaps a little strange that no perceptible reordering of this line of command took place. The ministries of enlightenment retained their republican status throughout, and seem only to have acquired new sections as their work-load increased.

The government machinery was, of course, supervised at all levels by the party apparatus. Major policy decisions about cultural matters have always been taken by top party leaders; general responsibility for the implementation of educational policy must in the early 1950s have lain in the Central Committee Department for Propaganda and Agitation. (No separate *department* for education was then, to my knowledge, in existence, so it must have been handled by some lesser unit.) Nominations to the most responsible, or 'nomenclature', posts in the educational hierarchy must have been supervised by the Department of Party, Trades Union and Komsomol Organs. Republican and lesser party offices were vested with supervision of the work of the departments of education in all local soviets. Khrushchev did not depart from these well tested principles, but he undoubtedly tried to strengthen party control. The most likely explanation for this lay in his reliance on party help to promote policies which encountered opposition from government officials or the public at large.

When a separate Central Committee apparatus was established for the RSFSR in 1956, it had its own Department of Higher Education and Schools, while a Department for Sciences, Schools and Culture appeared in listings for the parallel union republican apparatus. This duality was maintained until about 1965, when the Brezhnev leadership abolished them both and brought into being a single Department of Science and Educational Establishments for the country at large.[2]

A considerable stepping-up of the educational work of local party bodies was evident after the 1958 reform. By 1962 separate departments of science and schools had been established at the *oblast* and *krai* party offices, and this practice was subsequently extended to the district and town levels (*PZh*, 1962, no. 17, p. 10). Moreover, apart from supervising educational departments in the soviets, party officials had a say in school staffing policies (through the local nomenclature) and could give instructions to teaching and administrative staff who were themselves party members. CPSU membership amongst teachers in fact rose from about 18 per cent in 1956 to 25 per cent a decade later, by which time most schools had their own primary cells (Rigby, p. 437; *PZh*, no. 17, 1964, p. 7).

PROBLEMS OF CATCHMENT

The proper functioning of a complex educational system demands the registration of all children at an early age and their regular attendance at school. The growth of the general school in the USSR engendered ever-increasing problems of catchment, and it is to these and the measures devised to ease them that we now turn.

(1)   *Registration and Choice of School*

In the early 1950s children aged 7 by 1 September, when the school year began, were still registered for attendance on the basis of (RSFSR) instructions issued in July and December 1943. According to these all towns and rural districts were divided into strictly defined catchment areas, each with its own school. The problem of parental choice was thus, in the majority of cases, neatly solved: there was none. However, in practice a child might occasionally be allowed to enter another school by personal arrangement with the director, or on the pretext of fictitious residence with friends or relatives. The various ethnic minority and 'special' schools, which we shall discuss in due course, were the only significant exception.

The registration of urban children was done by the local education departments, which acted through the residents' housing offices or dealt directly with parents occupying private housing. In the countryside the matter was usually in the hands of the secretary of the village soviet, and the lists of children were checked by teachers after personal visits to their homes. Daily attendance was the responsibility of the school director, assisted by the teacher of the class to which the children belonged. Parents or guardians who failed to register a child, or ensure that he went to school regularly, incurred such penalties as the local soviet might establish (Abakumov *et al.*, p. 118).

The rules were tightened in the wake of the 1958 reform. An RSFSR law of 14 July 1959 moved the age of registration back to 6 so as to facilitate catchment procedures; stated that children who were under 16 but had not completed the eight-year school were to be traced and returned to the classroom; and enjoined members of 'education commissions' (which were sometimes set up to assist the education departments), state officials, housing officers and the public to participate more actively in the matter. Several instructions and decrees circulated afterwards were designed to reduce fall-out, expulsion and the transference of unsatisfactory pupils to part-time institutions (Abakumov *et al.*, p. 121; Deineko, p. 455). No detailed appraisal of the results of these measures seems to have been published; but there is good reason to believe that registration was on the whole reasonably efficient, except in cases where family circumstances, tradition or remoteness worked against it. The stringent rules for registering urban residence with the militia, the high proportion of working mothers and the pointlessness of keeping children out of school serve as adequate explanation.

When Khrushchev came to power, boys and girls in most large and medium-sized towns were taught separately from the seventh class onwards; indeed the two decrees of July 1943 which governed the practice stipulated that where possible the sexes should not even share the same building. The reasons given were differences in physical development, discipline and the requirements of military and labour training. With expanding enrolments, the implementation of these rules must have become increasingly difficult. A decree of 1 July 1954, quoting 'the wishes of the parents' and 'the opinion of school teachers', finally abolished the principle of separate instruction (Medynski, 1947, p. 74; Abakumov *et al.*, pp. 177, 192).

(2) *Assistance for Poorer Pupils*

Khrushchev showed a certain concern for the poor, and did something to improve their lot. Since material need was undoubtedly a major cause of parents sending their children out to work before completing the ten-year school (Shkaratan, p. 440), it is not surprising that some arrangements should have been made specifically to help the poorer pupil. Though limited in scope, they deserve mention.

In June 1956 the fees for attending the three senior classes of the general school, secondary special and higher educational institutions, which had been introduced in October 1940, were abolished (Abakumov *et al.*, pp. 192, 176). These fees, at 150–200 roubles a year for the first child, had initially been quite high in real terms, since the declared annual average wage was about 4000 roubles. True, poorer pupils had been exempted from paying them; the rate fell if there was more than one schoolchild in the family; and by the mid 1950s wage levels had more than doubled. Abolition was nevertheless a significant concession to many.

An RSFSR decree of 15 August 1959 officially re-established 'schooling assistance funds' (*fondy vse-obucha*) for 'needy' children in the first eight classes. These were modelled on a system which had existed in the 1930s (Medynski, 1947, p. 48). Although some schools had apparently continued to help the poor from their own, or local Soviet funds, the August decree put the practice on a more formal footing. The assistance funds were to equal at least 1 per cent of the school budget and were to be supplemented by contributions from local enterprises, co-operatives and trades unions. Money earned by the children's own activities could also be so used to this end. Payments from the funds were to be administered by a small commission headed by the school director and answerable to the local soviet (Kalinychev, p. 94; *Spravochnik dlya rabotnikov selskikh i poselkovykh sovetov*, 1970, p. 282). According to my interview sources, the teachers would sometimes propose that a child be helped, though occasionally a parent might make an application. As far as I know, no figures have been published, but it seems that assistance was very restricted. It usually took the form of clothes, footwear, textbooks, school dinner tokens or modest sums of money for the same purposes.

The provision of school meals had been common almost since the Revolution. Originally a method of alleviating famine among the most vulnerable age-groups, it became in many places a facility well suited to the needs of working parents. Thus school meals (like most low-priced catering in the USSR) came to be regarded as convenient, if inferior. It seems that by the early 1950s half of the urban schools and a tenth of those in rural districts were providing them. A decree of 11 August 1960 called for further expansion, but without much apparent effect. School meals were not free, though subsidies from local soviets and collective farms ensured low prices. It is noteworthy that no attempt was made at this time to provide free textbooks or school uniforms.

(3)   *Boarding Schools and 'Lengthened Day' Schools*

Boarding facilities for children of all ages have always been in great demand in the Soviet Union. Famine, war and mass arrest have made many orphans, while rural transport problems and the high employment rate among women have also generated continuous need. Clearly, the growth of school coverage demanded further development of this sector. Khrushchev favoured such schools particularly because he thought they would enable the state to play a larger role in the upbringing of the child, and inculcate attitudes which might not find favour in a family milieu.

In the early 1950s two main types of boarding institution were in existence – *orphanage schools* containing up to half a million orphaned and in some cases handicapped children throughout the USSR, and schools with *some boarding facility* (mainly rural), which served about the same number of children in the RSFSR (*Nar. khoz.*, 1958, p. 828; De Witt, p. 100). A USSR decree of 15 September 1956 established what purported to be a 'new type of educational institution – boarding schools designed to solve on a higher plane the task of training well rounded, educated builders of communism' (Abakumov *et al.*, p. 248). In fact, as the wording of the document showed, these closely resembled the older types and were intended to be a more efficient vehicle for 'polytechnisation'. Finance for running them was to come at least in part from the parents' pockets, for, surprisingly enough, fees had to be paid. Statutes approved on 13 April 1957 stated that local authorities were empowered to admit up to a quarter of all pupils free or, 'in exceptional circumstances', at a 50 per cent reduction (Deineko, p. 452, n. 5). Children with only one parent or invalid parents, and children who were orphaned or deprived, were to have first call on places. The actual scales of payment, as far as I am aware, were never officially revealed, and were the subject of some confusion among Western observers (De Witt, p. 98). A teacher with twenty years' experience in such establishments did, however, tell me that the full rate (as registered in the school accounts) was 540 roubles a month in the late 1950s, and that it had remained unchanged into the late 1970s, when she left. This would have been payable (to judge from nursery school practices) only for a child from a family with a per capita income of 1,200 roubles a month or more. But so high a standard figure implies that even with reductions many poor families' contributions were far from insignificant.

Khrushchev was nevertheless enthusiastic about the schools' prospects. The September decree had envisaged an enrolment of at least 1 million pupils by 1960; and the control figures for economic development approved in February 1959 allowed for an increase of up to 2½ million by 1965. However, by 1960 only 600,000 pupils had been enrolled, and some of these may well have been in the older institutions – for the relationship between the two types was never properly clarified.[3] By the spring of 1963 numbers seem actually to have dropped back somewhat (Abakumov *et al.*, p. 257; *NONK*, 1977, p. 80, derived), and in April of that year the Council of Ministers issued a highly critical decree which called for improvements in virtually all aspects of the schools' work. In 1961, it said, fees had been unpaid to the tune of 4 million roubles.

The reasons for this failure are not far to seek. The opportunity to send children to a boarding school could not have been particularly attractive to many parents; institutions traditionally designed for the underprivileged always tended to have a bad name. Then there was the question of cost to the family, which could be considerable. Thirdly, not only were the schools quite expensive to run but the burden of doing so was soon shifted down to the town and district authorities, who were often ill able to bear it (De Witt, p. 95; Deineko, p. 137).

The so-called 'lengthened day' schools offered a solution to another problem of school attendance, in providing extra supervision in the afternoon and evening so that parents could comfortably finish a full day's work. This practice was established by a decree of 15 February 1960, primarily for children in the first eight classes with two working parents. Although supervision was free, except in cases of need parents were expected to pay for additional meals. The official figures show that enrolment rose to a very respectable 2 million by 1964; so these facilities, unlike the boarding schools, must have been universally popular (*Nar. khoz. za 60 let*, p. 577; *NONK*, 1977, p. 80).

(4)   *Limitations on Juvenile Employment*

Most of the protection which the early Bolshevik labour codes afforded to non-peasant juveniles, including a formal ban on employment under the age of 16 and restrictions on the work they could undertake, was removed or forgotten by the early 1940s. Laws passed in 1940 and 1942, under the pressure of industrialisation and militarisation, equated youngsters under 18 in most respects with adult workers, and permitted hiring at 15 or, 'in exceptional cases', at 14 (Matthews, 1961, pp. 132 ff.).

Since opportunities for early employment encouraged early leaving, and a long working day inhibited part-time study, there was now a strong argument for changing the labour laws. An edict of the Supreme Soviet of 13 December 1956 stated that the starting age (outside collective farms) was to be raised to 16, though again 'in exceptional circumstances' 15-year-olds could be accepted. This at least favoured school attendance up to the eighth class. A number of other measures passed at this time re-established many of the post-revolutionary restrictions on labour, shortening the number of hours which juveniles could work and excluding them from certain heavy duties. All of these provisions were still valid, if not observed, in the late 1970s.[4]

Young people born in collective farms were always in a different category. Their involvement in agricultural activities from childhood was taken for granted, and they were more or less obliged to become farm members at the age of 16 (the legal position was not entirely clear).

Despite the large numbers involved, the Khrushchev leadership made no explicit change in these practices, and a proper procedure for joining the farm came only with the new statute in November 1969. Nevertheless, a March 1956 gloss on the existing document emphasised that collective farm members had a full right to education and that farms could send them to further-educational establishments, paying their stipends out of common funds (Kuznetsov *et al.*, p. 40).

(5) *Day Release for Part-Time Study*

Khrushchev was extremely enthusiastic about part-time study as a means of helping young workers and peasants to complete their general education. The options legally available to them in the early 1950s included exemption from overtime, paid day-release for final examinations and the right to arrange holidays to suit their study needs. These benefits were significantly improved in November 1959 by the right to obtain a day off with pay every week and to request even more if required.[5]

These generous provisions remained in operation into the late 1970s. There is no doubt that they were fundamentally admirable in intention, and matched good West European practice. Two points, however, need to be borne in mind. First, the relatively low standard of living in the USSR meant that many young people simply could not afford to go on to the reduced rates of pay (or students' stipend) which the new rules involved (see page 45); and secondly, we do not know how often managements refused to allow their employees any choice in the matter. Paying for time not worked could not have been popular in the finance divisions, while in the poorer collective farms any kind of concession must have been difficult.

The labour legislation still, in fact, contained much ambiguity. The changes suited Khrushchev's urge to encourage young people to study and improve themselves, yet allowed and even facilitated employment at an age which did not match the school-leaving requirements. The day-release provisions undoubtedly complicated labour schedules for managements and unsettled some youngsters, thus increasing unwanted labour mobility. Yet all the measures were undoubtedly liberal in intention, and it was unfortunate that, introduced hurriedly and without due compensation for employers, they caused (as we shall see) widespread difficulties of their own.

SCHOOL PRACTICE IN THE FIRST POST-STALIN YEARS

Most of the elements of Soviet general school practice at this time, as we have noted, were established in the 1930s, particularly by the decree of 3 September 1935. Overall responsibility for each establishment lay in the hands of a director, on the well-known Soviet principle of one-man control (*edinonachalie*); he (or she, for many were women) was assisted by a deputy director for study, another for organisation and equipment, the 'ordinary' teachers and an auxiliary staff. The director, deputy directors and teaching staff together formed a 'pedagogical council' which was (under the terms of the statute of 3 April 1943) at liberty to plan and discuss the work of the school, but could not override the director without the intervention of the local education office. Contact with the pupils' families was maintained by a 'parents' committee', but this was designed more as a support for official policies than a channel for outside influence. Its statute was approved on 2 November 1947 (*Direktivy VKP(b)*, pp. 119 ff., 177; Boldyrev, 1952, pp. 176, 201).

Each of the three parts into which the general school course was divided (classes 1–4, 5–7 and 8–10) was officially recognised as a benchmark of educational achievement. The curriculum had remained, in principle, highly standardised for all schools throughout the country, as indeed was the order of presentation of subject matter, so that a child finishing a school with only four classes in one district could continue unimpeded at another. Variation of content was permitted only at special schools for gifted or handicapped children, or where Russian was taught as a second language. Here an extra, preparatory, class might be organised, or the main course lengthened by a year to accommodate additional material. Soviet pedagogical theory continued to maintain that all children, in ordinary schools at least, should be taught in mixed-ability classes, without hint of streaming on the basis of ability or progress.

The school year normally lasted thirty-three to thirty-six weeks, according to the class and the number of examinations. There were short breaks over the 7 November national holiday, the New Year and at the end of March; these served to delineate two 'semesters' and four 'quarters' (Medynski, 1947, p. 53). Classes were held six days a week to provide a total of twenty-four to thirty-two hours, depending on the age of the pupils. The 'hours' were in fact periods of forty-five minutes, with regulation breaks between them. When possible teaching was completed by early afternoon, but a shortage of buildings necessitated the operation of a shift system in about half of the schools.

At the primary level each class had one teacher throughout the four-year course; in the middle and upper school, as the subjects became more complex, classes retained one teacher as 'class manager' (*klassny rukovoditel*) and were taught in turn by others. According to a 1925 regulation, the maximum permitted class size was forty. The teaching was based on officially approved textbooks and was very formal.

Strict discipline was required by the still valid ordinance of 2 August 1943, which stated that pupils had to conduct themselves at all times in a worthy manner (indeed, one of which the strictest Victorian peda-gogue would have approved). Apart from being clean, tidy, obedient, punctual, helpful and assiduous in their studies, they were to sit straight, refrain from leaning on their elbows, stand when the teacher entered the room and sit only with his or her permission. Marks were given for conduct as well as academic progress, a class journal and individual mark books being kept for this purpose. Each pupil from the fifth class up was issued with a numbered identity ticket which he was required to carry and present on demand (Abakumov *et al.*, p. 178).

The burden of homework was heavy – optima of one to four hours a *day*, according to class, were stipulated for the RSFSR in December 1951. The school regulations fixed a range of permissible responses to pupils' behaviour, from the issue of a certificate of merit down to exclusion or transfer to a Borstal-type institution. Corporal punishment was, however, still banned. Control of a more social kind was the concern of 'pupils' committees' which, under the terms of a statute of 4 August 1950, were elected at the level of the fifth class and above. The *Komsomol* and Young Pioneer organisations monitored activities of an ideological character.

Considerable stress was placed on tests and examinations. All progress, under regulations of January 1944, was measured on a five-point scale, whereby a mark of at least 3 was required to pass. Five was excellent, and 4, good; 2 showed insufficient, and 1, grossly insufficient, knowledge. Moving up from one class to another involved (except in the primary stage) passing tests, and failure to do so could mean repeating a year. To judge from ministerial comment, the results of this rigour were not altogether positive, for schools often came under unhealthy pressures from local education offices to mark performances up.

The final examinations in the seventh and tenth classes were both written and oral, and based on the 'ticket' system. This meant that pupils had to answer questions from a selection of cards, or 'tickets', containing questions which were known to them in advance and which had been approved by the local educational authorities or the school director. The difficulty lay in the fact that no examinee knew which cards he would pick up. Successful completion of the ten-year course entitled the pupil to a 'certificate of maturity' (*attestat zrelosti*) which carried the marks he achieved in Russian language and literature, mathematics, physics, chemistry, history, a foreign language and (for non-Russians) the native language and literature. Under rules insti-tuted in May 1948 pupils who finished with marks of 5, or in certain cases 4, were awarded gold or silver medals – honours which were highly prized because they facilitated admission to an institution of higher learning (Medynski, 1947, p. 82; Abakumov *et al.*, p. 182).

The question of failure at this point does not seem to have been treated explicitly in the published regulations, but the few reports I have had from experienced teachers suggest that it was virtually unknown. Children who could not be squeezed through on time were either given supplementary examinations in the autumn or kept back for an extra year.

The main RSFSR curriculum, by the late 1940s, contained the spread of subjects listed in Table 1.2 and the cycles totalled in Table 1.3. In the first three classes most of the time was spent on Russian and arithmetic; physical training and singing took up what was left. From the fourth class the range was gradually extended, but arithmetic, art and singing stopped after the fifth. The bulk of the curricular material was dealt with in the sixth to tenth classes. Under the terms of a decree of February 1933, all the textbooks used in the class were to be 'carefully examined' and approved by the collegia (i.e. inner councils) of the ministries of enlightenment. Of course, they were subject to the usual censorship regulations as well (*Direktivy VKP(b)*, p. 168).

To sum up, the nature of the Soviet school in the early 1950s can be judged from its organisational configuration, the subjects taught in it and what we know about cultural life under Stalin. It was a closely controlled institution, disciplined and academic in orientation, scientific in bias and demanding of time. The humanities as taught there were heavily impregnated with Stalinist ideology.

Obviously, this was a pattern which could have been modified in many respects when Khrushchev came to power. But he was very conservative about some matters, and at first left most of the detail of form and practice untouched. Neither were there any striking theoretical innovations. The first changes he attempted were rather in the sphere of curriculum content. The long-term stability here may be judged from the fact that of the sixty-one textbooks in use in 1958, eleven were very old and in their eleventh to nineteenth editions; ten were in their fifth to tenth editions, while thirty-five were 'current reprints' (De Witt, p. 308). Some destalinisation took place in the humanities, and outmoded textbooks were replaced by new ones in the sciences.

A more spectacular and far-reaching development was the reorientation of the curriculum towards polytechnisation, a trend which soon came to influence, if not determine, most other educational policies. It may aptly serve as a vehicle for further analysis here.

(1) *Polytechnisation in the Mid-1950s*

By the early 1950s the general school curriculum, on account of its academic orientation, was becoming progressively less appropriate to the needs of the day. The numbers of pupils in the senior classes were growing quickly and the school was becoming a mass institution, yet it still encouraged its charges to think only in terms of admission to an institution of higher education (or *VUZ*). At the same time there were no plans to expand the *VUZy* quickly enough to admit them.

Table 1.2   *RSFSR General School Curricula*
(selected years; ten-year totals for all classes, in hours)

	1947	1955	1959	1966	1978
Russian language and literature	3,003	2,788	2,926	2,584	2,584
History	710	660	728	642	498
Soviet constitution/ Social studies	66	33	70	70	70
Foreign language	743	660	726	572	572
Art	165	198	330	216	216
Music	132	198	287	252	252
Mathematics	2,112	1,980	2,139	2,077	2,077
Biology	—	396	511	428	392
Physics	478	544	631	568	568
Chemistry	346	347	407	355	355
Astronomy	33	33	39	35	35
Geography	545	479	434	394	394
Natural history	462	—	—	216	180
Military training (boys) }				—	142
Physical training	594	660	800	716	716
Machine drawing	165	132	71	107	107
Manual training and practicals	—	528 }	2,729	716	716
Excursions, production practice	—	188 }		185	185
Facultative (optional) subjects	—	—	—	638	461
TOTALS	9,554	9,857	12,828	10,771	10,520

Notes and sources: These are standard curricula for native Russian speakers.

The subject listings have been slightly simplified and rearranged for visual convenience. The totals for the years 1947 and 1955 are taken from different editions of Medynski (1947, p. 76; 1955, p. 84) and appear to be directly comparable.

The 1955 total contains an entry of 33 hours for 'psychology', which was short-lived, and has been omitted from the table. 'Manual training and practicals' included 198 hours for a type of labour lesson known as a *practicum*.

The 1959 column comes from De Witt (p. 591), whose figures have evidently been compiled by a method somewhat different from that used for 1947 and 1955. The large 'manual training and practicals' and 'excursions, production practice' totals included full school days which were supposed to be spent on these activities. It represented an ideal which was probably rarely achieved. The increases in the other totals in this column are explained by the proposed lengthening of the school course by one year.

The 1966 column was calculated from the weekly totals given in the teaching plan approved on 10 December 1966, and reproduced in Prokofiev *et al.*, 1967, p. 91; it contained no figure for military training, as this had been temporarily abolished; the 1978 column was derived from the teaching plan approved by N. V. Aleksandrov, RSFSR Minister of Enlightenment, on 19 January 1978 (Order 26-M). No annual totals for 1966 and 1978 have been found in Soviet sources; there is some doubt about how these weekly totals should be multiplied to compose a full school year, so I have used multiples of 35 and 36, according to class. The error, if there is one, should not be more than 3%.

'Excursions, production practice' totals were calculated from the number of days given in official sources. By 1975 the 'Soviet constitution' course had been replaced by 'social studies' (70 hours in the tenth class). A new course, 'Soviet state and law' (35 hours in the eighth class), was introduced in 1976, the hours needed being deducted from the 'facultative' component. Despite small discrepancies and the possible margins of error, the figures in the five columns are, I believe, realistic and closely comparable. A curricular distribution of subjects (by year of study) for the 1978 range is given on page 48.

Table 1.3   *RSFSR General School Curricular Cycles*
             (selected years; time inputs as percentages of annual total)

Cycle	1947	1955	1959	1966	1978
Humanities (including art and music)	50	46	40	43	42
Science (including geography)	42	39	32	40	40
Practicals (including PT and military training)	8	15	28	17	18

Note that the allocation of subjects to a given cycle is necessarily somewhat arbitrary. Facultative hours in the 1966 and 1978 curricula could be split among several, and have been omitted.
Source: Calculated from Table 1.2.

Moreover, the contingents of people in their mid-teens were due to fall as a result of the 'war dent', thereby exacerbating existing labour shortages. The economy required a supply of young people who would be content, for a few years at least, to work in unskilled or semi-skilled manual jobs. Similar situations were not uncommon in other industrialised societies, but the Soviet authorities prided themselves on their forward planning techniques and could not but be alarmed by the growing discrepancy.

The best solution appeared to lie not in restricting access to the senior classes of the general school, but in giving a new slant to the curriculum, so that the country's youth might acquire some basic knowledge of production methods, useful skills and indeed a more positive attitude towards manual labour while still at school.

As we have seen, such a response was well within the realms of Soviet experience. School courses had been heavily 'polytechnised' until Stalin restructured them in the 1930s. Concern was voiced about the 'abstract' nature of the curriculum even in the late 1940s; and the Nineteenth Party Congress, which took place in October 1952, called explicitly for a more polytechnical approach. This change was once again justified as being truly Marxist in conception, since the worker was called upon to fulfil many different functions, physical as well as mental, in a socialist society.[6] The new wave of polytechnisation was thus, somewhat paradoxically, Stalinist in origin. Initially, it involved three kinds of modification.

The first was the introduction, in 1954, of practical lessons in classes one to five. These comprised one hour of 'labour' per week in the first four classes, and a two-hour 'practical' in the fifth. Simple manual skills were taught at a school workshop or garden plot. The 1955 curriculum introduced two-hour practicals in agricultural, mechanical and electrical work in classes eight, nine and ten (Medynski, pp. 74, 84). These changes were mostly at the expense of Russian language, literature and mathematics, though the overall work-load was also increased by one hour a week from the fifth class onwards to accommodate them. By 1955 the proportion of practical and vocational instruction in the standard RSFSR curriculum had risen to about 15 per cent of school time, as against 8 per cent in 1947, when it had comprised only PT, military training and machine drawing (Tables 1.2 and 1.3).

Secondly, teaching of the sciences was made more practical and 'every-day' in its orientation. Physics and chemistry were particularly subject to change, being stretched to include the analysis of simple mechanisms, household equipment (such as electrical, heating and water systems) and explanations of technical and production processes in local enterprises. Work in mathematics became more concrete, while the economic and productive aspects of geography were stressed (Medynski, 1955, pp. 72 ff.). Thirdly, schools were expected to include production practice and excursions to works or farms in their extra-curricular activities. By 1955 virtually all schools in the RSFSR were said to have out-of-school circles of one kind or another, with 5 of the 12 million pupils who were old enough participating in them (*Kulturnoe stroitelstvo RSFSR*, 1958, p. 275).

The most distinctive – and troublesome – aspect of polytechnisation was training and practice in manual skills, because it could not be accommodated in lessons of the traditional type. The nature of such training varied both with the age of the pupils and with local conditions. The youngest children could only be expected to do childish handwork, but the rudiments of relatively advanced skills were attainable in the senior classes. In urban schools these ranged from instruction in service jobs or catering to pulling an old motor car to pieces. Sometimes the work was done at school, sometimes in premises belonging to a local enterprise. In the countryside, on the other hand, pupils were put on to simple agricultural jobs (like hoeing, weeding, planting). Since many agricultural enterprises – particularly the collective farms – were desperate for labour anyway, 'polytechnisation' was often just a new name for a well established practice. In fact, under *ad hoc* agreements reached between school and enterprise, pupils could legally be paid for their labour (Skatkin, p. 264).

A report from the Azerbaidzhani capital of Baku showed what, ideally, could happen in urban conditions.

We try to arrange things so that every child who leaves our school can go to a factory not as a pupil but as a trained workman [wrote a school director]. We had to co-ordinate teaching in school with production practice at the factory. The pedagogical council decided to form one class with production training among the 'parallel' classes of the eighth grade. Entry into this class was voluntary, but required the assent of the council. Twenty-eight pupils who desired to learn the trades of turner, fitter or milling machine operator, applied. The party bureau of the factory commissioned several engineers to work out a production programme . . . with the teachers. Saturday became 'factory day' for the schoolchildren . . . In addition, a period of practice lasting three weeks, with a four-hour working day, was organised for them in the summer holidays. (*Uchitelskaya gazeta*, 1 August 1956)

Further modifications of the curriculum were tried out in some localities. In 1956 the labour periods were replaced in the upper classes of about 500 schools in the RSFSR by a course called 'the principles of production'. This was designed to train children for certain skills specifically needed by industries near the chosen schools, and took up a whole day (Matthews, 1961, p. 51). In the Ukraine some school courses were for a time lengthened by a whole year to allow pupils to acquire training in a manual trade, partly in school hours and partly in extra-curricular circles.

The question arises as to what choice of skills the children in 'polytechnised' schools had. Parents, as we have seen, could not normally choose between establishments, so directors had a captive audience even to begin with. The matter does not appear to have been frankly discussed in published sources, but occasional Press reports and interviews which I had with school directors in Moscow at that time provided some indication. The practice seems to have been to allow choice whenever practicable. Both girls and boys had to be catered for, and facilities for training in one trade sometimes served for training in another. In larger schools the children learned different skills in different years of study; sometimes parallel classes offered different trades, or a choice between 'production' and 'non-production' classes, thus preserving some freedom of involvement. None of which, need I add, was supposed to lead to any formal streaming of the pupils by ability. There is little evidence that coercion was used to ensure participation within those schools which were polytechnised, though social pressures must have been palpable. The readiness with which children responded depended (according to some teachers) on the attractiveness of the skills taught. A few subjects, like motor mechanics and sewing, which could be useful regardless of career, were definitely popular. But many manual trades which could be practised only at a very menial level were not.

(2)   *The Initial Failures*

The success of polytechnisation in the mid-1950s may be judged by asking how far the proposed curricular changes were implemented (for mere publication of them did not mean that school directors were ready, or able, to comply); whether the pupils' overall attitude to manual labour was appreciably modified as a result; and whether their ensuing placement in jobs was made any easier.

As to the first point, by June 1958 about 75 per cent of schools in the USSR were still said to be using the 1954–5 unpolytechnised curricula, and 'training their pupils mainly for entry into a *VUZ*' (Shapovalenko, p. 133). The situation was apparently better in the Ukraine, where, as we have noted, a special effort had been made to polytechnise, and 88 per cent of the secondary schools were providing some kind of production training. Even here, however, only a quarter of the pupils were involved in it, and no more than 10–15 per cent of them were actually acquiring a recognised trade. And many of these, we may be sure, did not develop it further or use it when they started work (Matthews, 1961, pp. 52, 90). Implementation of the new curriculum depended in no small measure on the availability of equipment, workrooms and school plots. Figures for the RSFSR showed that such facilities were satisfactory for gardening and agricultural work but extremely disappointing for industrial specialities (Table 1.4). The extent to which industrial enterprises accepted pupils on the shop floor is unknown, but this practice was in any case not very efficient and was fraught with problems of its own.

Table 1.4   *RSFSR School Facilities for Manual Instruction, 1953, 1956* (percentages)*

	1953	1956
7-year schools:		
plots	65·0	93·0
workshops	1·3	7·5
10-year schools:		
plots	74·0	88·0
workshops	8·0	9·5

*Presuming one plot or workshop per school; urban and rural schools together.
Source: Kulturnoe stroitelstvo RSFSR, p. 308, adapted.

Furthermore, as a few contemporary studies of school leavers' intentions showed, there was little interest in manual jobs. One of the most interesting studies, conducted by M. A. Khomutova in the tenth classes of Moscow and Erevan schools, indicated that between 1952 and 1956 a '*VUZ* orientation' was shared by no less than 78–100 per cent of the several hundred children questioned (Matthews, 1961, p. 86; *Proftekhobrazovanie*, no. 3, 1957, p. 7). There was little doubt that in this respect, too, the polytechnisation drive was failing badly. 'The principal fault of our secondary and higher schools,' complained Khrushchev in September 1958 after four years of effort, 'is that they are isolated from life. Education and *VUZ* officials have often been criticised for this, but in practice the situation remains almost the same.'

THE DECEMBER 1958 REFORM

Astonishing though it may be, the failure only prompted Khrushchev to press on in the same direction. He was clearly convinced of the need for polytechnisation, could it be but properly implemented. The method he now chose involved restructuring the whole framework of school courses.

Public preparation for it was relatively elaborate, as the Soviet leader wished to convince everyone that it had everyone else's approval. He restated the problem strongly in a speech to the Thirteenth Congress of the *Komsomol* in April 1958:

As a result of the separation of the secondary school instruction programme from life, these young men and women [ten-year school leavers] do not know production. And so the problem of how best to use them, filled as they are with energy, arises. Many young people and their parents are dissatisfied with this position.

Furthermore, some young people, on finishing the ten-year school, are unwilling to work in factories, works, collective and state farms, considering that it is insulting for them to do so. This condescending, negligent and incorrect attitude to physical labour may be found in families as well . . . Some people turn physical labour into a sort of scarecrow for their children . . . The time has come, I believe, to restructure the education of the younger generation decisively . . . All the children who enter school must be trained for useful labour and participation in the construction of a communist society . . . The Soviet school is required to produce well rounded people who know their school subjects well but who are at the same time capable of useful labour; it must develop in young people an urge to be useful to society and participate actively in the production of the wealth which society needs. (*XIII S'ezd VLKSM*, 1959, p. 278)

On 21 September *Pravda* published a set of proposals for restructuring the educational system as a whole which Khrushchev, as First Secretary, claimed to have discussed with members of the Party Presidium. On 12 November these proposals were turned into 'theses' and embodied in a decree of the Central Committee. They were then debated at meetings throughout the land, and commented upon favourably in letters to the Press. An all-union law on the new educational structure was finally approved by the Supreme Soviet on 24 December 1958.

Some Western observers noted at the time that this law, in its final form, was a little less drastic than the theses, suggesting some effective opposition.[7] The most striking points of retreat, to jump ahead for a moment, were the omission of specific proposals that *all* children should start work after an eight-year education; that attendance at the Schools for Working and Rural Youth should be the *principal* channel for obtaining general schooling thereafter; that the senior classes of the general school be made more akin to a manual trade school; and that boarding schools should be regarded as an ideal type of educational institution.

The reform was launched in the union republics on the basis of detailed laws approved between 17 March 1959 (Latvia) and 28 May 1959 (Kirgizia). Since these laws differed from one another only in such phrasing as was needed to maintain a pretence of independent drafting, or matter of detail, we shall here confine ourselves to the RSFSR version. It covered not only course structure but also many associated arrangements.

With regard to the general school, the principal provisions were as follows. Clause 1 stipulated that eight-year schooling was to be obligatory for all children from the age of 7 to 15 (or 16, if need be). The existing seven-year course was thus in effect lengthened to eight, but the goal of a complete ten-year education for all, at least on a full-time basis, was omitted from mention. The eight-year school was renamed the 'incomplete secondary general labour polytechnical school', and its courses were to be modified over the ensuing three years so as to increase the practical element. Primary schools of four classes were to be retained only in small rural settlements, and the pupils transferred to the fifth classes of nearby eight- or ten-year schools when they were old enough.

Clauses 2–4 placed the onus of reform on the existing state apparatus and contained provisions for facilitating attendance which we have already commented upon, namely, improved registration, assistance for the poor, more boarding and lengthened day schools. A new eight-year school-leaving certificate was introduced, and special transport arrangements were proposed for children living over 3 kilometres from their school.

Clause 5 was of central importance in that it outlined the new senior school structure:

All young people from 15 to 16 years of age, after completing the eight-year school, engage in suitable social labour and acquire broad opportunities for completing their full secondary education through a combination of study and productive labour in educational institutions of the following types . . . (1) evening (shift) secondary general schools . . . (2) secondary general labour polytechnical schools with production training [which provide], in the course of three years [*sic*], secondary education and trade training for work in a branch of the national economy or culture . . . and (3) technical colleges (*tekhnikumy*) and other secondary special educational institutions.

The need not only to preserve but to extend the network of 'special' schools for gifted children was mentioned at this point; indeed, Khrushchev had laid particular emphasis on them in his theses. Encouragement of these schools may be seen as a corollary to the polytechnisation drive rather than as a contradiction of it, and as a move to protect the development of the nation's most talented youth.

So much for the basic proposals. With regard to the 'ordinary' general schools, three points deserve mention. First, as the reader may have noted, the provisions of Clause 5 contained an implicit contradiction: how could young people seriously 'engage in suitable social *labour*' (as opposed to training) if they were still at a full-time school as provided in points (2) and (3)? The ambiguity is in fact greater in the wording of the RSFSR version than it was in the original all-union law. Secondly, the full-time senior school was not only to be changed in character but was to become relatively less important, as may be surmised from the fact that it was listed *after* part-time study. Finally, the extension of the full general school course to eleven years (eight plus three) was intended not only to accommodate a bigger polytechnical element but also to discourage children from staying on full-time. The 'raw' general school leaver had for some years been facing increasing discrimination in *VUZ* admission procedures, anyway (see Chapter 5).

Clause 6 covered the development of boarding schools, a matter we have already considered. Clause 7 provided for the transformation in the course of five years of the existing ten-year schools into schools 'of different types' (presumably, those envisaged earlier in the text), without any reduction in overall facilities. Pupils already in the eighth to tenth classes were to be allowed to complete their courses following the existing curricula, but with some intensification of the labour content. The Council of Ministers of the RSFSR and lower executive bodies were enjoined to ensure that the change-over was smooth and thorough.

The next three clauses were concerned with organisational support from local authorities and employers, who, amongst other requirements, were called upon to release young people for study and assist the schools with their polytechnisation arrangements. Production training for schoolchildren was to be organised in 'instruction and production workshops at nearby enterprises, in state and collective farm pupils' brigades, on instruction plots and in school or inter-school instruction and production workshops'. The interspersal of instruction and labour was to fit the trades taught and the facilities available locally. The trades were to be determined, incidentally, not by the enterprise managements (which might be untrustworthy) but by local authorities; and these, together with the relevant ministries, were to ensure that the necessary workplaces and instruction were provided. Similar arrangements were 'recommended' for collective farms, which were held to be legally autonomous. The remaining clauses contained familiar exhortations for improvement and covered what might pardonably be termed background matters,[8] while the various republican enactments on the reform as a whole were followed by a plethora of laws designed to elaborate and implement their provisions.

The reformed RSFSR curriculum, published in August 1959, allowed for an enormous increase in the time devoted to manual training (Table 1.2). In the fifth to eighth classes it went up by two to three hours a week, while in the senior classes it was to occupy no less than twelve. This time had to come from somewhere, so the number of lessons given in the traditional subjects – principally Russian language and literature, mathematics, foreign languages and physical education – was reduced; the school week and the school year were lengthened and, as noted, a whole year was added to the ten-year course. (The difficulties presented by polytechnisation in areas where the school curriculum contained both a local language and Russian must have been particularly acute.) General 'overloading' was only slightly eased by the abolition on 9 February 1962 of military training for boys in the senior classes.[9] The balance of time devoted to the three cycles – humanities, sciences and practical activities – changed markedly in favour of the last, as may be seen from Table 1.3.

Further attempts were made to strengthen the ideological component. The old 'Soviet constitution' course was increased to two hours in the final year in March 1958, and then turned into a broader course called the 'fundamentals of political knowledge'. In 1962 this was renamed 'social studies' (*obshchestvovedenie*) and filled with a mixture of Marxist–Leninist texts, party documents and Soviet law. History-teaching presented a particular difficulty, in that the proposed switch to a basic eight-year course implied the exclusion of the post-revolutionary period, which came last. In the event the material was reorganised so as to ensure adequate coverage of these momentous years earlier in the curriculum.

The 'special' general schools covered in Clause 5 of the RSFSR reform law require separate mention. They included institutions where some subjects were taught in a foreign language, and schools with extra instruction for the 'most gifted' children in music, ballet and art. Khrushchev's theses had also mentioned special schools for children with particular aptitudes in mathematics, physics, chemistry and biology, and had proposed setting up instruction groups for them under the aegis of local *VUZy*. This variant, however, was omitted from the reform laws, presumably because it was still somewhat contentious. Local 'Olympiad' movements to encourage the scientifically gifted had in fact been going for many years.

The post-Stalin drive to expand the foreign language schools began with the decree of May 1961 which called for the establishment, over four years, of not less than 700 throughout the country, together with substantial improvements in language-teaching in ordinary schools. Some boarding schools were also to be reorganised for the purpose. According to one observer, the target was not achieved, as the total number of foreign language schools reached only 600 or so by 1970 (Dunstan, p. 92). Great emphasis seems to have been placed during these years on making English the most commonly taught language, the others being German, French, Spanish and a scattering of Eastern tongues.[10] It seems that foreign language instruction in the special schools increased to 30 or 40 per cent of the teaching time in the last two classes, as compared to 6–8 per cent in other establishments. The schools were said to be efficient but, of course, highly selective. Their continuing popularity was due partly to the fact that while fluency in a foreign language can be of great help career-wise, Soviet citizens could not send their children for instruction abroad, nor were foreigners freely available then any more than now for teaching purposes in the USSR.

Special schools for music, ballet and art, though much less numerous, also flourished. According to occasional data, the number of full-time secondary schools for children with outstanding gifts in music rose from five in the late 1950s to twenty-four by 1966; it is thought that the number of children in each numbered three or four hundred. Schools specialising in the fine arts increased from about five in 1958 to fifty in the late 1960s, and ballet schools from sixteen to eighteen over the same period.[11] The total of children in ordinary schools where extra musical and artistic training was provided, presumably outside school hours and certainly at parents' expense, grew from 216,000 in 1960 to no less than 490,000 in 1965. I suspect, however, that a rise of such magnitude did not really take place and that the official statistics reflected only the registration of schools where such teaching had been carried on informally before. So impressive a wave of artistic fervour is otherwise difficult to explain. The provision of extra-curricular facilities for children with a special interest in sport was also greatly improved (Riordan, p. 178).

An intriguing question is the degree to which the special schools were themselves 'linked with life'. There is evidence of a few attempts to find practical skills to fit the artistic training. But by and large the long practice hours which the arts demanded seem to have protected the pupils from the harsher rigours of artisan toil.

POST-REFORM SCHOOL PRACTICE

The reform was accompanied by certain noteworthy changes in school practice, over and above the arrangements for production work.

New and rather milder 'rules for pupils' were approved in November 1960. The text was now differentiated for children at the three levels of schooling; the old requirements about standing and sitting properly were dropped (though they evidently continued to be observed in practice) and there was no reference to the pupil's ticket or to expulsion for bad conduct. A great deal of emphasis was laid on involvement in labour, and there were new requirements for heightening 'cultural levels'. The rules also accommodated self-service provisions, approved in June 1959, which stated that schoolchildren were to participate in 'cleaning classrooms, planting trees and flowers, and looking after their work quarters, classroom equipment and books'. They could also do dining-room duties and a wide range of repairs. The aim of all this (like so much else) was to counter indigence and contempt for physical labour. The money saved was to be used for buying school utensils and improving material conditions (*SDSh*, p. 106).

There is some evidence that homework was quietly downgraded, and if that was indeed so it was probably explicable in terms of Khrushchev's disinterest and the increased work-load. In any case, homework found no mention in the major enactments of these years, and according to reports by former teachers it was for a time abandoned in the primary classes. The new school statutes approved in December 1959 revealed that passing-up exams, which had long been obligatory in the middle and senior classes, were now replaced by assessment of marks for work throughout the year.

September 1959 saw the issue of several ministerial orders requiring teachers in the RSFSR to improve pupils' achievement in Russian language and literature, which suggests that as a result of the new policies standards were falling. These orders were followed in the next few months by no less than eight instructions on the teaching of the traditional arts and science subjects, and as many more on general improvements in the quality of instruction, marking and verification (Deineko, p. 455, nn. 9, 18). A decree of 1 June 1962 limited the exclusion of pupils from the full-time general school, this having been a recognised method of dealing with imminent failures, at least in the senior classes. A teacher reported to me that about this time there was a marked increase of pressure on schools to achieve 100 per cent success rates, so that it became virtually impossible to give pupils a mark of 2, however much deserved.

Another acute problem was that of remuneration for the masses of pupils due to be injected into the productive enterprises. In 1960, for example, the last three classes of the urban general school contained nearly 1·3 million pupils: and if those not already involved in collective farm labour were to be brought into production, the financial implications could not but be considerable. In December 1959 statutes were published on paying pupils for their labour and enterprise instructors for teaching them. The gist was that the former were to be rewarded at the normal adult rates, providing their work was up to standard, while the latter got modest sums of 35–70 roubles per learner monthly, which, of course, had to be set against possible losses of output. The average industrial wage was then about 900 roubles. Thus was the 'economic' nature of pupils' labour enshrined in law (*SZAT*, 1965, pp. 172 ff.). The payments for instructors, though channelled through the enterprise, were ultimately set against the educational budget; but we have no means of knowing how well these rules were observed in practice.

THE REFORM OPPOSED

The last years of Khrushchev's tenure of office were marked by much criticism of, and some notable withdrawals from, his grandiose plans. Exhortations to remedy shortcomings have often been used in the USSR as a way of criticising a given policy while appearing to support it. The early 1960s saw an unusual proliferation of appeals of this type. In addition, a number of official decrees indicated directly that progress with the reform was, to say the least, disappointing.

On 30 May 1961 the USSR Council of Ministers issued a detailed decree on production training for pupils in the senior classes. Although, according to this, about half of all secondary general schools had introduced it and 53 per cent of the pupils in the ninth to eleventh classes participated, there were serious shortcomings in most aspects of the process.[12]

The remedies proposed involved in nearly all cases greater administrative pressure, but the second clause of the document was particularly interesting in that it contained what may have been the first significant modification of principle. After stating that the trades taught in each school were to be registered not with the local but with the higher *krai* and *oblast* authorities (presumably to ensure better control), it recommended that 'the training of pupils of each separate class should be conducted, as a rule, in not more than two specialisations'. This was at first sight a modest yet sensible proposal, aimed at avoiding administrative tangles. But in the average-size class many different preferences would normally be expressed and, assuming that one of the two choices now proposed was for boys and the other for girls, the operation of clause 2 would in effect preclude choice altogether. In other words, the great majority of young people were to have a manual trade imposed upon them, regardless of their wishes. This practice may have been not unknown before, but now it gained official approval. Only parallel classes in the larger schools could offer a real prospect of relaxation.

The switch-over to the new eleven-year curricula, it will be remembered, had been planned for completion in three years. A decree of the RSFSR Supreme Soviet of 25 July 1962 revealed that here, too, things were behindhand. Two-thirds of the secondary general schools in the republic had been reorganised into eleven-year 'secondary labour polytechnical schools with production training', but somehow no more than a start had been made in the rearrangement of the teaching. In some areas difficulty was being experienced in changing from the seven-year to eight-year school. These failures, it was said, 'bore witness to the fact that the [state bodies concerned] are weak in organisational matters, permit shortcomings in the selection and training of responsible staff, and do not involve the broad public sufficiently in the practical fulfilment of the law'. So, as usual, the blame was laid on the shoulders of ministerial and local officials rather than on those of the policy-makers in the CPSU. The solution proposed was, once more, closer adherence to existing rules and regulations.

We cannot, of course, know what was being said or thought about education in the top leadership at this time. But it is clear that opposition to the reform was considerable throughout the country, that the new measures were failing, and that Khrushchev himself was being confronted by other urgent problems, at home and abroad. Whatever the catalyst, there was a distinct switch in government policy towards the general school. Open admission of error in so weighty a matter was still out of the question, but two important enactments signalled the change to the public at large. On 10 August 1964 a joint decree of the Central Committee of the CPSU and the USSR Council of Ministers stipulated that from 1966 eight classes of full-time general schooling were to be followed by *two* more, and not the three stipulated by the reform. This returned to the full-time ten-year course the centrality which Khrushchev's reform would have effaced. The involvement of the Central Committee in the measure betokened opposition to the eleventh year in the highest party circles.

An even more forthright rejection of polytechnisation as Khrushchev envisaged it came in a decree of 23 February 1966. (Although a measure of the Brezhnev period, this is best mentioned here.) It stated that pupils in general schools would get trade training *'when conditions existed for it'* – in other words, such training was no longer to be considered mandatory everywhere. Local authorities were to draw up lists of schools where it was practicable and ensure that it was limited to the hours stipulated in the curriculum or done outside school time (Abakumov *et al.*, p. 219). This change was in fact reflected in the curriculum published for 1966 (Table 1.2).

And so the polytechnisation plans for the general school were never fully implemented. Manual instruction was not organised on the scale Khrushchev envisaged: and as was revealed later, only a small proportion of the school leavers who acquired trades actually used them when they went to work.[13] As far as the problem of altering attitudes was concerned, the many sociological surveys of school leavers' intentions conducted in the mid-1960s continued to show a widespread desire for early admission to a *VUZ*.[14]

Why did Khrushchev's plans for polytechnisation fail twice in the course of a decade? The failures had far-reaching political as well as social implications, and undoubtedly contributed to his fall. I would suggest three major reasons, around which many lesser ones could be grouped: polytechnisation, in the forms then envisaged, was administratively impracticable, socially unacceptable and inadequately financed.

The administrative difficulties need no further elucidation. Production and education establishments are so different in organisation and function that any kind of liaison between them cannot but present problems. A really successful link-up between the Soviet productive sector and the school, on the scale required by the 1958 reform, would have needed a significant reorientation of enterprise priorities and multiple instruction agreements between any given school and a number of enterprises, so as to satisfy a majority of pupils' tastes and career intentions. This usually proved to be quite unworkable in practice.

The educational and indeed social interests ranged against polytechnisation, though not always explicit, were powerful. The state educational officials were undoubtedly aware of the pitfalls, and must often have felt very reluctant to proceed. Directors of schools were badly hit by the administrative complexities, while teachers had grounds for objecting to the intrusion of such subjects as manual training and enterprise visits into the curriculum, since they bore responsibility for any consequent fall in educational standards. The more academically oriented pupils disliked having the manual lessons thrust upon them, especially if there was little or no choice of trade. The reactions of their parents must have been similar, few of whom could have welcomed the extensions of the school course by a full year for this purpose. Production work by itself did not change anyone's attitudes. On the other side of the fence, managers of production enterprises were often reluctant to provide training facilities for groups of uninterested and possibly frivolous adolescents. 'It is no secret,' an authoritative article stated in the spring of 1963, 'that people at some enterprises approach production training in an irresponsible manner. Schoolchildren are either not given work or are put in the most neglected and dirty spots with antediluvian and broken-down equipment, and no care is taken to organise their labour. What, in such circumstances, can they, the children, get out of it?' (*PZh*, no. 5, 1963, p. 49).

Finally, the problems of finance, though perhaps of less immediate interest to us, were by no means negligible. Although expenditure on general education was apparently rising, sufficient funds were not forthcoming for the extra needs of polytechnisation. The introduction of an eleventh year at school, the establishment of school workshops or garden plots and the provision of an entire army of labour instructors were all potentially expensive operations (Noah, p. 168). Khrushchev perhaps wished to lighten this burden (of which he must have been well aware) by popularising part-time study and some degree of self-financing. He may also have thought that the induction of children into the production process while they were still at school would offset some of the costs of training them later. In fact, part-time study remained relatively inefficient, while the economic gain from teaching manual skills to schoolchildren was more apparent than real. All in all, polytechnisation as envisaged by Khrushchev was exceedingly short-sighted in conception and sluggish in implementation. The surprising thing is that it was pressed so hard and for so long in the forms described.

JOB PLACEMENT FOR SCHOOL LEAVERS

It is no exaggeration to say that the regimentation of the labour market and the refusal to recognise unemployment, which was so characteristic of Stalinism, forced the specific problems of placing school leavers out of sight. Anyway, the creation of vast numbers of new jobs in industry and the existence of various recruiting agencies (see pages 67–79 below) meant that in a crude sense there was never any difficulty about finding work – of one kind or another.

By the time Khrushchev came to power not only had the old agencies ceased to function adequately but new employment difficulties were springing up. Indeed, as I have indicated, the reform of the educational system was not unconnected with them. The matter was soon authorised for open treatment in the Press; and the arrangements then devised for facilitating the transition from school to work lend themselves to easier analysis.[15]

Youth unemployment was first admitted to be a serious social problem by A. N. Shelepin, First Secretary of the *Komsomol*, in April 1954, and in the course of the next three years a spate of newspaper articles threw a great deal of light on it. The most common type may be loosely termed 'involuntary', in that it arose from the refusal of managers to hire. Part of the trouble was that the labour protection laws of the mid-1950s made juvenile labour relatively unattractive. Under-18s became more difficult to fit into work schedules, and managers, it seems, were usually expected to carry the burden of employing them without a commensurate reduction in their production or financial commitments. So except when shortages of labour were really acute, adults were hired in preference. Press reports criticised managers for this practice and also for ignoring the legal restrictions on juvenile labour.

Further difficulty was caused by the improved conditions of

employment for part-time students. Many managers, it was said, were reluctant to hire any persons who looked as though they might register for part-time courses, for the release provisions to which they became entitled could cause great production difficulties. A third source of trouble was the fact that many young applicants for jobs, especially those with ten classes of general school behind them, had no intention of staying long in any case. They went to work merely to pass the time until re-sitting the *VUZ* entrance examinations, or to obtain a certificate of employment which allowed them to take advantage of preferential admission rules (see p. 154). Managers naturally looked askance at these aims. The result of the various frictions was that whenever the demand for labour slackened, juveniles and part-time students were the first to suffer.

The youth unemployment of these years was not, however, only of an involuntary kind. Increasing numbers of ten-year school leavers – Khrushchev contemptuously called them 'white-hands' – were unwilling to work, and dreamed only of going straight into a *VUZ*. The authorities clearly hoped, at least initially, that the polytechnisation movement would prove an adequate remedy for these woes, and would turn school leavers into trained (or, more accurately, partially trained) workers who were both eager to toil and eminently acceptable to enterprise managers. Ideally, the proposed links between school and enterprise would ensure not only the availability of production practice but also effortless placement when it was complete.

There were, nevertheless, early signs of more direct state intervention. A decree of the USSR Council of Ministers of 2 August 1954, though concerned mainly with low-grade technical schools, enjoined the republican councils of ministers to ensure 'the widespread participation of local soviets in affording all possible help to young people from the ten-year schools in choosing a suitable trade and obtaining work' (Malin and Korobov, vol. 4, p. 250). In the next two or three years some local soviets set up permanent 'placement commissions' to gather information about vacancies and offer young people assistance in filling them. Moscow City Council, for example, devoted a good deal of attention to the problem, and such commissions were reported to be operating in about a dozen other large towns. Their activities did not, at first, attract much public support or interest, but the failure of polytechnisation as a placement mechanism eventually prompted the authorities to back them more strongly.

A decree of September 1957 entitled 'On the Placement of Ten-Year School Leavers in Industrial and Agricultural Production' stipulated that state authorities, from the republican councils of ministers down to local soviets, were to co-operate with the State Planning Authority (*Gosplan*), the State Labour Reserves and the newly established regional economic councils 'in fixing, within the labour plans of associated enterprises, a quota (or *bronya*) for hiring and training ten-year school leavers and juveniles'. Within this framework, the local soviets would direct school leavers to local managers, who would then be obliged to accept them. The actual business of deciding who went where was to remain in the hands of the placement commissions.

The quota system, which had many antecedents in Soviet labour history, may be seen as part of the plan to integrate the general school with the youth labour market. Its social and economic implications were potentially profound, for if fully implemented it would have involved making something like 1½ million initial placements by 1958. But the fact that Khrushchev decided to proceed with the December reform strongly suggests that the quotas were not, in themselves, of much use.

The last effort to improve the system under Khrushchev took the form of the decree of 4 December 1963, 'On Improving the Placement of Juveniles'. This fixed quotas for hiring juveniles at between 3 and 5 per cent of enterprise labour intakes and obliged local authorities to compile statistical reports on youth unemployment, or 'juveniles who are not studying in educational institutions nor engaged in production', as the phrase went. The measure may best be regarded as an attempt to salvage an employment scheme which was not working properly. Given the economic disadvantages of hiring juveniles, it is difficult to see how it could. Khrushchev did not evince much interest in it anyway, and as far as we can tell he never forfeited his faith in polytechnisation as the best path to the world of work. The establishment of a regular youth employment service became possible only after his dismissal.

TEACHERS AND THEIR WELL-BEING

The Soviet teaching profession grew in size and qualification level in the Khrushchev years, but the policies of innovation and reform inevitably subjected it to extra strains and stresses. We may well ask how its practitioners fared in consequence.

Teachers' terms of employment were covered by sets of rules approved in the late 1930s and 1940s. These stipulated (in general terms) that the directors and the teachers of senior classes in ten-year schools were to be appointed and released by the education offices at the *oblast, krai* and autonomous republic levels. Most other administrative and teaching posts were controlled basically by the town or district offices, while the appointment of such personnel as military and PT instructors, pioneer leaders and school doctors required reference to the relevant outside organisations. School directors themselves were empowered to hire only technical and cleaning staff (Danev, p. 59).

The changes registered under Khrushchev may be summarised as follows. In June 1960 party supervision of the hiring process was somewhat increased,[16] and in November the employment of *all* teachers was made the personal responsibility of the heads of district and town education offices. This may be viewed either as a variety of decentralisation or as a reasoned response to the increase in the numbers involved: in any case, it probably made for greater administrative flexibility. In October 1957 the teaching staffs of all educational institutions, regardless of level, were brought into one vast national union, and there was a modest re-activation of trades union functions.[17] The old system of annual confirmation of tenure was now abandoned, and this may have given some teachers better job security. They acquired, however, no important new rights, and their employment records were still, like those of all other workers, registered in a work book.

Working conditions and pay were still, in the early 1950s, governed by instructions approved in June 1948. Teachers had a basic work-load of twenty-four hours in the first to fourth classes and eighteen in the others, plus marking and supervision. Their pay scales ranged from 441 to 935 roubles a month; directors earned from 635 to 1,412 roubles.[18] Teachers were not paid for any extra-curricular help they gave to children or for involvement in propaganda and cultural activities, some of which were time-consuming and considered as state impositions. Teachers' well-being may be judged from the fact that the average wage for workers and employees outside the peasant sector was about 640 roubles (1950); the figure for *all* persons employed in teaching and cultural establishments was 680 roubles, or some 6 per cent higher.

The Khrushchev period was not a particularly happy one in that by 1964 this wage, at 79 new roubles, had fallen to a point 13 per cent below the national average. It was only in July of that year that this trend was reversed. As a result, the average wage in teaching and cultural services rose to around 94 roubles a month, which was again just above the national average.[19]

The spread of wages in the profession seems to have been retained much as before: teachers received between 65 and 137 roubles a month, directors between 82 and 208. Experienced staff in large urban schools had the best opportunities for high earnings; those employed in rural areas were at the bottom of the scale and often had to tolerate bad material conditions as well. It is true that under laws passed in 1948 and 1954 their local authorities were required to provide them with free accommodation, light, heating and a garden plot (*SDSh*, p. 312). But such benefits could be meagre in the extreme, and hardly compensated for the disadvantages of rural living. The flight of teachers from rural schools was a well recognised consequence of their neglected state.[20]

NOTES

1   The material for this outline has been drawn from a number of well-known sources, so I have dispensed with specific references. The main sources are Bowen, Counts,

Fitzpatrick, Florinsky, Medynski, Prokofiev and Skorodumov. The relevant decrees and statistical compendia have also been consulted.

2 See Fainsod, p. 201; *XXIII S'ezd KPSS*, vol. 2, p. 576. 'The Department of Science and Educational Establishments of the Central Committee', wrote a Soviet specialist recently, 'works out the principal proposals regarding the further development of education, and exercises systematic control over the implementation of party and government documents, providing everyday assistance for the educational organs' (Panachin, p. 88).

3 Panachin, p. 98. De Witt claimed that the 2½ million also included extended day school enrolments, of which more in a moment, but the text of the control figures is explicit (De Witt, p. 101; *XXI S'ezd KPSS*, vol. 2, p. 531). Possibly the issue was deliberately confused by opponents of the boarding schools, so as to re-interpret government policy in a manner favourable to themselves.

4 As far as *hours of work* were concerned, adolescents aged 14–16 were guaranteed a four-hour day and those aged 16–18 a seven-hour day (edict of the Supreme Soviet of 15 August 1955). An edict of 26 May 1956 further shortened the working day for adolescents aged 16–18 to six hours. Both *overtime* and *nightwork* were banned for the under-18s by the decree of the Central Committee and Council of Ministers of 8 August 1955, while the decree of the Council of Ministers of the USSR of 26 May 1956 fixed the pay of adolescents working a shortened day at approximately the same level as that of adults, even if they were on piecework (*SZAT*, 1958, pp. 336–8).

5 The decree of 5 November 1959 gave pupils in the ninth to eleventh classes of Schools for Working Youth a day a week off, or the equivalent during the school year, while pupils in Schools for Rural Youth became entitled to two days off, with a maximum of thirty-six days for each category. They could have 50 per cent of their normal pay during this time, though not less than the state minimum. Extra time off (one or two days a week) could be taken without pay at the management's approval.

   It will be noted that these benefits were limited to pupils in the senior classes but could be offered to other successful pupils at the discretion of the management. The earlier twenty-days' release provisions for the final examination were apparently retained and collective farms were again encouraged to release and assist any members who studied at this level (*SZAT*, 1965, pp. 169–74). The thirty-day release scheme for final exams was extended to pupils of part-time *PTU* about the same time (13 October 1960). For a summary of comparable legislation for *VUZ* and *SSUZ* students, see page 150, note 14.

6 The actual resolution read: 'In order to increase the socialist educational significance of the general school as much as possible and guarantee the conditions necessary for a free choice of profession for school leavers, it is resolved to start introducing polytechnic instruction into the general school and adopt measures necessary for the transition to general polytechnic education.' 'The idea of polytechnical education was scientifically grounded by Marx and Engels,' wrote I. A. Kairov, President of the RSFSR Academy of Pedagogical Sciences. 'The development of heavy machine production is accompanied by constant changes in technology, under the influence of which changes take place in the social division of labour and the functions of the workers. The nature of heavy industry demands an all-round development of the worker and the capacity to adapt himself quickly to the constantly changing conditions of production. One means of promoting such all-round development should be, according to Marx and Engels, polytechnical instruction, which acquaints pupils with the general scientific principles of production and arms them with the skills necessary to handle the most widely used tools' (Kairov, p. 124).

7 See, for example, the article by J. J. Schwartz and W. R. Keech in *American Political Science Review*, vol. 62, 1968, pp. 840–51.

8 Clauses 11–20 may be summarised as follows: special schools for the physically and mentally handicapped were to be adapted to the new scheme as far as possible (Clause 11); ministerial control was retained over the school year, teaching programmes and textbooks (12); there was to be strict supervision of safety and

health provisions during production practice (13); teaching equipment was to be improved and more use made of such resources as films and television (14); the right to instruction in a non-Russian native tongue was formally reaffirmed, parents in minority areas retaining in principle the right to send their children to a Russian or a non-Russian school (15); the importance of improving moral and ideological upbringing was emphasised for both teachers and parents (16); the certificate of maturity was to be retained as a 'certificate of secondary education' and supplemented in suitable cases by a manual skill certificate (17); measures were to be worked out for improving the equipment and building of schools maintained by local soviets, while collective farms were 'recommended' to improve school facilities in rural areas, although no extra financial aid was mentioned for this purpose (18); teachers were to be retrained for polytechnical work and their living and working conditions improved (19); and finally, pedagogical research was to be reoriented so as to further the reform (20).

As far as further legislation was concerned, both the new 'eight-year school' and the 'secondary general labour polytechnical school with production training' got their (RSFSR) statutes on 29 December 1959, incorporating the new legislation and laying particular stress on production training. The old Schools for Working Youth, Rural Youth and Adults were renamed Evening (Shift) and Correspondence Secondary Schools, and were likewise textually incapsulated in December 1959 and May 1962. Statutes for boarding schools and lengthed day schools were promulgated on 14 September 1960 and 18 October 1962, respectively (Tarasov and Trutneva, pp. 45, 55: *SDSh*, pp. 37, 43; Abakumov *et al.*, p. 197).

9   The new range of hours was from thirty-four in the eighth class to thirty-eight in the eleventh, while the school year was lengthened by three weeks (De Witt, pp. 589, 591). The longer hours may in fact have been compensated for by a reduction in regular homework. Military training for girls and younger schoolchildren had been abolished by a decree of 13 August 1946, and its further abandonment in 1962 accorded with a much publicised reduction in the Soviet armed forces.

10   A decree of the RSFSR Council of Ministers issued in February 1963 declared that by 1971 the proportions should be English – 50 per cent, French – 20 per cent, German – 20 per cent, Spanish and others – 10 per cent in the fifth classes of ordinary schools (when language-teaching began). The proportions in secondary and higher educational establishments were, incidentally, to be 45, 20 and 15 per cent for the first three languages respectively, 15 per cent for Spanish and 5 per cent for other languages (Abakumov *et al.*, p. 218).

11   Western authorities who have provided this data (D. Levin, G. Z. F. Bereday, M. Morton, M. Bryce and D. Glowka) are listed with references in Dunstan, p. 73, nn. 1–7.

12   They included discrepancies between training plans and enterprise needs; inadequate equipment; lack of workplaces for pupils at enterprises; slow provision of separate workshops or agricultural plots; shortages of raw materials; inadequate attention to safety rules and to the physical capabilities of the schoolchildren. Furthermore, teachers of manual skills were not being trained in sufficient numbers (Abakumov *et al.*, p. 214).

13   Sonin, p. 267; Nazimov, p. 55. Figures of between 10 and 18 per cent were given in these sources.

14   These surveys have been analysed in detail in several Western sources and require no further elaboration here. See, for example, Matthews, 1971, pp. 262 ff.: Lane and O'Dell, p. 112. For a Soviet listing of important studies see *SI*, no. 3, 1978, pp. 111, 112; Titma, p. 112.

15   I have in mind here employment for normal able-bodied youngsters. Local soviets had long been empowered to make *ad hoc* arrangements for orphans, invalids, ex-servicemen, delinquents and former prisoners. The background to juvenile unemployment is discussed in more detail in Matthews 1972.

16   In fact the overall responsibility for deciding which office should nominate the

directors and teachers of primary and eight-year schools was passed to the union republican *party* authorities (Kalinychev, p. 57), which could only have meant greater politicisation.

17 *Spravochnaya kniga o profsoyuzakh*, p. 309. After its formation in 1919 the teachers' union had a chequered history, and existed for many years as a group of republican organisations. It was reconstituted as the Union of Workers of Enlightenment, Higher Schools and Research Establishments, for 'workers of general schools, pre-school and extra-mural institutions of the ministries of enlightenment; for pupils, students, workers and employees of *MinVUZ* higher and secondary special educational institutions . . .; for research workers and all scientific, assistant and administrative staffs of Academy of Sciences . . . research establishments and of the USSR Academy of Pedagogical Sciences.' In the USSR most people eligible to do so join a union: in 1967 this one had 6·2 million members.

18 Any given wage depended principally on (1) the locality in which the school was situated, (2) the teacher's level of training, (3) the level at which instruction was given, (4) the number of years of service, (5) the actual number of hours of class work undertaken (which could be more or less than the stated norms) and (6) extra administrative duties (Noah, p. 229).

19 *Trud v SSSR*, p. 139. During these years there was some piecemeal improvement in the wage rates of some categories of employees. In March 1960 teachers in part-time schools had their salaries raised by 15 per cent, to equal that of their colleagues in full-time institutions, and school inspectors also benefited from a 15 per cent rise (Abakumov *et al.*, p. 472). Teachers were largely exempted from Khrushchev's squeeze on second jobs (under the law of 10 December 1959), and in October 1960 there were some rises for school directors and their administrative deputies (Deineko, p. 463, n. 37). For details of the July 1964 rise mentioned in the text, see *Reshenia*, vol. 5, p. 479, and *SDSh*, p. 271.

20 A most interesting account of a rural teacher's professional life at this time, based on personal experience in the Ukraine, has been provided by D. Tiktin(a) (see Bibliography).

2
General Education under Brezhnev

The strong interest in educational reform and especially polytechnisation, that had been characteristic of Khrushchev's leadership was not, at first, shared by Brezhnev. In any case, the new leadership permitted the quiet abandonment of the most unpopular aspects of the December 1958 reform and thereby, no doubt, earned the gratitude of many.

Yet the general school had numerous other problems for which solutions had to be found. The growth in coverage, which had continued so steadily since the 1940s, was now reaching a plateau, with important social implications. The Brezhnev leadership exhibited a liking for bureaucratic centralisation, in education as elsewhere, and this was to affect not only school administration but also the placement arrangements for school leavers. The curriculum required further adjustment, both in form and content. The most interesting developments, however, and the ones to which we shall devote particular attention, were the introduction of some choices into the senior school course and the reappearance of polytechnisation as a major issue. The Brezhnev years, if less eventful than the preceding ones, were by no means devoid of change.

THE PATTERN OF GROWTH

The principle of providing a general ten-year education for every child was firmly embraced by the new leadership, and duly expressed in a resolution of the Twenty-Third Party Congress in April 1966. The number of pupils in full-time general school continued to rise, reaching a peak of 49·2 million in 1970 (Figure 1.1, page 7). The subsequent decline was due not so much to government policy (though the expansion of other types of school may have affected numbers in the senior classes) as to a fall in the overall number of children, when the offspring of 'war dent' parents came of school age. In any case, the total of full-time ten-year school leavers rose quite dramatically from about 900,000 in 1965 to 3 million in 1978.

The coverage of the relevant age-groups improved correspondingly. Eight classes had been made obligatory, it will be recalled, for all Soviet children under the terms of the December 1958 reform. As may be seen from the width of the middle band in Figure 1.1, page 7, enrolments in the eight-year school increased quickly until the end of the 1960s, and then remained more or less constant. By the early 1970s over 90 per cent of the children were said to be attaining this level, and by the end of the decade, almost all.

The provision of ten-year education was a more difficult proposition. The Twenty-Third Congress stated that universal general education was to be 'in the main' achieved by 1970, but this target was not met. Thus by 1976 only about 60 per cent of the children leaving the eighth classes of schools in the RSFSR went into the ninth classes, which implied that only about half of the relevant age-groups were finishing all ten on a formal full-time basis (*PMP RSFSR*, no. 26, 15 February 1977).

To judge from comment in the ministerial decrees available, constant efforts were made to raise this figure. But it was also part of government policy to expand intakes into vocational and secondary special institutions offering equivalent levels, so the slight fall which occurred in the size of the ninth and tenth classes after the mid-1970s was partly due to this. In any case, of the schoolchildren (some 40 per cent) who left the RSFSR general school after eight classes in 1976, 11 per cent went into secondary special educational institutions, 14·5 per cent into the 'secondary' *PTU*, and about 13 per cent were said to have joined evening or correspondence classes while at work. Throughout the USSR as a whole, 91·2 per cent of all children 'admitted in the relevant years to the first classes of the general school' (a phrase intended to cover children repeating years) were said to have obtained full secondary education by one means or another. The least satisfactory figures for coverage were, not surprisingly, in the Muslim republics where cultural factors militated against educating girls (Tadzhikistan, Kazakhstan and Azerbaidzhan achieved only about 80 per cent), and in the remoter parts of the country (*NOb*, no. 5, 1977, p. 11).

A special effort was made to improve the coverage of the village school, where the biggest difficulty lay. Between 1965 and 1978 the number of rural children staying on in the ninth and tenth classes increased by half, as against a rise of only a few percentage points in the towns: the village, as a result, must almost have caught up in this respect (*Nar. khoz.*, 1978, p. 467).

The number of teachers remained reasonably stable, at about 2·3 million, though the decline in the number of pupils in successive age-groups must have meant temporary improvements in the teacher–pupil ratio. The quality of the teaching staff (at least as reflected in their educational levels) continued its inexorable rise, and by 1978 nearly 70 per cent were said to have higher education.

The part-time general schools continued the transformation started under Khrushchev. Although the total of pupils in them changed little, the size of the last two classes grew from 3·1 million in 1965 to 4·5 million in 1978 (against 6 million children, full-time), while that of the first eight classes dropped from 1·7 million to 257,000 (*Nar. khoz.*, 1978, p. 486). This sector came to serve more as a fall-back for younger people who had dropped out of school after eight years, and less as a remedial system for older folk.

The network of full-time schools also underwent some striking changes (Table 1.1, page 8). The number of ten-year schools rose, but the overall total of units was reduced to 137,000 in 1978, catchment areas increasing accordingly. The fall was mostly at the expense of primary and incomplete general schools, in both town and country. The differences between the two sectors nevertheless remained substantial, and the abundance of tiny primary units in the countryside continued to constitute a problem.

The extension of general school facilities had certain foreseeable social consequences. Ten-year schooling, as such, finally lost its uniqueness; the senior classes no longer functioned primarily as a reservoir of *VUZ* applicants; and the development of other types of specialised institution for 15- to 18-year-olds meant that fewer youngsters started their careers, however modest, without any vocational training whatever.

The growth of facilities meant more work for the administration, and here the Brezhnev leadership made a number of modifications. In August 1966, 'in accordance with the wishes of the union republics', the republican ministries of enlightenment were upgraded to union republican status and acquired, in M. A. Prokofiev, a minister for all schools throughout the USSR. The republics may indeed have pressed for this change in the hope that it would give them better access to central funds but to judge from the RSFSR it did not entail any significant internal reorganisation or change of function.[1] The new USSR ministry contained a Council for School Affairs which was to 'take full account of the peculiarities of the union republics in solving matters of school development'. The stability of the new order was exemplified by the fact that Prokofiev was still at his post fourteen years later. Also in 1966, the Academy of Pedagogical Sciences was upgraded from RSFSR to all-union status with the declared aim of 'increasing the role of pedagogical science . . . and co-ordinating pedagogical research'. The voluntary Pedagogical Society, founded in 1960, was provided with its statute in March 1970 (Abakumov *et al.*, pp. 491, 503).

The permanent commissions established in the USSR Supreme Soviet in August 1966 as part of an effort to involve deputies more actively in legislative functions have been the subject of much comment. Two such commissions, one for each chamber, were in fact formed to deal with 'education, science and culture'. Like their sister organs in the republican supreme soviets, they met a few times a year for discussion, the drafting of new laws and supervising the practice of old ones. We have yet to see firm evidence, however, that they had any notable impact on the formulation or implementation of policy, over and above that which their members would have commanded as deputies or professional educationalists (which many, apparently, were). For instance, the July 1973 Fundamental Law on Education in the USSR, said to be one of the commissions' major achievements, was an extremely conservative document and did little more than systematise existing legislation in a single text. The establishment of such low-powered bodies for educational matters was very characteristic of the day (page 110).

At the same time there was no relaxation of party control. We have already noted the appearance of a single Central Committee Department for Science and Educational Establishments about 1965. S. P. Trapeznikov, reputedly a friend of Brezhnev and a man of exceedingly dogmatic views, was put in charge of it, and he too retained his position for a decade and a half. The services of the local party offices and the primary organisations were perhaps not required to the same extent as under Khrushchev, since there was less hurried innovation; but 'schools departments' evidently continued to be set up at the town and district level after he fell (*PZh*, no. 18, 1973, p. 64). Local party offices still, of course, had their nomenclature lists and the right to decide what educational posts were included in them (Khaldeev and Krivoshein, p. 309). As for the primary organisations within the schools, they were encouraged to be more active by the conferment on them, in April 1971, of the 'right of supervision (*kontrol*)' over the work of the school administration. It is by no means easy to judge the impact of this particular rule, but three new foci of activity were mentioned in connection with it, namely, the expansion of out-of-school activities, the promotion of polytechnisation and the re-attestation of teaching staff, all matters I shall discuss in due course. The proportion of teachers in the Party remained at about 25 per cent, its 1966 level.

PROBLEMS OF ATTENDANCE

The growth of numbers in the ten-year school involved (to risk a tautology) bringing into the classroom older, and ever less able, or accessible children who might not otherwise have appeared there. To ensure this the authorities continued to rely on the system for registering children which we have already described, while improving other inducements.

Assistance for poorer pupils was extended somewhat. The general measures for alleviating poverty, including rises in the state minimum wage, reductions in income tax for the lower paid, improvements in pensions and financial assistance for low-income families, must have benefited many children of school age.[2] More specifically, a number of improvements were effected in the administration of the schooling assistance funds, including, in June 1972, extending them to cover the senior classes, which had hitherto been excluded (Abakumov *et al.*, p. 239). The fact that older schoolchildren – whose upkeep bore most heavily on parents – had been ineligible for help for so long is in itself noteworthy.

School meals services were improved by a number of measures on public catering and by the expansion of lengthened day schools (of which more in a moment). A decree of 7 January 1972 stated that hot meals were to be provided in *all* schools, though by 1975 only about 40 per cent of the schools in the RSFSR had their own dining-rooms and buffets. The large towns evidently did best: in Leningrad, for example, over 90 per cent of the pupils were said to be so nourished. The cost of meals was exceedingly modest (35 kopeks was the price of dinner in a Leningrad school in the late 1970s) but even this apparently presented difficulties for parents in the villages.[3] A decree published on 6 July 1973 stipulated that in cases of need free meals could be provided for up to 27 per cent of the children in rural boarding schools, and a 50 per cent reduction could be allowed on the cost to the remainder.

Two other relatively small matters may be mentioned at this point. In July 1965 the Supreme Soviet of the RSFSR decreed that children should not have to pay fares on their journeys to or from school, while rural authorities at the *krai* and *oblast* level had to ensure that school transport was available when needed. The abolition of fares, which were little more than nominal, was not of great moment, but the provision of vehicles could often have been. Unfortunately, the capital and running costs of this service had to be found from local budgets; and although, under the terms of another decree (2 July 1973), state farms were to be provided with buses from republican funds, collective farms were still expected to buy their own. As a result, progress was slow and by 1975 only 46 per cent of the village children in the RSFSR, that is, presumably fewer than needed it, had been provided with transport (*PMP RSFSR*, no. 283, 24 June 1976). Secondly, children's textbooks have always been heavily subsidised in the USSR, though the cost of them for poor people was never negligible. A decree of 24 November 1977 finally introduced the principle of 'free use' of these texts, henceforth to be made available through school libraries.

The Brezhnev years saw a more cautious effort to expand the network of boarding schools, and by the beginning of 1976 the number of children in them had apparently risen to 1·5 million, with 750,000 more in orphanages proper (Ivanov, 1976, pp. 29 ff.). The authorities released little information about these institutions, following the wave of interest in the 1950s, and one can detect no important changes in their activities. The reason for official reticence may lie in a growth in the number of orphans or in the difficult living conditions which seemed characteristic of all boarding establishments.

Ministerial complaints concerning whole *oblasts* have in fact been frequent, and I quote the following by way of example:

> In 1976 there were again cases of illness in [five named] boarding schools and in certain others. The cause in all cases was lack of hygiene . . . violation of regulations on cleanliness in catering blocks and unsatisfactory water supply and sanitation. The Aleksandrov boarding school in Sakhalin *oblast*, for instance, was not prepared for the school year in good time; the hot water system was not working, the catering equipment and refrigeration were out of order . . . As a result of faults in the guttering and drainage water flooded the bedrooms and basement. The children could not maintain personal hygiene; they had no soap or toothbrushes and drank water from the tap. (RSFSR ministerial statement, no. 524–M, 27 December 1976)

As for lengthened day schools, the network continued to grow rapidly, particularly in rural areas. By 1978 the total enrolment had quadrupled that of 1964 and had reached a massive 9·9 million (*Nar. khoz.*, 1978, p. 466).

Part-time schooling was encouraged by a few organisational changes. In November 1964 the school year in the RSFSR was made more flexible, and arrangements were introduced to permit smaller and 'parallel' classes. Day-release provisions were slightly improved in December 1969, to give time off for revision; and the Evening (Shift) Schools were granted a new statute in January 1971. This last, however, appears to have been little more than a tidying-up operation.[4]

The Soviet authorities always made much of the benefits available for part-timers, although, as we have noted, it was for a long time not clear what advantage was taken of these benefits. The mystery was partly solved in 1975 by the publication of a few results from a survey of 2,022 young workers employed in thirty-seven widely scattered enterprises (S. G. Vereshlovskii and L. N. Lesokhina, in *SI*, no. 2, 1975, p. 90). The data showed that of the 842 persons who were studying part-time, only 221 took advantage of day-release provisions regularly and another 181 intermittently. The unwillingness of the remainder to do so was not explained, but less than a fifth of the sample were actually prevented from study by their work obligations – family, academic or personal reasons being most commonly cited. My interviews with former schoolteachers have in fact suggested that many young people, if they can be persuaded to study at all, prefer to avoid the cut in pay which proper day-release may bring.

It is noteworthy that during these years the Evening (Shift) Schools did not rid themselves of many long-term failings. A check-up by the RSFSR financial organs in 1977 showed that the fall-out rate was running at 16·2 per cent a year (which gave a figure of 40 per cent over a three-year course). A USSR Ministry of Enlightenment inspection in

Moscow, Leningrad, five *oblasts* and a Baltic republic in 1976 revealed that in only half the schools did the pupils have all the prescribed textbooks, up to 70 per cent missed classes, and the level of achievement was low, since 63 per cent of the pupils were weak in Russian spelling and punctuation (USSR Ministry of Enlightenment letter, no. 55–M, 8 September 1976, referred to in *PMP RSFSR*, 28 September 1976 and 21 July 1977). Such results, it seems, caused a great deal of inaccurate reporting by directors anxious for their establishments and staff salaries. But a school course which annually demands some 700 hours of study from people who are working, and possibly not too highly motivated, can hardly produce a high rate of success.

NEW SCHOOL POLICIES

Although it was not allowed to crystallise, the need for further change in the character of the general school had been recognised while Khrushchev was still in office. Discussions of what should be done started in the Academy of Sciences in October 1964; and a decree on general education passed on 10 November 1966 incapsulated the most important proposals to emerge. This measure profoundly affected the drafting of the new School Statute of September 1970, and M. A. Prokofiev was still describing it in March 1976 as 'one of the most essential achievements in the history of the Soviet school' (*XXV S'ezd KPSS*, vol. 2, p. 180).

Although the decree did not cover all developments, it may serve as a good starting point for analysis. Six of its points were in fact of particular significance. Some of the course material, it stated, did not reflect the 'contemporary level of scientific knowledge' (a number of textbooks had still not been thoroughly revised since the 1930s); the teaching material needed redistribution by year of study, so that it could be presented to the pupils more consistently; there were too many obligatory lessons, which led to 'superficial learning' and damage to pupils' health; and academic standards needed to be improved through modification of the examination system. The other two points, which we shall need to discuss in separate sections, were that teachers were not (in a cryptic phrase) paying enough attention to the use of the collective for developing pupils' 'individual abilities', and that there was still a need for manual and polytechnical training.

(1)   *School Organisation and Practice*

As far as the teaching materials were concerned, new sets of textbooks (ninety titles in the RSFSR alone) were indeed introduced, but the process took ten years rather than the four originally anticipated. A proper analysis of the new texts lies far beyond the scope of this volume; but according to a subsequent (if not altogether convincing) report, the result was to modernise them, improve their theoretical content and systematise interdisciplinary links.[5] A 'Brezhnev' orientation certainly penetrated the humanities; and the sciences, too, were deeply affected, the object here being to remove the cruder 'production' examples of Khrushchev provenance without undermining too obviously the polytechnical value of study. The primary school programme now came to be fitted into the first three classes (witness the broken curve in Figure 1.1, page 7), although reordering of lessons was avoided. This change allowed some of the material to be taught sooner and children to be transferred from small schools to large ones at an earlier age.

The number of hours in the new 1966 curriculum was sharply reduced, but it remained, ironically, greater than it had been under Stalin, while the balance between the arts, science and practical cycles reverted approximately to where it had been in 1955 (Tables 1.2 and 1.3, pages 19, 20). If 'superficial learning' was an indirect reference to the old evil of too many subjects, then of alleviation there was none. In fact the new 'facultatives', or optional courses, and the reintroduction of military training (mainly for boys), implied further loading.

The military component is distinct enough to merit an extra word of explanation. It was reintroduced (in the ninth and tenth classes) under the Conscription Law of October, 1967 and the Military Service of June, 1968. The training involved took up two hours a week, with five days' field training after the ninth class, and carried its own mark in the certificate of maturity. By October 1977 the schools and pedagogical institutes together employed more than 50,000 military instructors, while 40 per cent of the establishments had their own shooting ranges! Some schools also introduced a fifteen-hour course in civil defence for pupils in the fifth class (*SDSh*, p. 157; *PMP USSR*, no. 140, 24 October 1977; *PMP RSFSR*, no. 419–M, 11 October 1978). A new concern with physical training, which became apparent at this time, no doubt had martial connotations. In any case this too was promoted by a string of instructions, covering both curricular and extra-curricular activities. Out-of-school physical training groups were given their own statute in August 1967.

The efforts at improvement so far described, though pursued for years, were not sufficient to avert sharp criticism in another, major, decree which was promulgated on 22 December 1977. The course content was still, it said, not adequate to develop the pupils' ideological and moral qualities or prepare them for life, and parts of the curriculum and textbooks were overloaded with 'excessively complicated secondary material'. It is difficult to know whether these points should be taken at their face value or whether they were intended to smooth the way for the new move towards polytechnisation, which was by then under way.

But in any case they lay behind some modification of the RSFSR 1978 curriculum (shown in full in Table 2.1). This reduced class work to a range of 25–32 hours a week, as against 24–36 hours previously; and slightly cut the total of hours, mainly at the expense of history, natural history, biology and facultative subjects (Table 1.2, page 19).

The examination system had been regarded as a *sine qua non* of high

Table 2.1   *RSFSR Curriculum for Primary, Eight-Year and Complete Schools, 1978–9*

	No. of hours per week in classes									
Subject	1	2	3	4	5	6	7	8	9	10
1 Russian language*	12	11	10	6	6	4	3	2	—	—
2 Russian literature	—	—	—	2	2	2	2	3	4	3
3 Mathematics	6	6	6	6	6	6	6	6	5	5
4 History	—	—	—	2	2	2	2	3	4	3
5 Fundamentals of Soviet state and law†	—	—	—	—	—	—	—	1	—	—
6 Social studies	—	—	—	—	—	—	—	—	—	2
7 Nature studies	—	1	2	2	—	—	—	—	—	—
8 Geography	—	—	—	—	2	3	2	2	2	—
9 Biology	—	—	—	—	2	2	2	2	1	2
10 Physics	—	—	—	—	—	2	2	3	4	5
11 Astronomy	—	—	—	—	—	—	—	—	—	1
12 Technical drawing	—	—	—	—	—	—	1	1	1	—
13 Chemistry	—	—	—	—	—	—	2	2	3	3
14 Foreign language	—	—	—	—	4	3	3	2	2	2
15 Art	1	1	1	1	1	1	—	—	—	—
16 Music	1	1	1	1	1	1	1	—	—	—
17 PT	2	2	2	2	2	2	2	2	2	2
18 Labour	2	2	2	2	2	2	2	2	2	2
19 Primary military training	—	—	—	—	—	—	—	—	2	2
TOTALS (weekly)	24	24	24	24	30	30	30	31	32	32
20 Practical work (in days)	—	—	—	—	5	5	5	—	22	—
21 Options	—	—	—	—	—	—	2	3	4	4

Notes (as given in the original):

* In schools where there is a need to perfect the senior pupils' knowledge of the Russian language, the RSFSR Ministry of Enlightenment recommends the introduction, for the ninth and tenth classes, of optional lessons based on the programme published in 'Optional Lessons in the Humanities', and the allocation of one hour (of Russian) a week in the classes indicated.

† One hour a week is allotted for the study of the 'fundamentals of Soviet state and law' in the eighth class, with a corresponding reduction (from four to three hours) in the optional lessons envisaged for this class.

Source: Approved by N. V. Aleksandrov, RSFSR Minister of Education, on 19 January 1978 (Order No. 26–M, in *Sbornik prikazov i instruktsii ministerstva prosveshchenia RSFSR*).

standards under Stalin. Khrushchev had simplified it, and his attempts at polytechnisation had evidently depressed standards. The attractiveness of the gold and silver medals, which represented the peak of attainment, had in any case been dimmed by certain changes in the *VUZ* admission rules. Although I have not traced any regulations on restructuring, the new leadership seems to have put more emphasis on tests and examinations. It also moved to reactivate the medal system. A decree of 18 December 1968 replaced the silver one by a certificate, tightened up the rules for issuance and removed the Khrushchevian requirement for prowess in production work (Abakumov *et al.*, p. 225). At the same time another shift in the *VUZ* admission rules restored to such awards much of their old importance (see page 156). Inevitably, there were reports of startling improvements in schoolchildren's performance as a consequence, and at one point the minister Prokofiev felt it necessary to criticise the old evil of inflated marking. The policy of keeping all children at school meant, of course, more pressure on teachers to pass borderline cases.

Given the known proclivity of the Brezhnev leadership for discipline, it is not surprising that some school practices should have been modified in that direction. The 1970 General School Statute simplified the range of marks given for conduct to 'exemplary', 'satisfactory' and 'unsatisfactory', presumably with the object of making them more effective. A satisfactory mark required, apart from observance of the school regulations, active participation in social work and practical labour, while an unsatisfactory mark in the last class could lead to the withholding of the school-leaving certificate.

A new version of the Rules for Pupils brought out in February 1972 followed its predecessors in most respects, but again with a few changes. The new instructions were more direct and concise; regard for labour and practical work was backed by more references to the observance of safety regulations; declared obedience to the pupils' 'self-governing' bodies (of which more in a moment) and respect for 'useful traditions' got specific mention; pupils were now required to protect the environment; and readiness to defend the socialist motherland was also mentioned. It is perhaps just worth noting that whereas both Khrushchev's and Brezhnev's ideal pupils were modest, honest, polite, perspicacious and neatly dressed, the former were 'truthful' while the latter were only 'principled'. One may speculate whether the epithet was altered for stylistic reasons only.

New provisions for homework, issued in April 1970, retained the 1951 range of one to four hours a day, yet concern continued to be expressed about amounts and irregular imposition. According to a circular letter of the RSFSR Ministry of Enlightenment of 30 April 1970, children in the first class often got from one and a half to three hours a day, and those in the tenth class, five or six hours. Teaching staffs were called upon to improve the quality of their lessons so as to obviate the need for so much extra effort, while inspectors and local authorities were required to keep the matter constantly in view (*SDSh*, p. 154; Korotov, p. 288).

The dominance of Russian as the medium of instruction for the Soviet peoples had long been beyond question, although Stalin had always permitted instruction in the most important minority tongues. Khrushchev on the whole adopted rather liberal policies towards the nationalities, and his school reform supplemented children's explicit right to instruction in their native language by instruction in any 'freely chosen' tongue. A number of observers (Kreindler, Lewis) have, however, suggested that the new formation was intended to facilitate the use of Russian.

It is impossible to form a complete picture of language use in the Soviet general school at any point in time, because proper statistics are rarely published. Yet there is no doubt that the 1960s and 1970s saw the end of teaching through a few minority languages, its restriction in others to ever lower age-groups, and more intensive instruction in Russian for non-Russian children (Silver, p. 29). By 1974–5 64·3 per cent of the children in the full-time general schools of the USSR were said to be taught in Russian, while Russian-speakers comprised no more than 52 per cent of the population. In the RSFSR the respective figures were 96 and 80 per cent (Kuzin and Kolmakova, p. 102). It may well be that even in schools officially designated as non-Russian (and in some several languages were used) the senior classes were in fact conducted in Russian.

Social activities in the general school received an unusual share of attention. The Brezhnev leadership was intent on introducing a semblance of democratisation in several spheres of public life, and this was one of them. I mentioned parents' committees in my outline of Stalinist practices. These bodies continued to function, with some local encouragement, during the Khrushchev years (Deineko, p. 456), but were not, it seems, the object of any marked concern. In December 1970 they were granted new statutes, which could have implied some re-activation. But they remained small elective bodies, with no power to change internal school practice or control the director's activities.

An annual meeting of parents was empowered to elect representatives, which met for discussion and called parents together at least four times a year. Its chairman had a seat on the school pedagogical council. The new parents' committees, like the old, could only make 'recommendations', but the Brezhnev regulations did play down the director's dominance and allowed the committee to appeal to the local education office in cases of disagreement with him.

The committees retained their old functions of promoting good attendance, ensuring out-of-school supervision, supporting cultural activities and helping with the maintenance of the school premises. To these duties were now added support for pupils' production work, vocational guidance, help with school dinners and in boarding establishments. More specific activities mentioned to me by former schoolteachers included collecting money from parents for school textbooks, spring-cleaning the school, organising the presentation of small gifts to teachers (a very regular practice in the USSR) and keeping any eye on delinquent families. I have heard very positive attitudes expressed towards the parents' committees, though the value of their work depended much on local enthusiasm.

More pupil participation in school affairs was encouraged by the promotion of 'pupils' committees'. These, too, were an older institution, covered by a statute of August 1950; it was replaced by a very similar one in July 1978. The pupils' committee was elected at the beginning of each school year by a general meeting of all the pupils from the fourth class up. It worked under the specific supervision of the teaching staff and the *Komsomol*, and co-operated with the Young Pioneer organisation; any decisions it made required the ultimate approval of the director. Its main tasks were to help in all officially approved measures, review attendance, make general repairs to school premises, run the self-service system (which still enjoyed strong encouragement) and promote good discipline. Given the presence in the school of teachers who were also class managers, of the *Komsomol* and the Young Pioneers, it is perhaps difficult to see the need for yet another organisation. The reports available on the committees give no clear indication of their usefulness.

(2) *A Choice of Subject for Senior Pupils*

The possibility of allowing pupils to choose their subjects of study, though on occasion openly discussed, ran quite counter to the spirit of the Soviet school. The exclusive role of the standardised, 'core' curriculum, and absence of any mechanism for 'dropping' subjects, made it impracticable. Polytechnisation, it is true, had involved a choice for some, but a choice of a very specific nature. The admission of this principle with regard to other subjects, albeit in a limited form, was one of the most striking innovations of the November 1966 decree.

Two kinds of arrangement were envisaged. Under the first, schools were allowed to introduce from the seventh class onwards 'facultative' or optional classes according to the pupils' wishes, 'for a deeper study of physics, mathematics, natural sciences and the humanities, and also to develop pupils' various interests and capabilities' (Clause 4). The options were supposed to 'reflect more fully . . . the contemporary achievements of science, technology and culture, and to take account of the local peculiarities of each school'; they could permit important additions to be made to the content of education without changing the basic course content. The detailed ministerial instructions which were sent out to directors in April 1967 recommended introduction for the following school year (*SDSh*, p. 129). In the event the 1966 curriculum contained an allotment of from two to six hours a week for this purpose, depending on level, or over 600 hours for the course as a whole (Table 1.2, page 19). Options in most subjects of the school curriculum, including PT and many manual skills from electro-technology to typing, were permitted. Regulations emphasised that options were to be completely voluntary, and that their introduction was to depend on pupils' wishes and the presence of facilities. If places were short, preference was to be given to the most enthusiastic applicants (*SDSh*, p. 133).

In practice the movement spread quickly. An official writing in December 1970 claimed that options had been established in all the ten- and 82 per cent of the eight-year schools, the position in the countryside being least satisfactory. The number of children involved was said to have reached about 5 million in 1970 and 8½ million in 1975.[6] The spread of options in this manner might have betokened more than mere curricular shift. Although children were still obliged to go to the single establishment serving their catchment area and could not be formally streamed by ability, options must in some cases have provided a restricted substitute for streaming and a flexibility from which many benefited. If pursued, it could have led to a real change in the nature of the general school.

The second kind of arrangement covered by the November decree involved 'a certain number of schools and classes with a more profound theoretical and practical study, in the ninth and tenth (or eleventh) classes, of mathematics and computer technology, biology and agrobiology, the humanities, etc.' (Clause 7). Interest in schools of this type had, as we have noted, been great for a number of years, and indeed some were already functioning experimentally. Khrushchev included provisions for them in his 1958 theses, but they had not appeared in the republican reform legislation.

A circular letter sent out in July 1967 contained details on how such 'profound study' was to be organised (*Spravochnik rabotnika narodnogo obrazovania*, 1973, p. 121). An essential step was the establishment of links between the school and a suitable enterprise, research institute or *VUZ*, together with the hiring of qualified outsiders to help with the teaching. The schools concerned were to be released from the usual catchment rules and serve whole districts and *oblasts*. The fortunate pupils were to be selected by interview, with due regard for the marks they had obtained in the eight-year school. Such a procedure was, apparently, publicly justified by the need to verify the applicant's ability to bear the extra scholarly stresses. The USSR Academy of Pedagogical Sciences was enjoined to work out suitable programmes and prepare the necessary textbooks.

Clearly, the transformation of an ordinary school to 'special' status was a much more serious matter than the introduction of options. Such status could, anyway, be sanctioned only by a union–republican ministry of enlightenment. No consistent data have been published on the extent of transmogrification, and even M. A. Prokofiev, writing in 1977, quoted figures that were 7 years old. Be that as it may, in 1970 the RSFSR possessed 155 schools with a 'profound' study of mathematics and computer technology, eighty-one for physics and radio electronics, thirty-seven for chemistry and chemical technology, and some eighteen others – a total of 291 in all (*NOb*, no. 10, 1977, p. 13). The sociologist F. R. Filippov gave, without quoting his source, a figure of 254 for the school year 1973–4 (1976a, p. 59).

It is significant in this context that the older schools for gifted children did not come under any palpable adverse pressures. The language schools retained their role as show-pieces of the system. The 'ordinary' music, art and choreography schools continued to expand, the numbers of pupils rising from 489,000 in 1965 to just over 1 million in 1975 (*NONK*, 1977, p. 141). Contingents in schools providing extra courses for children with a special aptitude for sport rose from about 839,000 in 1967 to 1·6 million by the same year. The Olympiad movement for children gifted in mathematics, physics and other sciences achieved all-union (as opposed to regional) status in 1967, and attracted many thousands. It is regrettable that so little precise information is published on this fascinating sector of the Soviet school system.

The development of the various 'special' facilities in the general school can be explained by social and economic pressures which are by no means unique to the Soviet Union. Indeed, the absence of some specialisation, even in a purportedly egalitarian school, would be sorely felt. Yet the emphasis placed on it in 1966 was particularly interesting. The notion that differences in the levels of educability of schoolchildren, though socially conditioned, were not destined for early disappearance, was well recognised by Soviet sociologists. There was doubtless a demand, particularly in the upper layers of society, for more selective and protected schooling. The rapid and apparently enthusiastic spread of options suggests, for example, that there was an initial consensus about their desirability in the CPSU apparatus, in educational and managerial circles among the parents and indeed children themselves. For a year or so after Khrushchev's fall liberal policies were pursued in several sectors, and slight differentiation in the senior school curriculum could be categorised as one of them.

Yet, particularly in its 'option' form, the movement was soon to lose momentum. The time needed for military training in the ninth and tenth classes seems, from the beginning, to have been drawn from this course, so as to avoid lengthening the school week yet again. In May 1969 the RSFSR Ministry of Enlightenment sent out a circular letter forbidding schools to institute optional courses without authorisation, and tightening the rules for registering them – which suggested official unease about their popularity (*SDSh*, p. 142). There is every likelihood that the new trend towards polytechnisation, which we shall consider in a moment, tended to impinge further upon optional courses. In any case, by the mid-1970s the fund of time available for options had been reduced by nearly 30 per cent, to some 460 hours.

The retreat from the options policy raises as many questions as did its introduction: in the absence of an official explanation, I can only suggest it was downgraded partly because it contradicted the growing conservatism of the Brezhnev leadership and partly because other concerns tended to overshadow it. Compared to the considerable variety of courses which can be found in the school systems of other lands, it was, of course, but a small enterprise from the beginning.

(3) *Further Developments in Polytechnisation*

We have already discussed the restrictions imposed on the polytech-nisation movement when its impracticalities became evident. 'As a result of an absence of teaching time and finance for production training,' wrote two experienced Soviet economists in 1974, 'teaching workshops were closed down in an overwhelming proportion of schools' (Sonin and Zhiltsov, in *Kommunist*, no. 14, 1974, p. 37). Yet the general school was still required to teach its pupils about production and prepare them for manual jobs; and once the break with Khrushchev's experimentation had been made clear, renewed emphasis on polytechnical training was probably inevitable. The 1966 curriculum retained labour instruction periods, and the options policy did not exclude the teaching of manual skills.

As time went by, a concern to encourage artisan leanings was expressed ever more forthrightly. An RSFSR ministerial circular sent out in June 1967 stipulated that schools with an adequate 'production base' were to be allowed to retain a deputy director for production instruction. Emphasis was laid, in an instruction of 22 May 1969, on teaching village children to handle agricultural machinery, so as to alleviate the continuing shortage of skilled labour in agriculture (*SDSh*, pp. 56, 140). The decree of 20 June 1972 moved the polytechnisation process forward again, by requiring local education authorities to set up, with the help of industrial and agricultural enterprises, 'school and inter-school instruction and production' workshops. (This followed rather similar moves to improve training facilities for young workers on the job; see p. 181). It also stipulated that learners' production brigades, forestry groups and other 'pedagogically sound' forms of involvement should be encouraged and perfected.

In August 1974 local authorities were empowered to establish, where conditions permitted, inter-school instruction and production *combines* 'for labour instruction and the professional orientation of pupils in the ninth, tenth (and eleventh) classes'. The instruction offered by the new combines, which had evidently evolved from the 1972 facilities, was to 'acquaint pupils with labour processes and the content of enterprise labour, effect the professional orientation of pupils with the object of preparing them for a considered choice of work, and instruct them in the basic skills of their chosen job'. This instruction was to accord with the local demand for workers and the existing production base (*SPR*, 1975, p. 370).

The overall effectiveness of these measures was not altogether clear. By the mid-1970s it seems, half a million pupils in the last two classes of the general school were doing automobile mechanics (in preparation for the long-awaited car age) and nearly half a million more were learning to drive tractors, combine harvesters and agricultural machines. Undisclosed numbers were learning typing, shop work, weaving techniques, electrical and metal work, and other skills. As for the teaching combines, their numbers grew to over 800 by 1978 (*Kommunist*, no. 9, 1978, p. 26).

The combines clearly had considerable educational potential, designed as they were to concentrate skilled instruction in recognised centres. But in general, in terms of quality there was still a long way to go. Manual training in the senior classes, according to a special decision of the School Council of the USSR Ministry of Enlightenment of March 1977, 'had not been perfected on a countrywide scale', while the quality and effectiveness of vocational guidance 'were not sufficiently high'. The three specific reasons given for failure were the ineptitude of the labour teachers (in four peripheral republics only 9 per cent of them had higher education), the lack of equipment and the low participation rate of pupils in out-of-school circles (*NOb*, no. 3, 1977, p. 19).

There was also more general criticism of the curriculum as a whole.

With the transition to universal secondary education [proclaimed *Pravda* on 23 March 1977] four-fifths of the general school leavers now get jobs immediately after graduation. Yet the thrust of the school programme – that is, the content and scope of the curriculum – remains virtually the same. In fact the 'modernisation' of instruction that has been carried out in the last few years has intensified this one-sidedness. Is there any wonder that many pupils, teenagers especially, display indifference towards learning and the grades they receive, declaring, 'I won't get into an institute anyhow, and I don't need high grades to get a job . . .' The times dictate that we redefine the pedagogical aim of present-day general secondary education.

The article mentioned readers' suggestions that the general school be reorganised to produce workers only, since 'courses of various kinds, lecture bureaux, the preparatory divisions of higher schools and widespread . . . private tutoring already perform the task [of preparing young people for the *VUZ*]'. The implication was that the school should achieve a cautious balance between the two extremes.

The school-leavers, moreover, were still reluctant to take jobs which fitted such manual training as they got at school. We know (to look ahead for a moment) that the popular orientation towards further study remained strong, that school experience was not important in helping pupils to choose a career and that manual jobs remained quite unprestigious. A study conducted in Orlov in 1972–3, for instance, showed that of 288 children who took a 'manual option' in one of sixteen trades, only forty-four wished to find work in it, and of these twenty-six had learnt driving, which was probably popular because of its wishful associations and the chances it gave for earnings 'on the side' (Shishkina, p. 83). In village schools there was the longstanding problem of the drift from the land.

So polytechnisation continued its inexorable course. The next major decree on general education – that of 22 December 1977 – was devoted almost entirely to the problems of manual training, and strongly reiterated the familiar gamut of possibilities, from curricular modification to school–enterprise links.[7] It showed that the authorities were again tending to emphasise the role of the senior school primarily as a mechanism for providing the economy with workers of a suitable occupational complexion.

The decree retained the principle of optional subjects, but contained the implication that obligatory instruction in manual skills could take up some of the option hours. (The experience of past years had not been entirely forgotten, however, in that much stress was laid on adequate teaching arrangements.) The introduction, by an order of 9 January 1979, of mass training for school 'labour inspectors' was hardly coincidental; neither was the publication of a statute on school–enterprise relations a few days later. The legal status of school workshops was similarly codified in March. There is, incidentally, some evidence that the new drive was not altogether approved by the educationalists. M. A. Prokofiev, discussing the December measure in *Kommunist* in June 1978, seemed intent upon saying as little as possible about its strong polytechnical bias, and emphasised that the general school 'could not take upon itself the functions of specialised trade schools'.

The resurgence of polytechnisation explains the unprecedented inclusion of a few data on it in the USSR 1978 statistical handbook (p. 467), showing that some 74 per cent of the full-time general schools were providing instruction in manual skills. This figure is, however, less impressive than might at first appear, since only about 38 per cent of pupils in all possible classes throughout the country were covered. Thus in arithmetical terms only one pupil in every two at schools where such instruction was given was actually involved.

Finally, it must be borne in mind that polytechnisation was always closely integrated with a number of other practical activities, including self-service and the use of child labour during holiday periods. The first we have already commented upon and needs no further explanation.

Holiday work seems to have been, if anything, more actively encouraged during the Brezhnev years than before.[8] In late July 1976, for instance, no less than 83 per cent of the children in the seventh to ninth classes of the general schools of the Moscow *oblast* were drawn into it, the main forms being 'work and holiday camps', 'pupils' (agricultural) production brigades', 'school forestry units', 'repair groups' and 'brigades working in industrial and public service enterprises'. Throughout the RSFSR about 1·7 million children participated annually in the agricultural brigades alone. The periods of labour seem to have varied from two to six weeks, with a four- to six-hour day, depending on the children's ages.

SCHOOLCHILDREN'S ASPIRATIONS: DISTINCTIONS BETWEEN SCHOOLS

Beyond the administrative problems of matching general school education with national or local needs there lay, as Khrushchev had found to his cost, that of modifying social attitudes. The most careful planning could easily be undermined by adverse public response. Studies of pupils' career intentions in the mid-1960s, not to mention the existence of voluntary youth employment, provided ample proof that polytechnisation was having little impact on popular attitudes and expectations. The question arises as to whether any shift can be detected over the Brezhnev years, and social surveys again provide the most convenient yardstick.

One of the most revealing studies to come to my notice involved 792 ten-year school leavers in the Cheremushki district of Moscow in 1973 (Kozyrev *et al.*, p. 52). The figures from this, reproduced in Table 2.2, speak for themselves. They show that, despite all that had been done by way of school reform, only about 16 per cent of the respondents actually wished to go out and work, which, to judge from the 'achievement' figures, was greatly at variance with the requirements of the labour market. The study further showed that of the 83·8 per cent who planned to continue their education, the overwhelming majority (nearly 70 per cent) wished to go into *VUZy*; about 10 per cent aimed at

Table 2.2   *Career Intentions of Ten-Year School Leavers (792 respondents, Cheremushki district, Moscow, 1973; percentages)*

Career type	Plan	Achievement
Study	83·8	44·4
Work	2·9	36·9
Work and part-time study	12·6	15·8

Source: Kozyrev *et al.*, p. 44. Small percentage shortfalls are unexplained: that in the 'achievement' figures was possibly due to respondents being 'lost' for survey purposes after leaving school.

secondary special educational institutions and a few per cent looked to vocational training in *PTU*.

It could be argued that these results were untypical, in that Cheremushki is a rather favoured locality, being close to the numerous *VUZy* of the capital. There is also the difficulty of estimating the gap between what school leavers think and what they say they think: many in this case must have known that their chances of higher education were more slender than those of older brothers and sisters, but were unwilling to admit it. Nevertheless, the Cheremushki figures are convincing in that they approximated closely to those produced by many other comparable surveys. Of the twenty-five listed by Yu. N. Kozyrev for the years 1965–72, for instance, no less than twenty showed 78–91 per cent of the respondents anxious to continue full-time study (*Vysshee obrazovanie*, p. 24).

It is not altogether clear how far the pattern changed later in the decade. The preliminary results of a country-wide survey by the Academy of Sciences Sociology Institute to hand at the time of writing appeared to indicate that the proportion of would-be *VUZ* applicants among school leavers had fallen to about half (F. P. Filippov in *SI*, no. 2, 1977, p. 48). This fall could have been a consequence of improved opportunities for trade training or of a popular reassessment of the value of *VUZ* study. On the other hand it may have been more apparent than real; 73 per cent of the children covered still said they wished to go on to full-time technical education of some kind, and only 15 per cent wished to start work immediately. I have not yet come across a proper analysis of the latest trends.

The Cheremushki study, incidentally, provided some rather rare data on differences in aspiration patterns between children in different types of general school. Table 2.3, which presents these data, appears to confirm what might have been suspected. 'Work' was unpopular everywhere, but children in the special schools (not to mention their parents) were least orientated towards it and in fact entered employment less frequently than anyone else. The boarding schools, where underprivileged children presumably predominated, showed the highest achievement in this respect. The figures for full-time 'study' revealed, by and large, the opposite trend, though this orientation was strong even among the boarders. The 'work and study' figures were more variable, probably because the study component could take several forms, but except among boarders they were still quite disappointing.

PLACEMENT PROCEDURES AND PROFESSIONAL ORIENTATION

Placing school leavers at suitable enterprises, particularly in the towns, had, as we have seen, caused considerable concern under Khrushchev. The matter assumed greater urgency in the mid-1960s, when the official faith in the power of polytechnisation temporarily weakened

Table 2.3   *Career Intentions by Type of General School*

	Special general	Ordinary general	Polytechnised general	Boarding general
Work				
pupils P	1	4	4	2
A	26	37	42	54
parental choice	—	1	4	—
Study				
pupils P	85	82	78	62
A	58	44	34	12
parental choice	89	91	85	65
Work and Study				
pupils P	13	13	7	36
A	19	17	18	17
parental choice	10	8	11	35

Source: Kozyrev *et al.*, p. 46. P = plan; A = achievement. All figures are percentages of pupils and parents for each given type of school. The small percentage discrepancies are probably due to rounding; the larger shortfalls of 11% in polytechnised school pupils' plans, and up to 17% in certain 'achievement' groups, are unexplained.

and the abolition of the eleventh class (in 1966) meant that two contingents of school leavers had to be placed simultaneously. Moreover, school leavers were now becoming absolutely dominant among new entrants to the labour force, as against housewives and rural migrants. So the danger of unemployment, if not the evil itself, was quite taken for granted. Youth unemployment figures for this period are rare indeed, but T. R. Zarikhta, writing in 1973, stated that the number of unemployed school leavers equalled 1–2 per cent of those working or studying, and that, owing to employment regulations, young people looking for work before the age of 16 were most vulnerable (p. 343). In addition, the problem of job-changing continued to be particularly acute. An immense study of 125,000 young people employed in seventy-three towns of the RSFSR in 1971–2 apparently showed that only 27 per cent intended to stay at the enterprise where they were employed (Kotlyar, p. 173). All of which easily explains the attention now devoted to the administrative mechanisms for placement.

Under the terms of a decree of 2 February 1966 the 'placement commissions' which had been established in the 1950s were turned into a cohesive nationwide network attached to local soviets. They were charged with two basic functions (Matthews, 1972, p. 328). The first was to administer the old quota system, which meant drawing up annual placement plans and transmitting them to enterprise managers for implementation. The rights of managers were now made a little more specific, in that they could vary the proportions of jobs they gave to young people between 0·5 and 10 per cent of hirings, as expedient. Also, the presence of learners was allowed for in the enterprise productivity plans and output norms somewhat reduced (*SZAT* 1970, p. 75; *Sotsialisticheskii trud*, no. 8, 1973, p. 138). Secondly, the commissions were empowered to issue work vouchers to back school-leaving certificates, thus ensuring immediate employment for the holders. The placement of certain specific categories of children, particularly orphans and delinquents, remained as before under the control of local 'commissions for youth affairs'.

The elaboration of placement procedures for school leavers was an integral part of a more general reorganisation of the labour market. An RSFSR State Committee on the Use of Labour Reserves was set up as a kind of country-wide employment agency early in 1967, and this opened 'placement and information bureaux' – the first such offices to appear since 1933 – in many large towns. These bureaux were specifically concerned with the placement of young people, though not first-time work-seekers (Matthews, 1972, p. 327).

Another change came in April 1969, when a set of statutes on the placement of general school leavers and other young people was approved for the RSFSR. These empowered the 1966 commissions to co-operate with republican State Committees on the Use of Labour Reserves and *Gosplan*. Verification of the readiness of enterprises to receive young workers, the correct use of juvenile labour and the development of training facilities were also part of their work.

The authorities have not, to my knowledge, released any general data on how these arrangements worked out in practice. But results from the RSFSR survey just mentioned help put them into some numerical perspective. Of the youngsters questioned, only 9 per cent had found their jobs through placement commissions, while 53 per cent had done so on their own initiative. Most of the remainder had been placed through other state channels (Kotlyar, p. 189). In some areas, indeed, young people could apply to a commission only if their own efforts to find a job had failed (Mriga *et al.*, p. 196).

The development of placement mechanisms for school leavers was accompanied by the introduction (or re-activation, after decades of neglect) of a recognisable system of vocational guidance (Nazimov, p. 57). In June 1968 provisions were made for the establishment of 'Councils for Professional Orientation' (to use the Soviet term) in all towns and districts of the RSFSR; these councils were to be supervised by the local education departments and the placement commissions, organising talks and production outings for school leavers. Their aim, however, was not so much to develop children's own abilities as to encourage interests which fitted local needs, and to persuade children to take the jobs actually available (Matthews, 1972, p. 330).

In December 1969 a large-scale conference was held in Leningrad to promote the movement. The participants concluded that experience gained in such places as Latvia, Lithuania and Leningrad should be used in building up the system with instructors, methodological literature, psychological research and other aids. The matter continued to receive considerable publicity, including mention at the Twenty-Fourth and Twenty-Fifth Party Congresses.

Even so, vocational guidance was not to enjoy the success anticipated. In December 1974 Yu. Averichev, head of the Labour Instruction and Professional Orientation section of the USSR Ministry of Enlightenment, cautiously criticised it as being 'in many cases' abstract, unrelated to local needs and confined to sporadic campaigns. Academician S. Batyshev, writing in December 1975, said that the consultation points envisaged by the scheme were still few in number, which 'negatively affected' the use of labour reserves. He suggested, amongst other things, that a short vocational guidance course should be introduced into the eighth to tenth classes of the general school, though it never appeared as a basic subject (*Sotsialisticheskii trud*, no. 12, 1974, p. 76; no. 12, 1975, p. 82). The December 1977 law laid particular stress on the need for improvement here.

It would be rash to affirm that the service will always be so ineffective, for the future may prove otherwise. Nevertheless, many surveys have shown that most Soviet schoolchildren look to other sources for advice on their careers. The example given in Table 2.4 is quite typical of the genre, and provides yet another illustration, albeit inadvertent, of how little the trappings of polytechnisation could influence young people's choice of a workplace.

Table 2.4 *Young Workers' Reasons for Choosing their Jobs, RSFSR, 1971–2 (percentages)*

Source of information on, reason for, choice of job	Young workers in	
	industry	construction
Parents' advice	15	11
Friends' example	20	20
School recommendation	2	3
Similarity to training received	7	6
Place where skill was acquired	4	4
Possibility of work–study	10	7
Place of preliminary practical experience	8	11
Enterprise notice	16	13
Placement commission recommendation	3	5
Closeness to home	16	7
Availability of hostel accommodation	8	13
Pay	6	8
Other reasons	17	23

The totals exceed 100% as more than one source/reason was sometimes named.
Source: Kotlyar, p. 173.

TEACHERS AND THEIR WELL-BEING

The Brezhnev leadership, to judge from the legislation available, was as neglectful of the teaching profession's living standards as was its predecessor. The July 1964 pay increase, as noted, lifted the average salaries of persons employed in the sphere of education and culture to a little over the national wage. Although these salaries had risen another 88 per cent (in monetary terms) by 1978, they again ended up some 17 per cent below it. Teachers had a pay rise in September 1972 which worked out at about 13 per cent, but this was again less than the average rise for the country. Not surprisingly teachers were reported to be anxious, when possible, to take on extra classes with pay. Although the closure of small village schools tended to reduce the numbers in the lowest wage groups, most teachers could still not hope to attain more than a modest standard of living.

Sociological investigations of their time-use conducted in the mid-1960s revealed a heavy work input, which, I believe, did not change much in the years that followed. Teachers in Novosibirsk and Sverdlovsk, for example, had a working week of well over fifty hours, compared with one of just over forty for industrial workers, though the extra burden was to some extent eased by the school holidays (Kolesnikov *et al.*, p. 320). Data from a sample of 434 respondents at urban and rural schools in and around Sverdlovsk in 1965 and 1966 showed that primary and village schoolteachers, particularly men, worked longest (Sergeev *et al.*, p. 324). Only about half of the time was, however, spent in the classroom (Table 2.5); the rest went on preparation, marking and meetings.

No wonder, in the circumstances, that a fairly high level of dissatisfaction should have been recorded. An analysis of the attitudes of 732 teachers in the Novosibirsk area revealed that only about half were positively disposed to their work; a fifth to a quarter were critical of it and the remainder were indifferent (Belyaeva, p. 375). There was not much difference, it seems, between the responses of men and women. The attitudes of teachers in town and country were also similar, and thus did not cast light on the problem of rural desertion.

The Brezhnev years saw a concerted effort to improve efficiency. The decree of June 1972 on general education stipulated the need for the 'systematic attestation' of general school teachers so as to 'stimulate a constant growth of teaching skills and creative initiative'. This was turned into a regular five-yearly process by a decree of 16 April 1974. The local commissions charged with the task were supposed to review teachers' work and qualifications and had the right to promote, transfer or dismiss them, though in the latter case appeal was possible to the ministry. The results set out in Table 2.6 suggest that the most palpable consequences of this exercise were the recognition of merit, and more rigour in promotions. Very few teachers suffered to the extent of losing their jobs.

Table 2.5　*Time-Use among Sverdlovsk Teachers in the Mid-1960s (working hours and minutes, per week)*

Time-use	Town	Village
Instruction and educational work	26–59	28–56
including: lessons	19–54	23–41
extra lessons	2–00	1–31
class management	4–29	1–52
'circle' work	0–36	1–38
Preparatory work	25–17	24–58
including: lesson preparation	12–18	14–00
marking, etc.	9–01	6–13
'circle' preparation	0–42	1–03
'methods' meetings	0–48	1–38
pedagogical council meetings	0–35	1–52
work with parents, social duties	1–53	1–31
Breaks	3–06	3–50
TOTALS	55–22	57–44

Source: Sergeev *et al.*, p. 327, adapted.

Table 2.6　*RSFSR Teacher Attestation Results, January–May 1976*

Total teaching staff covered	252,200
Attested	163,700
Exempted from attestation	88,500
Recognised as fully efficient*	125,400
including those deserving of reward	37,900
Recognised as conditionally efficient	38,200
including those:	
requiring further training	9,600
currently raising qualification	16,100
on whom no details given	12,500
Left because of inefficiency	748
Declared inefficient	70

* The Soviet term is 'corresponding to the position occupied'.
Source: Decree of the RSFSR Ministry of Enlightenment, 27 August 1976, No. 242.

A thorough investigation of the prestige of occupational trades and professions conducted among Leningrad schoolchildren in 1964 and 1965 gave schoolteachers an average ranking, with those in primary schools measurably below their confrères in the senior classes (Osipov and Shchepanski, p. 48). There seems to be no doubt that the profession was in need of a little social uplift. The introduction of state honorifics was, as we have seen elsewhere, very characteristic of the Brezhnev period, and educational workers were in fact particularly favoured. Beginning in 1965, a whole series of titles and awards was created for the first time, or introduced in union republics where they had been unknown before. They were capped in December 1977 by the all-union title of Honoured Teacher of the USSR, which surpassed all the republican awards existing.[9]

THE QUESTION OF STABILITY

Concern with development and change in the general school over the quarter of a century following Stalin's death, though perfectly justified in itself, should not distract attention from the stable elements in the system. All Soviet leaderships since Lenin have, in one way or another, been intensely conservative, and general education under Khrushchev and Brezhnev proved to have many relatively permanent features. A summary of them is not inappropriate at this point.

In the realm of educational aims and theory it is difficult indeed to see any substantive shifts. Of course, any change in the running of a school or in the content of the teaching has its philosophical implications, and the developments we have examined so far are no exception. However, the essential Marxist principles regarding the education of communist man remained intact. Both Khrushchev and Brezhnev tended, in my view, to embrace Stalinist, rather than Leninist interpretations of them, for the post-Stalin school remained closer in important respects to the pattern of the 1930s than that of the 1920s. Polytechnisation was admittedly an exception, but even Stalin was prepared to reintroduce this. There was no significant narrowing of the gulf between Soviet and 'liberal' theories on education or on the role of the school in society.

Strict political control of the system continued to be taken for granted. Some observers might be tempted to argue the contrary, pointing to changes in the pattern of administration and the political shifts we have documented. But none of these affected the overriding dominance of the Party and central government. What evidence was there, we may ask, that the Department for Science and Educational Establishments of the Central Committee lost any significant powers? At the same time, the stream of detailed ministerial instruction flowed unabated through state channels and showed little change. The educational budget and methods of financial control seem to have been remarkably stable, though there were refreshing gleams of concern with economic efficiency. School directors did not acquire or lose any important powers, nor was there any obvious delegation of authority within the school.

Many intra-school arrangements, such as the pattern of attendance, hours of instruction and classroom procedures, are to a large extent fixed by the physical capabilities of the children, and not easily altered.

But beyond this, much in Soviet school practice was preserved with exceptional care; and many so-called innovations, as I have been at pains to show, only marked a return to practices well known in the past.

Teaching remained controlled and formal, despite the increasing use of modern aids and appliances. The examination system retained its rigidity. A narrow Marxist, anti-Western slant was as characteristic as ever of the course content. Science remained supreme, and (apart from the polytechnical elements) the range of subjects taught in 1978 was virtually identical to that of 1947. Such experimentation as took place in individual schools had remarkably little impact upon the standard curriculum, and the fate of the options was disappointing. There was a continuing refusal to authorise differentiation or selection of the basic courses to suit pupils' differing abilities – though the 'special' sector was allowed to flourish.

The placement of leavers was a subject much discussed. But here, again, such changes as were made were very centralist in spirit; the school was still expected to train rather than educate children – if not for further educational establishments, then for factory or farm. The notion of schooling as a preliminary to dedicated toil explains the recurrent concern not only with polytechnisation and placement but also with vocational guidance and holiday work.

The old balance between the school, the 'social organisations' and society at large was also scarcely altered. The rule of the *Komsomol* and Young Pioneer organisations in running in- and out-of-school activities was upheld in both theory and practice. The degree of influence allowed to parents' committees remained very restricted. Parents, by and large, gained little or no choice in the matter of schooling for their children or say in what they were taught. And finally, public attitudes towards general education seem, in a strange way, to have been very resilient. Complete general schooling was for many years regarded as the pathway to the *VUZ*, and thence the middle and upper reaches of society. The latest social surveys available illustrate how tenacious that attitude proved to be. Such differentiation of the school as was allowed can be explained both as an attempt to improve the system and as a way of bolstering well recognised social distinctions.

NOTES

1   The available listings of RSFSR Ministry of Enlightenment departments for 1965 and 1977 are identical. These included an Equipment Directorate, a Main Directorate for Higher and Secondary Pedagogical Educational Institutions, a Directorate of Evening Schools, a Directorate for Pre-school Education, a Staffing Directorate, a Directorate for Capital Construction, a Curriculum and Methodology Directorate, a Main Directorate for the Supply and Sale of Textbooks and Teaching Equipment, a Main Directorate for Teaching Equipment Enterprises, a Main Schools Directorate, a

Directorate of Boarding Schools and Orphanages, and an Artistic and Technical Council for Toys (*Moskva – Kratkaya adressno-spravochnaya kniga*, 1965, p. 42; ibid., 1977, p. 73). It is noteworthy that by 1977 the ministries of enlightenment had a staff of 14,000 school inspectors (Panachin, p. 145).

2   The Soviet authorities have never been reticent about their alleged concern for public welfare. A detailed selection of laws may be found in Chernenko and Smirtyukov.

3   See, for example, the circular letters of the RSFSR Ministry of Enlightenment, 27–8 July 1976 and 11 January 1978, in *Sbornik prikazov*.

4   For details see Balov, p. 72; Mriga, p. 105; Abakumov *et al.*, p. 399.

5   Kuzin and Kolmakova, p. 62. See also Abakumov *et al.*, pp. 224, 227; *Vospitanie shkolnikov*, no. 2, 1976, translated in *Soviet Education*, November 1976, p. 34. The new Brezhnev-oriented party history, a textbook for general use, made its appearance in 1969, with further editions later.

6   *Uchitelskaya gazeta*, 22 December 1970, 1 January 1971; *NOb*, no. 7, 1971, p. 5; *Sovetskaya pedagogika*, no. 4, 1971, p. 43. A partial breakdown of subject options for the RSFSR in the early 1970s, by proportion of children involved, was: mathematics – 24 per cent; literature – 12·8 per cent; biology, geography – (not more than) 2·5 per cent; social studies, machine-drawing, astronomy – 1·5 per cent. This left about 60 per cent of the classes unaccounted for, a few of which were devoted to labour training.

7   It included the following points: (1) effective labour instruction and professional orientation were to be arranged with an eye to local employment; (2) 'social planning', a fairly recent innovation, was to be extended to cover the careers of all children leaving the eight-year school; (3) the amount of time devoted to labour in the ninth and tenth (eleventh) classes was to be increased from two to four hours 'within the confines of the curriculum' (since no indication was given of where this time was to come from, and it was not reflected in the 1979–80 curriculum, I assume that it took up optional classes); (4) all facilities for labour training (provided via channels such as enterprises, *PTU*, school workshops, laboratories, garden plots, inter-school production combines and instruction brigades) were to be used to the full; (5) new programmes for labour instruction were to be worked out; (6) better training was to be arranged for the instructors; (7) extra inspectors were to be attached to local soviets for checking training arrangements; (8) closer ties were to be developed between individual schools and enterprises; (9) republican councils of ministers were to select enterprises at which teaching workshops would be established and (10) help local educational authorities extend inter-school instruction; (11) the ministries of enlightenment and the Academy of Sciences and Pedagogical Sciences were called upon 'to introduce changes into the curricula, timetables and textbooks so as to include . . . the fundamentals of the necessary sciences, and guarantee a polytechnical, labour and educational direction in the subjects studied, together with their accessibility, internal consistency and logical order at all levels'.

8   If legal enactment is a measure of official interest, then it must have been intense, for the pupils' brigades got their statutes in February 1969, while summer practical work was similarly graced in April 1973 and the work and holiday camps in May 1976.

9   The title of Honoured (*zasluzhenny*) Teacher was now introduced in most union republics; formerly only Armenia and Azerbaidzhan had possessed it (Zhaleiko, p. 81). Between July and September 1967 the authorities introduced a Certificate of Honour for 'success in the development of education in the USSR, and instructing and educating the younger generation in a communist manner', thirty 'N. K. Krupskaya' medals for staff who had particularly distinguished themselves in the same way, and an Outstanding Educational Worker of the USSR badge for good work (Abakumov *et al.*, p. 476).

3
Low- and Middle-Grade Technical Schools

Vocational training of different kinds is an essential aim of educational systems in all advanced societies. Before the Revolution, as I have mentioned, Russia had a variety of schools and courses for this purpose. During the first months of Bolshevik power there was a great deal of contention about what should be done with them, for the broad reach of the new unified labour school was thought by many to render them superfluous. However, in June 1919 Lenin signed a decree setting up a department for professional (that is, vocational) and technical education in the *Narkompros*; and thereafter their right to a separate existence was beyond question.

The schools themselves were soon divided into two main categories. The 'secondary special' institutions, such as the *tekhnikumy*, usually offered a four-year course for children who had been taught in the second stage of the unified labour school. Lower-grade schools, including the new factory and works apprentice schools, or *FZU*, courses and workshops, provided much more limited training for the less able or ambitious. Both networks grew at respectable rates during the 1920s, but the *SSUZy* (as we shall call the secondary special type) expanded exceptionally fast during the 1930s too. By the time the Soviet Union entered the Second World War there were almost a million pupils in the *SSUZy* and a quarter of a million in the *FZU*. Even so, most young people were still acquiring manual skills directly on the job.

The two groups of institutions are best treated separately, and I shall devote the first part of this chapter to the low-grade vocational network. Consideration of the *SSUZy* will then, more conveniently, precede the chapters on higher education, and training on the job will be relegated to Chapter 6. Vocational training of the more elementary kind underwent a thorough organisation in 1940, when a unified country-wide system called the 'State Labour Reserves' was established. This is a good point at which to pick up its unduly neglected history.

THE STATE LABOUR RESERVES – CREATION AND CHARACTER

The Main Administration for State Labour Reserves was set up by a decree of the USSR Council of People's Commissars (*Sovnarkom*) on 2

October 1940. The development of industry, the preamble declared, demanded 'a constant flow of new labour into the mines, transport enterprises and factories', and the state had the task of 'organising the training of new workers from the urban and rural population, and creating the necessary labour reserves for industry'. Hence the peculiar appellation.

This explanation was not really adequate, however, as trained workers had been needed in great numbers since forced industrialisation began in the late 1920s. Many more specific factors may be discerned. These included the extra demands of the third Five-Year Plan, especially in heavy industry; the comparative inefficiency of the old *Orgnabor* system of recruiting new workers, primarily from the peasantry; the casual nature of much training on the job; the failure of the existing *FZU* schools to provide enough skilled labour (graduations having fallen off considerably after the early 1930s) and the virtual abandonment of polytechnical training in the general school. The establishment of the SLR must also be viewed against the increasing regimentation of the labour market and the fact that trainees of the *FZU* schools, *SSUZy* and *VUZy* had been subject to state direction for many years.

The main provisions of the 1940 decree may be summed up as follows. It gave the Council of People's Commissars the right to call up or mobilise annually between 800,000 and 1 million youths aged 14–17. Collective farms had to provide two recuits for every hundred able-bodied members, while the local soviets had variable quotas which were to be fixed centrally. Soon afterwards girls aged 15–18 were also made liable to the draft. Mobilisation, *ipso facto*, excluded the possibility of entrance tests or minimal standards of learning, though entrants were supposed to be physically fit.

A totally new school network could not, of course, be set up overnight, and many of the 1,500 establishments which the system comprised were taken from other sources. Some 900 *FZU* schools, for example, were transferred in this way (those left outside the SLR serving mainly the light, textile and food industries). The newly formed establishments trained workers in 800 or so manual skills; during the war years, the majority of trainees appear to have gone into defence and heavy industries. Between 1946 and 1950 – the first years for which more precise figures are to hand – three-quarters were directed into heavy industry, mining and construction. Nearly 70 per cent of them were fitters, turners, carpenters, masons, plasterers or electricians (Veselov, p. 352; Matthews, 1961, p. 249; *Nar. khoz.*, 1961, p. 589).

In organisational terms the SLR establishments were of two distinct types. The first were the trade, railway and mining *uchilishcha*, which provided two-year courses in the more advanced skills, mainly for young people with seven years of general education. The second were the factory, works and mining schools (*FZO*), with simpler courses lasting mostly six to ten months. Naturally the curricula in both types placed strong emphasis on practical learning, as the breakdown in Tables 3.1 and 3.2 shows. Young people who completed either type were considered to be still legally 'mobilised' and obliged to work for four years at the direction of the main administration, on normal rates of pay.

Table 3.1 SLR Uchilishcha *Curricula*
(*selected years; total courses in hours*)

	1940	1945	1951	1957
Production instruction	2,880	2,225	2,220	1,948
Special technology	324	286	364	318
Materials	—	60	108	—
Metal technology	96	—	—	120
Drawing	168	138	160	140
Basic mechanics	—	—	134	120
Basic electrics	—	—	52	60
Physics	144	138	—	—
Mathematics	240	207	108	80
Russian language	—	190	—	—
PT	180	164	164	140
Political studies	—*	164	160	140
	4,032	3,572	3,470	3,066

* The variant of the 1940 curriculum given by F. L. Blinchevski and G. I. Zelenko includes 194 hours for political studies and 358 hours for military training, with a total of 4,584 hours.
Sources: Veselov, p. 389; Blinchevski and Zelenko, p. 69.

Table 3.2 FZO *School Curriculum for Metal Workers, 1940*
(*total courses in hours*)

Production instruction	1,026
General and special technical information	116
1) Introduction to production	(10)
2) Safety precautions	(10)
3) Materials	(22)
4) Reading drawings	(28)
5) Machine-setting	(20)
6) Basic concepts of technical process	(14)
7) Arranging the work and workplace	(8)
8) Labour law	(6)
Military training	106
TOTAL	1,248
Political studies (extra curricular)	52

Source: Blinchevski and Zelenko, p. 70. Note that the sub-totals for the second entry add up to 118 hours; this discrepancy is unexplained.

The SLR schools were clearly meant to draw young people from the least privileged sections of society. The general educational content of the courses was small or non-existent. Draftees were offered few inducements, even judged by the harsh conditions of the day: free dormitory accommodation, food and uniform. They were not entitled to a formal wage or pocket money, but did in practice receive some remuneration for their production efforts. It was hardly coincidental that on the day the SLR were established, *Pravda* announced the introduction of fees for enrolment in the upper classes of the general schools, the *SSUZy* and *VUZy*, together with a reduction of some student maintenance grants. The balance of social priorities so revealed requires no comment.

(1)   *Administration and Planning*

The Main Administration for State Labour Reserves was a powerful body in that it had all-union status and was directly attached to the *Sovnarkom*. It established offices throughout the country, with the usual pyramidal system of subordination; the first mobilisation order that it issued covered no less than seventy-two republics, *kraya* and *oblasti* (Rachkov, p. 38).

The administration was headed by a director, assisted in the usual way by a collegium of officials. The departments in Moscow, which were never, apparently, listed, handled overall planning, control and implementation. The local offices bore detailed responsibility for the schools in their districts, and drew up their own recruitment plans within the national framework, passing them up the hierarchy for correction. They were then approved by the *Sovnarkom* and passed down the chain again for implementation; the actual recruitment on the spot was carried out by 'mobilisation commissions' consisting of representatives of the executive committee of the local soviet and State Labour Reserves office, a *Komsomol* secretary, a medical officer and a representative of the local trades union council (Rozofarov, pp. 3, 8, 40, 51).

The placement of trainees, to turn to the other end of the process, was a comparatively simple matter, since they were usually sent to the enterprises with which their school was linked. Plans for this operation, too, were drawn up by the local SLR offices and forwarded to the central authorities, to be approved or modified in the same way as mobilisation orders. Other checks were, of course, kept on the flow of young workers via the enterprise labour plans. We may assume, given the number of trainees involved, that much lateral co-operation was needed between SLR offices and local enterprises to fix estimates and smooth over difficulties.

(2) *Intakes, Placement and Coercion*

The first contingent of SLR trainees, enrolled in October and November 1940, numbered about 600,000 (different data were given in different sources). About half went into the *FZO* schools and half into the *uchilishcha*: three-quarters of them were boys and nearly two-thirds came from the villages. Enrolments, as suggested by Figure 3.1, were evidently rather ragged during the war years (despite at least twenty large-scale recruitment drives), and by September 1945 there were about 800,000 pupils in 2,750 establishments. In fact, in the course of hostilities the SLR trained 2·5 million workers; but, impressive though this figure was, it must be set against the 11·3 million instructed directly on the job. The relative merits of the two methods were for a long time a matter of dispute.

The response to the initial recruitment effort was hailed as a splendid illustration of the willingness of Soviet youth to acquire useful and well taught skills. *Pravda* announced (on 10 October 1940) that 1,100,000 applications had been received, and that in some regions there were several times as many candidates as there were places. Yet figures published in the newspaper *Trud* on 23 November cast doubt on this claim: indeed, the degree of compulsion which recruitment involved was, in social terms, one of the most disturbing aspects of the whole undertaking. According to this source, only 409,405 – or 71 per cent – of the 568,564 recruits were volunteers, which meant that over 159,000 had been drafted against their will. Even so, some of the schools were apparently not quite full, and many recruits were unsuitable. According to an unpublished decree of the main administration circulated in December 1940, trainees were sometimes physically unfit for work; below the prescribed age and educational standards (for example, without even primary schooling); and unaware of their responsibilities under the terms of the mobilisation orders (Rachkov, p. 52).

Mobilisation implies the existence of sanctions against persons who fail to comply, and SLR recruitment orders were sometimes said to have 'the force of the law'. Yet, surprisingly, there do not appear to have been any legal instruments specifically for dealing with refusal. 'Even the call-up into the trade [*uchilishcha*] and *FZO* schools was by no means mobilisation in the true sense of the word,' wrote Yu. P. Orlovski, a legal scholar, in the easier days of the 1950s, 'since there was no established judicial responsibility on the part of the persons concerned for refusing to appear before a call-up committee.' Furthermore, if they did appear but failed to go to the appointed school, they still did not break the law. According to a directive letter of the USSR People's Commissariat of Justice of 11 September 1943, recruits refusing to show up at an SLR establishment were to have the laws relating to mobilisation explained to them and their parents, and were to be subjected to measures of *social* pressure (Orlovski, p. 80). It is not easy to judge what actually happened at this distance in time, but such pressure, social or other, could not have been negligible. Hence the great emphasis placed on 'explanatory work' by local State Labour Reserves offices and other organisations which had access to possible recruits.

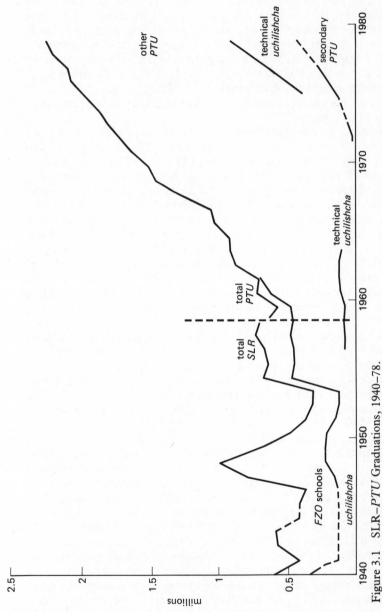

Figure 3.1 SLR–PTU Graduations, 1940–78.

Sources: Nar. khoz., relevant years; 1941–5 *uchilishcha* – average figures (Veselov, p. 373); 1944–5 *FZO* schools and totals are residual averages; 1946–58 from Matthews, 1961, pp. 249a, 250a.

Notes: Categories cumulatively arranged. Discrepancies of a few thousand in pre- and post-1958 data are due to an unexplained change in indices. No separate statistics are available for the technical *uchilishcha* between 1963 and 1976.

The legal position was, however, quite clear with regard to trainees once they were in the schools. A draconian edict of the Supreme Soviet, dated 28 December 1940 and entitled 'On the Responsibility of Pupils for Unauthorised Departure from the State Labour Reserves', stated that flight from a school, as well as 'systematic and crude violation of discipline, leading to expulsion', made the culprit liable to a sentence of up to one year's hard labour in a work colony. The harshness of this penalty may explain why, as an internal instruction of 1943 revealed, SLR directors did not always prosecute (Orlovski, p. 80). In any case the December edict appears to have remained in force at least for the duration of the war.

The legal position of young people who started their four-year posting was also hardly in doubt. Desertion at this stage was regarded as 'unauthorised quitting' and punishable under another edict – that of 26 June 1940 – which stipulated two to four months' imprisonment. SLR trainees remained on an official list throughout their period of mobilisation, and were liable for military service only after their four years were up (Aleksandrov, p. 132).

THE STATE LABOUR RESERVES – POSTWAR DEVELOPMENT

By the end of the war the output of the SLR system was down to about 400,000 trainees per annum, which was much less than in the best war years (Figure 3.1). The reasons for this fall lay in the destruction of a large number of schools during the German advance, the disruption caused by transferring others to the east, and, no doubt, the system's general unpopularity. A decree of 25 August 1945 revealed that there was also 'a sharp fall in the quality of training [it] provided'.[1]

Yet, faced with the enormous tasks of postwar reconstruction, the authorities decided not only to retain the SLR, but to promote massive expansion, concentrating on the *FZO*. The main administration was instructed to turn out, in the course of the 1946–50 Five-Year Plan, 4·5 million workers, as against the 7·7 million trained directly on production, and a campaign was started to improve the administration's work all round. As a result, the numbers of young people finishing at SLR establishments increased to a peak of 1 million in 1948, but this could not be maintained and it declined again quickly thereafter. The requirements of the original fourth Five-Year Plan (I say original, because it was revised downwards) were under-fulfilled by some 24 per cent, and only 3·4 million workers were trained by the SLR in the course of it. On the other hand, over 11 million workers acquired new skills at the bench (*Trud v SSSR*, pp. 303 ff., 320). Significantly, no firm figures were given for growth in the five-year plan which followed. The official reactions to this failure ranged from deprecation to defensive assertions that the SLR had, in any case, met the immediate demands imposed on them (Kurov, p. 111; Matthews, 1961, p. 252).

The instruction provided by the SLR changed in a fairly predictable way. The main shifts in the *uchilishcha* curricula may be appreciated from Table 3.1. The production element initially took up 70 per cent of the time, and this is said to have risen even higher during the war. In 1945, however, it was cut back to about 63 per cent, and remained at that level through the 1950s. The Russian language was taught for a while, presumably for remedial purposes. Most of the time originally devoted to physics and mathematics was transferred progressively to technical subjects (perhaps because the trainees' rising general educational levels made the former superfluous). Physical training and political studies, however, maintained their fixed allotment. The drop in the total of hours spent on production after 1951 should no doubt be regarded as a positive trend. The *FZO* courses in 1940 consisted mainly of manual instruction, with military training and a few extra items thrown in (Table 3.2). No subsequent curricula are to hand, but there is no reason to believe that they changed much in length or content. Although the intakes into both *uchilishcha* and *FZO* fell steadily after the late 1940s, the former institutions, with their much fuller courses, proved rather more resilient to decline.

The short-lived revitalisation of the system involved a strengthening of its organisational base. On 28 December 1947 the main administration was elevated to the status of an all-union ministry, and the *Orgnabor* recruiting offices were put under its control. A description of the new structure showed that while the old offices at the republic and lower levels, with their pyramidal system of subordination, were retained, no less than thirty departments monitored work at the centre. Five new regional boards were established to co-ordinate activities in the localities (Matthews, 1961, p. 257; Rozofarov, p. 365).

The SLR retained their ministerial status until March 1953, when, in the course of an amalgamation of central ministries, they were turned back into a main administration, under the scarcely appropriate aegis of the Ministry of Culture. This was when their fortunes, in terms of enrolments, were at rock bottom. But at the end of the year they were charged with the important task of training agricultural 'mechanisors', or machine handlers; so when de-amalgamation came in March 1954, the main administration was attached directly to the Council of Ministers. There it found shelter until it was finally dissolved in 1959.

(1)   *Intakes and Coercion*

The *uchilishcha* and *FZO* schools faced rather different recruitment problems, and are best dealt with separately. As may be seen from Table 3.3, recruitment to the *uchilishcha* was 50 per cent voluntary in 1946 (which meant conscription for at least 125,000 trainees) but had become completely voluntary by 1951.[2] This change may have been promoted by improved selection methods or more attractive living conditions, but the overall fall in enrolments was certainly relevant. The authorities, finding compulsory recruitment the least efficient way of filling the longer courses, may have simply abandoned it. The term 'call-up' was not, in any case, used in legislation after 1953 (Orlovski, p. 79). The formal abolition of mobilisation for the *uchilishcha* came only on 18 March 1955, as part and parcel of Khrushchev's drive to liberalise labour law. The fact that this particular decree lay unpublished for a whole year after it had been passed doubtless reflected the authorities' continuing touchiness on the matter.

Table 3.3   *State Labour Reserves: Involuntary Recruitment, 1946–54 (thousands and percentages)*

	1946	1950	1951	1952	1953	1954
Uchilishcha						
Involuntary recruits, totals	125	3	—	—	—	—
Percentage of intakes	50	2	—	—	—	—
FZO Schools						
Involuntary recruits, totals	165	151	79	70	63	68
Percentage of intakes	70	56	38	38	35	30

Source: Figures compiled by Lemelev (p. 173) from the notes of the Mobilisation Department of the State Labour Reserves, and adapted.

The *FZO* schools were far less popular than the *uchilishcha*. Only 30 per cent of the persons trained in them in 1946 entered of their own accord (which meant 146,000 conscriptions), and by 1950 the proportion had reached only 43·7 per cent. The jump to over 60 per cent by 1951 was again, no doubt, linked with a sharp fall in enrolments; but the rise in intakes after 1954, due to the transfer to the SLR of the agricultural mechanisor schools, could only have been effected by an *absolute* rise in enforced recruitment (to about 68,000). No mention was made of *FZO* schools in the March 1955 law, so they presumably retained formal powers of conscription. The voluntariness of recruitment certainly varied according to region, trade and other factors. Figures fortuitously available for the important *FZO* mining schools of the Voroshilovgrad (formerly Stalingrad) *oblast* well illustrate the point (Table 3.4). Here intakes were at first almost entirely involuntary, but after 1950, when they were for some reason cut back, conscription went down to about half.

We have noted that recruitment was conducted by 'mobilisation commissions' and that drives were at times frequent. In view of the element of compulsion sometimes involved, it is interesting to see how they were actually managed. The SLR offices were, it seems, responsible for little more than posting public notices: beyond that matters were mostly in the hands of the *Komsomol*. In October 1940, for instance, its

Table 3.4   FZO *Mining Schools, Voroshilovgrad* Oblast – *Involuntary Recruitment*
(*selected years*)

	1947	1949	1950	1952	1953
Total intake (thousands)	57·3	40·9	17·9	13·6	6·1
Involuntary (thousands)	54·2	38·6	9·8	6·1	2·9
Involuntary (percentages)	94·6	94·4	54·7	44·8	47·5

Source: Sokolov, p. 128. Compiled from materials of the Voroshilovgrad *oblast* Administration of State Labour Reserves.

Central Committee sent a circular letter down to the localities, asking for their active co-operation. *Komsomol* agitators were delegated (as one authoritative source put it) 'to seek out young volunteers desirous of entering *uchilishcha* and *FZO* schools', and to take 'an active part in the organisation and technicalities of the call-up and in getting the teaching and work premises ready'. Trades union officers were expected to lend a hand when possible (Rachkov, p. 34).

Co-operation of this kind was, as one might expect, renewed in the postwar years, and it became particularly important around 1948, when it took the form of four major recruiting drives (Kurov, p. 90). The local *Komsomol*, at the instigation of their central committees, arranged talks, concerts, exhibitions and even broadcasts. Sports competitions were held under State Labour Reserves auspices, and trainees were asked to send letters to their friends extolling the advantages of inscription. *Komsomol* meetings were used actively for recruitment purposes, as shown by M. N. Kurov:

A meeting of *Komsomol* members of trade *uchilishche* no. 19 in Leningrad passed resolutions which stated that all *Komsomol* members were to help fill the *uchilishcha* with a new contingent of pupils, and for this every member had to persuade at least one person to apply. The *Komsomol* committee was to keep a personal account of the fulfilment of this instruction . . . Groups of the best *Komsomol* members were to be appointed for duty at mobilisation points, where they were to talk with recruits individually, and decorate the premises with exhibitions of SLR trainees' work. They also had to post recruitment notices up throughout the town (p. 102, from the archives of Petrograd District Committee of the *Komsomol*, Leningrad).

It may be assumed that as recruitment shed its coercive character such operations became less necessary; but the *Komsomol* continued to play its part in the solution of other placement problems.

(2)   *The Quality of Instruction and Living Conditions*

The popularity of the state labour reserves depended in great measure on the living and working conditions in them, and complaints about these were continuous. As early as December 1940, a meeting of the SLR collegium was reported to have considered shortcomings which encouraged desertion; and a series of detailed, if ineffective, instructions for improvement followed. Living conditions were commonly described in such terms as 'extremely inadequate', 'particularly bad', 'not well prepared for the winter'. There was criticism of staff members who had a 'negligent and careless attitude towards instruction and towards pupils' everyday needs'.[3] It was as a result of these failings and of poor training prospects that 119,000 trainees left the system in 1945, including 77,000 (possibly a sixth of the enrolment) without authorisation (*Direktivy KPSS i sov. prav.*, vol. 3, p. 98). Although no more comment of this kind appeared in major enactments after 1948, there is little doubt that poor conditions contributed to the decline of intakes right into the early 1950s.

In social terms, the SLR continued to cater for the underprivileged, especially poorly educated boys from the countryside. The proportion of male recruits to all SLR establishments rose from about two-thirds during the war years to over 90 per cent by the early 1950s. The *FZO* schools took three-quarters or more of their entrants from the village, and the *uchilishcha* over half. But the two types of institution differed rather more in the educational levels of their trainees. In 1953 two-thirds of *FZO* and mechanisor school entrants still had less than seven classes of general schooling behind them, as against a quarter of the entrants to *uchilishcha*. Over the next two or three years both levels improved; the proportions dropped to a half in the *FZO* types, while the *uchilishcha* were able to switch almost entirely to seven-year school leavers.

In 1943 special four-year *uchilishcha* were introduced for the country's numerous orphans. The numbers enrolled rose from about 11,000 in 1944 to over 41,000, or nearly 13 per cent of all trainees, in 1952 (Bulgakov, p. 71; Blinchevski, p. 74). It was partly as a result of this sad function that the establishments acquired a reputation for delinquency.

(3) *Legal Control of Trainees and Placement*

In the immediate postwar years the 'desertion' law of 28 December 1940 was still valid, though, it appears, badly enforced. Several cases of schools failing to prosecute runaways were, for instance, recorded in the legislation of 1947, when the authorities were making yet another effort to reduce fall-out. Sometimes directors tried to conceal desertion, or were slow to bring it to the notice of the local militia. SLR offices ignored infringements of the rules, and courts were known to pass light sentences or none at all. A July 1947 order of the Ministry of State Labour Reserves, and several others, brought in more restrictions (Matthews, 1961, p. 276). School directors and enterprise managers who did not provide suitable conditions for trainees, or who failed to report desertion, were made liable to prosecution. The deserters themselves were to be sought out and punished. However, these pressures seem to have eased towards the end of the decade; since more reliance was placed on volunteers, such severity became self-defeating.

I have not found, in Soviet sources, any detailed instructions covering the actual placement procedures. The statutes of *FZO* schools and *uchilishcha* approved on 29 December 1946 stated merely that pupils were 'obliged to take the final examinations on completing the course . . . those who passed received a leaving certificate . . . showing their trade and qualification'. Such succinctness was in striking contrast to the flood of regulations elsewhere. The implication is that SLR leavers were presumed either to have made their choice when they entered the SLR or to have surrendered their right to one altogether.

In fact, most youngsters continued to be sent to work in the enterprise to which their school was attached – for instance, the proportion directed to other *oblasts* did not, in the early 1950s, rise above 15 per cent (Lemelev, p. 184). Leavers were dispatched to enterprises in batches, on a single drafting order. Any who left their jobs before their four-year term had expired were still punishable under the law on unauthorised departure of June 1940. Yet concessions were certainly made for personal circumstances. 'The desires and interests of the young workers themselves,' wrote one observer, 'should be taken into account when directing them to enterprises: in particular, they should be sent to work . . . near their families, if this is possible. Experience shows that in the overwhelming majority of cases the bodies which handle direction take into account leavers' desires regarding location' (Astrakhan *et al.*, p. 42).

The controlled placement of such large contingents of youth labour was no easy matter, and here again there were wide gaps between plan and fulfilment. On occasion whole ministries were unable to accept quotas of trainees which they had ordered; in 1953, for instance, six major branches of heavy industry, transport and construction were said to be 'unprepared' for about 33,000 leavers, ranging from 14–28 per cent of the planned intakes. Sometimes the SLR leavers were dispatched to enterprises other than those for which they had been trained, and sometimes managers refused to accept them because other workers had been trained in their place. In 1948 nearly 9 per cent of the SLR trainees, employed in over 5,000 enterprises, were said to have been given jobs in the 'wrong' trades (Sokolov, p. 213). The official figures for leavers who were actually left unemployed were relatively low, for example, 2–4 per cent in 1952–4, but obviously concealed many other difficulties. Official concern about them was expressed at regular intervals.

Despite the restrictions on desertion, many SLR leavers did not stay at their appointed posts. Departures, expressed as a proportion of the total number of young people under mobilisation orders, ran at 18–27 per cent between 1950 and 1953, though about half of them had some sort of permission to leave, if that meant anything. In the Ukraine the rate fell from 40 per cent in 1947 to just over 16 per cent in 1950 (Matthews, 1961, p. 283). Such figures are not, in my view, surprising, given the natural mobility of youth labour and the difficult conditions of placement.

To sum up, the facts available suggest that for all the propaganda that surrounded them in the first decade of their existence, the State Labour Reserves never became a universally attractive form of training. Many hundreds of thousands of trainees were conscripted against their will, the schools themselves were often of poor quality and the system of placement which followed them relatively inefficient. If any justification is to be offered for preserving them into the 1950s, it must be sought primarily in the country's acute need for trained labour.

LOW-GRADE TECHNICAL SCHOOLS UNDER KHRUSHCHEV

When he came to power, Khrushchev was certainly aware of the State Labour Reserves' disappointing performance; but he still hoped the system could be improved and better utilised, if only on a piecemeal basis. The failings of agricultural administration and the severe shortage of skilled labour on the farms, which suddenly became matters of great political moment, gave him an opportunity to try. In the course of 1954 a number of mechanisor schools hitherto run by the Ministry of Agriculture and Supply were transferred to the SLR's control. As a result, graduations from the SLR as a whole leapt from 324,000 to 690,000, and remained at about that level until 1958. The output of the mechanisor schools was held steady at about a third of a million. However, government policy regarding the future role of the SLR was not decided at this point, the proposed polytechnisation of the general school and the fall in the size of the relevant age groups serving as complicating factors. The SLR system, it will be remembered, had been established in part to compensate for de-polytechnisation in the 1930s.

Growth was to start again only when the system of vocational education was reorganised following the December 1958 reform, and it then (to glance ahead) continued uninterrupted through the 1970s. The part-time sector which was established in it also throve. By 1978 the total annual output of the 'professional and technical *uchilishcha*', or *PTU*, was over 2·2 million, including 441,000 part-timers; and by the mid-1970s the new system was training about a third of the young people who took manual jobs. The proportions of *PTU* leavers sent to different branches of the economy are shown in Table 3.5. As time went by, industry as a whole gained over agriculture, and significant numbers of youngsters began to be trained for light industry, food-processing and trade.

Table 3.5   PTU *Trainees by Branch of the Economy, 1960 and 1975 (in thousands; full-time institutions)*

	1960	1975	*Factor of change*
Industry	172·0	535·3	3·1
including:			
metallurgy	(11·5)	(35·4)	3·1
chemicals and oil	(8·3)	(38·8)	4·7
machine-building	(83·3)	(237·3)	2·8
wood-processing	(11·2)	(21·6)	1·9
light, and food-processing	(21·6)	(124·4)	5·8
agriculture	339·5	615·1	1·8
transport and communications	40·2	85·0	2·1
building	119·0	307·1	2·6
trade, catering, other local services	—	92·8	—
TOTALS	689·0	1709·8	2·5

Subtotals in brackets.
Source: NONK, 1977, p. 149, adapted.

(1)   *The Innovations of the Mid-1950s*

The modifications effected in the system up to 1958 were, with the exception of mechanisor training, rather minor. Individually, they served newly recognised economic need, brought the SLR schools more into line with the general school system, and were designed to efface the negative image of the past.

In August 1954, technical *uchilishcha* offering one- or two-year courses in advanced skills were established to cater for the growing number of young people who had already obtained a general school-leaving certificate.[4] When, in January 1955, the government launched a campaign to improve and modernise animal husbandry, arrangements were made to teach the mechanisors skills like electrical work and plumbing which could be used in a modern cowshed. A decree passed in August 1955 called for the expansion and strengthening of the establishments which taught building trades (*Direktivy KPSS i sov. prav.*, 1958, vol. 4, p. 472).

In 1956 some Latvian *uchilishcha* began to include material from the part-time general school in their courses, so that trainees had the chance to obtain a general school-leaving certificate as well as a trade. The practice was said to have been relatively popular, and was to be much extended later (Batyshev, p. 96). In 1957 the government opened *uchilishcha* with twelve-year courses, to improve the SLR provision for orphans (Veselov, p. 373). These institutions were in most cases boarding schools, offering both a full general education and a trade.

The March 1955 abolition of compulsory recruitment to the SLR *uchilishcha* was undoubtedly meant to improve their status. The introduction in the RSFSR of such minor honorific titles as Master of Professional and Technical Education and Honoured Teacher of Professional and Technical Education, on 18 July 1956, indicated concern over the standing of the staff (Zhaleiko, p. 57 ff.).

None of this tinkering, however, did much to improve the schools' work, and in 1956 a public debate started between representatives of the managerial fraternity and SLR officials about whether they were needed at all. Sweeping criticisms of the system, reminiscent of the critical decrees of the 1940s, were made by I. Kiparenko in the labour journal *Sotsialisticheskii trud* in February of that year. There was, he wrote, a gulf between the schools and the enterprises which they served, a lack of co-ordination in the delivery of trainees and a failure to provide training in the skills required. The quality of instruction was poor, the pupils' fund of knowledge small, and production practice insufficient. Training on the job was a better and more flexible solution (notwithstanding criticism by the SLR officials).

Kiparenko nevertheless proposed changes which he thought would make the State Labour Reserves more viable. The first involved considerable decentralisation of control, a concept very much in vogue at that time. The size of intakes, he said, should be decided by the enterprise managements and the SLR *oblast* offices. The main administration and the recipient ministries should issue only general figures, in accordance with the state plans, leaving individual orders to be directed in other parts of the country. Secondly, production training should be reorganised so as to give SLR trainees more practical experience and (by implication) earning opportunities. Thirdly, the amount of money spent on trainees' subsistence and maintenance should be reduced. Fourthly, courses should be made more flexible, so that trainees could be switched to other trades if it became necessary. Fifthly, they should be recruited from areas where they would later work; the existing situation, in which no less than 63 per cent of the SLR trainees had to live in hostels, would thereby be alleviated. *All* new workers, he concluded, should get their theoretical training in the SLR schools, but the main administration should not control the enterprise plans for hiring and training, as some people suggested. Clearly, these proposals called into question some hallowed SLR principles, such as centralised planning, detailed control and the assumption that as a training system it was unsurpassed.[5]

In the course of 1957 G. I. Zelenko, head of the SLR, published two articles refuting Kiparenko's arguments and restating the advantages

conferred by his empire (*Pravda*, 7 May; *Sotsialisticheskii trud*, no. 8).
After expressing regret, in his *Pravda* article, over the relative
stagnation of the SLR in the 1950s and the faults in planning, he wrote
warmly about the changes resulting from the imminent establishment
of regional economic councils. Within this new administrative structure, the SLR could become much more efficient. But there were other
good reasons for retaining the system: a longer period of training was
necessary for young people who would be engaged in automated(!)
production; the SLR schools gave consistent ideological and political
education; and they were still useful as a means of transferring labour
from one economic region to another. 'It is quite clear,' he concluded,
'that the State Labour Reserves system is the form of training and
directing qualified labour . . . most suited to present-day conditions.'

In his *Sotsialisticheskii trud* article he repeated the well-known
shortcomings of training on the job, namely, its poor quality, its
superficiality (which led to indifference on the part of trainees) and its
tendency to encourage managers to accumulate pools of apprentice
labour not envisaged by plan. He conceded, however, that different
kinds of apprenticeship had different requirements and that the
enterprise should provide training in low-grade skills that were, as he
put it, 'little needed'. Then there would be 'a correct combination of
the two types of training of new workers – the basic form, in permanent
state labour reserve schools, and the auxiliary form', that is, directly on
the job.

This defence of the system was, to judge from its history, anything
but well founded. But it was intended to satisfy several powerful
lobbies – the central planners who wanted maximum control, the
professional ideologists who naturally preferred a formal class situation
for their work and, most significantly, the body of educationalists who
had a genuine interest in improved training.

(2)   *The Establishment of the Professional and Technical* Uchilishcha

When the December 1958 reform came, the low-grade vocational
schools were very much a part of it, albeit in a changed form. To this
extent the 'preservationists' won out. The schools had their own section
in the law, entitled 'Professional and Technical Education', the word
'professional' again being used in the broad, Soviet sense. The future
was not without its shadows since the law restated the old principle that
the schools were to be self-financing – which meant instruction still
being subordinated to output. But in the event this principle was
muted, and, as the figures in Appendix C suggest, the *PTU* came to be
relatively well provided for.

The Main Administration for State Labour Reserves was finally
disbanded on 11 July 1959, and replaced by the USSR State Committee
for Professional and Technical Education attached to *Gosplan*. The

functions of the new body were surprisingly narrow, and restricted to such modest matters as the compilation of teaching programmes, methodology and equipment norms, the purview of trades taught, inter-republican transfer plans and the control of such foreign relations as existed. The schools themselves, together with the local offices and various subsidiary organisations, were handed over to the councils of ministers of the union republics. The short- and long-term planning procedures (extended in 1957 to include general school leavers and learners on the job), finance and school construction were decentralised in like manner (*SZAT*, 1965, p. 144).

Under the terms of new statutes published for the RSFSR in May 1961 and March 1962 (for full- and part-time institutions respectively), the old SLR establishments, together with a few more of the *FZU* schools, were turned into 'professional and technical *uchilishcha*' designed to take pupils from the now obligatory eight-year general school.[6] The urban *PTU* were to operate on a full-time or evening basis and offer courses of four to five years; in the countryside the courses were to last one or two, and be oriented towards agriculture. In practice some urban *PTU* also ran shorter courses, depending on the specialisation. The change-over was to be implemented over three to five years, depending on locality. The *PTU* took over the 1,100 or so specialisations in which the SLR schools had provided training, but a comprehensive revision of the various curricula had to wait until 1967 (Batyshev, pp. 155, 188). The new schools retained the main organisational characteristics of those they replaced. They were still closely associated with their base enterprises for purposes of production, training and placement, and were expected to be partly self-financing. Their directors were appointed by republican or provincial offices of the State Committee of Professional and Technical Education, and had fairly comprehensive powers. Teaching staffs were, as before, divided into 'production masters' who taught trade skills and 'teachers' who handled the general subjects.

No noteworthy changes were made in recruiting procedures, and entrance tests were not introduced. The main requirements for applicants were that they should be living locally, have completed the eight-year school and be in a reasonable state of health. If there were more applications than places, selection was made on the basis of school marks, though orphans and underprivileged children continued to have priority. Rather surprisingly, the December 1958 law had envisaged the partial abolition of maintenance grants for trainees, except in cases of particular need. Under a decree of 21 October 1960, however, the grants were re-confirmed, suggesting that the trainees' low earning power made abolition impracticable. The new statutes declared openly that trainees' output, during their periods of production practice, was to be paid for at standard rates, and the money earned either given to them directly or paid to the *uchilischcha*.

Trainees who passed the qualification exams at the end of the course received a certificate; those who did extremely well in both their general subjects and production work could gain a distinction and laudatory mention. The problem of placement was, as previously, solved largely by institutional attachment to local enterprises. There was no stipulation as to the length of time *PTU* leavers were required to work at their place of posting, but the time spent at the *PTU* was considered to be part of their work record, and early departure must have entailed the usual interruption of social insurance benefits.

THE *PTU* UNDER BREZHNEV

The system had not been reorganised long before the Brezhnev leadership came to power, bringing with it further changes.

The first area to receive attention was administration. Under the terms of a decree passed on 9 September 1966, the State Committee for Professional and Technical Education was granted most of the powers which it had been deprived of at its formation. This amounted to a massive re-centralisation of the system and an extension of the trappings of control over the whole youth labour market.[7]

A change of potential, if not immediate, importance was made in the status of the schools themselves. A decree of 2 April 1969 stipulated that they were to be 'gradually' transformed into 'secondary' educational institutions, based on the eight-year school, and provide instruction in subjects from the general school programme. This recalls the older Latvian experiment of the mid-1950s. Trainees who successfully finished such courses would get a 'complete general education diploma' as well as their trade certificate. In June 1972 a 'distinction' category was added, and the most successful trainees acquired the right to apply for a place at a full-time *VUZ*, like the best *SSUZy* graduates (Abakumov *et al.*, pp. 130, 240). The *PTU* with complete secondary education were designed to admit the more aspiring eight-year school leavers and teach them rather advanced skills.[8]

Given the general educational policy of these years and the need to refurbish the image of the *PTU*, this was a realistic move: but as S. Ya. Batyshev, an expert in such matters, revealed, there was another, less apparent, reason for it. By the early 1970s about a third of all *PTU* pupils were also engaged in part-time general education, the figures ranging from about 52 per cent in Moscow to 29 per cent for thirty-five *oblasts* of the RSFSR. 'This path,' said Batyshev (p. 95), 'could not be considered a rational one. Study at two institutions simultaneously increases the study load of 15- or 16-year-olds to fifty-six hours a week. This, of course, has a negative effect on their health, lowers their marks and causes a big fall-out from the evening schools. Neither must it be forgotten that the *PTU* do not by any means get the most capable young people.' The secondary *PTU* were evidently meant to ease this problem.

In the event, the new establishments proved quite popular. Their initial intake was set at 50,000, with a planned rise to 300,000 by 1975: in fact, by then it surpassed half a million. There were plans to make these *PTU* the dominant type in some districts by 1980 (Batyshev, p. 63). The growth of *PTU* based on the older technical *uchilishcha* for children who already had ten years of general schooling behind them was also encouraged. A decree passed in September 1977 reiterated that *most* ten-year school leavers should now get their vocational training by this means, and stipulated that intakes should rise to 800,000 by 1980 (*Pravda*, 11 September 1977).

By the late 1970s, therefore, the *PTU* had acquired a variety of forms. The three basic types were one- and two-year schools providing the simpler trades for all comers; the secondary *PTU* with longer courses for eight-year school leavers; and the one- or one-and-a-half-year technical *uchilishcha* for ten-year school leavers. In addition there were the part-time and boarding establishments, with most types further differentiated by branch of the economy.

The configuration of the *PTU* school year depended on the length of the courses. Those lasting one year were continuous, except for a two-week winter break, and finished in time for trainees to take the equivalent of an employee's annual holiday before starting work. The shorter courses lasted ten months of the year, with the normal 'school' winter and summer holidays. Production periods took up the greater part of the semesters, except in the timetables for *PTU* offering complete secondary education. Here it was limited for most of the course to twelve hours a week, with the last three weeks of the school year being devoted exclusively to production. A week was allowed every year for examinations.

As numbers grew, the *PTU* curricula received increasing attention and, following a decree passed in June 1972, further revision. The principal features of four courses, as taught in the middle of the decade, are shown in Tables 3.6 and 3.7. The first three, which cover 'ordinary' *PTU*, bear a strong resemblance to the curricula of the former State Labour Reserve establishments, particularly in the dominance of production instruction and the composition of the technical cycle. But the shorter courses now included extra social science topics. The secondary *PTU*, on the other hand, absorbed the bulk of the senior general school programme, which meant a greatly expanded 'general' cycle. The 1972 decree in fact lightened the weekly teaching load in these institutions from thirty-nine to thirty-six hours a week, modified the teaching of the general subjects so as to facilitate follow-on from the eight-year school, and removed some of their overlap with the old technical cycles (Batyshev, p. 262).

The upgrading of the system brought renewed efforts to improve the

Table 3.6   PTU *curricula, mid-1970s*
        (totals in hours)

	One-year course*	Two-year course†	Three-year course‡
Production instruction	1,184	2,034	3,072
Special technology	157	253	399
Tolerances and measurement	—	39	—
Materials	40	—	95
Equipment	—	—	—
Garment formation	—	—	270
Electro- and metal technology	—	173	—
Drawing (design)	54	110	129
Safety precautions	45	—	—
Labour and production economics	—	30	30
Political economy	69	—	—
Social studies	—	110	110
Soviet law	25	25	25
PT	54	110	188
Primary military training	—	140	140
Consultations	40	75	75
Examinations	18	24	26
TOTALS	1,728	3,123	4,647
Aesthetic education	50	60	60

* Repair fitter and servicing operative, oil–chemical industry.
† Repair fitter.
‡ Tailor, women's and children's clothes.
Source: Bulgakov, pp. 162–7, adapted.

standing of the staff. In April 1969 those teaching general subjects in secondary *PTU* were transferred to a system of pay and conditions similar to that enjoyed by their confrères in the general school, while in June 1972 the production masters were brought under the same attestation procedures (Abakumov *et al.*, pp. 130, 242).

SOME SOCIAL DIMENSIONS

The *PTU* retained the predominantly male complexion of the SLR, though the proportion of men fell from 86 per cent in 1955 to 72 per cent in 1970. This was in part due to the increased number of trainees for light industry, where female labour was common. There was an overall lowering of the age of the trainees, at least in full-time institutions, as the *PTU* increased their intakes. Between 1960 and 1976 the proportion of those aged 18 or more fell from 54 to 25 per cent. The urban/rural ratio remained almost constant, with about 60 per cent of the trainees coming from the countryside (Batyshev, p. 47; Bulgakov, p. 107; *Trud v SSSR*, p. 307).

Table 3.7   PTU *Curriculum with Complete Secondary Education,*
            Mid-1970s* (total courses in hours)

Vocational and technical cycle (total)	2,975
Production instruction	2,088
Special technology	223
Tolerances and measurement	39
Materials and machine-building technology	117
Drawing (design)	112
Labour and production economics	46
PT	210
Primary military training	140
General cycle (total)	1,525
Russian language and literature	230
Mathematics	349
History	245
Social studies	70
Geography	39
Biology	43
Physics	319
Astronomy	20
Chemistry	210
Overall total of cycles	4,500
Consultations	90
Examinations – no total given	
Options	
Foreign language	140
Aesthetic training	50

* Lathe operators, metal-workers, instrument-makers.
Source: Batyshev, p. 266, adapted for comparison with Table 3.6.

The improvement in general educational levels throughout the country was inevitably reflected among *PTU* trainees. Consecutive data from the mid-1950s are not to hand, but the proportion of trainees with a full ten years of general schooling behind them is said to have risen from 5 per cent in 1965 to over 31 per cent in 1976. Yet there is no doubt that the *PTU* took the less able pupils, even from the ten-year school; extensive studies conducted in the mid-1970s showed the *average* school-leaving mark of *PTU* trainees to be barely above the pass level. Attainment in general and theoretical subjects inside the *PTU* was also, it seems, poor. The lack of a proper system of entrance examinations meant that there was usually no minimum standard; the modest career prospects and the difficulty of going straight into a full-time *VUZ* after leaving a *PTU* undoubtedly deterred the more aspiring (*SI*, no. 1, 1977, p. 97; no. 4, 1978, p. 91).

The relative unpopularity of the *PTU*, especially among the more favoured groups in society, sprang not only from these long-term disadvantages and their peculiar history. There were also the social problems. A 1976 survey which was intended to be representative, and covered 908 *PTU* pupils of Moscow and four other towns, revealed that '52·5 per cent of the pupils miss classes without good cause, 26·8 per cent may come late and 18·1 per cent leave classes without authorisation. Nearly one pupil in every six has had some violation [of discipline] reported to his parents.' There was also insufficient participation in organised cultural and social activities. One of my interviewees, who taught in a *PTU* in Odessa in the early 1970s, stated that drunkenness was common amongst his charges.

Moreover, results obtained from a study of 2,255 *PTU* trainees conducted in Nizhni Tagil in 1975 showed that they hardly made better or more stable workers than those who had taken jobs straight after leaving the general school. As far as promotion was concerned, the key factor seemed to be advanced general schooling rather than a *PTU* background; such schooling was not common among *PTU* contingents over most of the period analysed. The same study did, however, reveal that youngsters from the secondary *PTU* were more successful, and there is evidence that these institutions outshone immediate employment as an option for some (*SI*, no. 3, 1977, p. 47; no. 4, 1978, pp. 87, 96). *PTU* of different trades, as other interview reports have shown, varied, like all other institutions, in their popularity and drawing power.

The placement of trained labour continued to be regarded as an integral function of the system. One would, for obvious reasons, expect *PTU* placement to be more efficient than that of general school leavers but less so than that of graduates of secondary special and higher educational institutions, who were still subject to detailed legal curbs. The authorities have been as reticent on this question as they have on others: but the findings of the above-mentioned 1976 survey regarding career intentions were, to say the least, disconcerting. Of the *PTU* trainees questioned, only 48·7 per cent intended to work in the trade they had learned; most of the remainder wanted to change their specialisation or proceed to further study, or had simply not decided. Attendance at *PTU* evidently did not bring about the kind of orientation in trainees' attitudes which was essential for the really successful operation of the system. So in this respect, again, there was a gap between the aim of official policies and the social response.

SECONDARY SPECIAL EDUCATIONAL INSTITUTIONS

Soviet secondary special educational institutions (*SSUZy*) are designed to train what might be called semi-professional personnel such as technicians of various kinds, nurses and para-medics, teachers for kindergartens and primary school classes, librarians, office and retail trade workers and supporting staff in the arts. As an element in the educational scheme, they are extremely important: yet we may pardonably claim that most lack any really distinct character. In some organisational respects which relate to the age and experience of their pupils, the *SSUZy* are like the general school: they bear a resemblance, which is becoming increasingly marked, to the more advanced *PTU*. Yet in many administrative matters they are run like higher educational establishments, and have long been subordinate to the same ministry. Study at them, for the great majority of the pupils, precludes admission to a full-time *VUZ* course for a number of years, so they are, in a sense, an educational cul-de-sac. Alone they might justify expansive treatment, but if we are to avoid a great deal of repetition they must be dealt with fairly briefly.

The courses of training offered by *SSUZy* vary in length. The simplest last two years or so, and are designed for ten-year school leavers. The more complex are of up to four years duration, with a considerable general studies cycle, and are mainly for those who left school early. The part-time courses take up to an extra year to complete. As in the *VUZy*, up to a score of subjects must be studied, and there is a comparable system of examinations and tests. Technical and agricultural *SSUZy* are required to provide a qualification in a vocational skill, so up to a third of the course may be devoted to practical instruction (Ushakov and Shuruev, p. 17). *SSUZy* have the same type of application procedures as the *VUZy*, though, of course, with different standards; their graduates obtain a middle-grade diploma (possibly with excellence) and a trade qualification, and are subject to a form of state posting. Together with these similarities go profound differences. The *SSUZy* are much smaller and simpler units, for, although they have in the aggregate almost as many students as the *VUZy*, they outnumber them by about five to one. They have a departmental rather than a faculty structure, and lack research facilities. They have a 'pedagogical' not a 'learned' council; 'lessons', not lectures; and 'pupils', not 'students'. Although the majority of the pupils are eligible for stipends, the rates have always been much lower than in the *VUZy*. Yet it is doubtful whether *SSUZ* pupils eat less than their more elevated brethren.

(1) *The Pattern of Growth*

In terms of growth the *SSUZy* have shown, like most types of educational institution, remarkable vigour. The number of pupils rose overall from 1·8 million in 1954 to 4·7 million in 1978, which was little less than the increase registered by the *VUZy*. The growth followed roughly the same pattern (Figure 3.2). Full-time intakes fell from a peak of 453,000 in 1954 to a low of 358,000 in 1957, a trend also observable at *VUZ* level (see page 101 below). Subsequently intakes rose steadily, reaching 812,000 by 1969 and 934,000 by 1978, which was evidently something like optimum capacity. The *SSUZy* have always had fewer people on part-time courses, but the proportion grew from around 15 per cent in the early 1950s to 37 per cent in the late 1970s.

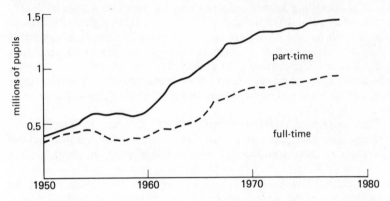

Figure 3.2 Intakes into secondary special educational institutions, 1950–78.
Source: Nar. khoz., relevant years.

Here, too, the expansion of general school facilities affected the educational levels of youngsters admitted, but in different ways. According to official data, the proportion of *all SSUZ* intakes with ten years of general schooling fell steadily from about half in 1957 to a quarter in 1965; perhaps the pressures on the senior classes of the general school prompted more parents to switch their children to *SSUZy* after the eighth class, so as to be sure they got at least the technical equivalent of a general education. In 1966, no doubt as a result of the double graduation from ten-year school, the proportion of *SSUZ* entrants with a general school certificate jumped to nearly 40 per cent, and reached 57 per cent by the mid-1970s. This change favoured the development of shorter courses.

It is difficult to judge the efficiency of the full-time institutions in terms of student retention, since no flow statistics have been published for them. Graduations have in some cases far exceeded the corresponding admissions two to four years before, implying either that 'repeaters' were swelling the numbers or that extra students were being taken on after courses had begun. But if we stoutly assume such aberrations to be fairly constant, there seems to have been a distinct fall in the efficiency of the *SSUZy* between 1959 (when it was around 90 per cent) and 1965, when it was something over 70 per cent. Should this indeed have happened, Khrushchev's educational policies must once more take the blame. By the late 1970s full-time retention rates seem to have risen again, and reached a level comparable with those of the *VUZy* (see page 149, note 4). The problems of student drop-out were also said to be remarkably similar.

Finally, a word on the branches of the economy which the secondary special educational institutions have served. In 1975 some 40 per cent of the intake trained for industry and construction, 17 per cent for agriculture, 13 per cent for law and economics, 11 per cent for health, physical culture and sport, 9 per cent for education and the residue for transport and other needs. The main change in this balance, as compared with the early 1950s, was a shift towards industry and agriculture at the expense of education, since more schoolteachers were trained in pedagogical *VUZy*.[9]

(2) *Organisational Development*

Throughout the post-Stalin years the *SSUZy* were administratively subordinate to the Ministry of Higher Education on the one hand and the agencies which employed their graduates on the other. Their internal development paralleled that of the institutions of higher education.

The first major enactments which concerned them after Khrushchev came to power (in particular the decree of 30 August 1954 and the ensuing ministerial order of 9 September) contained numerous general criticisms of their work, from the planning stage right through to the employment of graduates in production.[10] The *SSUZy* were said to be producing too few trainees and, like the *VUZy*, they had too many narrow specialisations. The decree called for improvements in all respects and an increase in graduations, so that two to four times as many middle- as high-grade specialists would be trained, depending on the branch of the economy. This kind of expansion, as the figures show, was not achieved, but the *SSUZy* were at least assured of growth in the longer term. Between 1955 and 1957 the number of specialisations offered was reduced from about 1,000 to 349, though the growing complexity of demand caused it to rise again to 450 by 1967 (Prokofiev *et al.*, p. 293). Not surprisingly, the more advanced ones tended to be reserved for entrants with a school-leaving certificate.

The secondary special educational institutions seems to have escaped most of the experimentation of the mid-1950s. They were also the least affected by the December 1958 reform. It may be that they were closer to Khrushchev's notion of an ideal educational establishment than either the general school or the *VUZ*; certainly they were less in need of renovation than the State Labour Reserve schools.

As it was, under the terms of the April 1959 RSFSR reform law, *SSUZ* courses for seven-year school leavers were modified to suit eight-year school leavers; the practical content of the full-time courses was increased (which in fact entailed lengthening them by up to a year); part-time facilities were expanded; and provision was made for the introduction of what we would call sandwich courses. On 22 June 1959 the Ministry of Education was turned into the Ministry of Higher and Secondary Special Education and although, under its former title, it had contained a whole directorate for the *SSUZy*, the new appellation reflected their increased importance. They were granted a new statute in March 1961, to codify the main changes which had occurred since the promulgation of the previous one in 1944. The other major enactment concerning these institutions in the Khrushchev years was the decree of 9 May 1963, which covered very much the same ground as that of August 1954 and does not, for our purposes, require detailed scrutiny. Though the *SSUZy* and *VUZy* were again criticised in parallel terms, the former seemed to come off more lightly.

The Brezhnev leadership treated the *SSUZy* in a cautious manner. The most important decree which concerned them during these years, that of 22 August 1974, resembled a July 1972 enactment on the *VUZy* and touched on similar administrative problems.[11] It established an 'all-union council' for secondary special education within the ministry, and *SSUZ* directors' councils in the localities. These bodies were supposed to explore better ways of running the institutions and improve co-ordination between them. The decree called for a reduction in the number of ministries which shared control over the *SSUZy*, narrower specialisation in each establishment and better definition of the functions of middle-grade specialists who graduated. Inspection procedures were to be intensified, the training of teaching staff improved and a system of quinquennial attestation introduced. The text also contained a number of familiar clauses urging, for example, further growth, better instruction, equipment and cultural facilities. It dwelt particularly on the need to increase party control and activate trades union and *Komsomol* organisations.

There were two minor provisions concerning the well-being and career prospects of the pupils. They now obtained the right to receive stipends while on production practice, so as not to be dependent on payment for their output, as before; and the proportion of graduates of any particular establishment who could apply for *VUZ* entry immediately after graduation (with, incidentally, a reduction of up to one year in the *VUZ* course) was increased from 5 to 10 per cent. In a word, the 1974 decree seemed designed to promote further expansion of the system and strengthen bureaucratic control, yet make the *SSUZy* a little more attractive as an educational option.

(3)   *Status and Selection Problems*

That the average secondary special educational institutions have always had much less appeal than *VUZy* may be taken for granted. There are obvious reasons for it. Young people who go to *SSUZy* may lay claim only to middle-grade jobs; their passage to a full-time *VUZ* directly after graduation is highly restricted; and lower state expenditure per pupil (as compared with *VUZy*) expresses itself in lower standards all round. The word 'average' is central to these remarks, for a few *SSUZy*, like the Moscow Conservatory and the Moscow Academic Choreographic *Uchilishche*, are extraordinarily prestigious, while others – KGB and Ministry of Defence establishments, for instance – may also enjoy a kind of privileged status.

The comparatively undemanding admission rules meant that many poorly prepared youngsters applied.[12] The most revealing account of selection problems to come to my notice was produced by an admissions commission in Leningrad for the year 1969 (Tsarkov and Korolev, p. 36). First, there was the lop-sided demand for places.

The greatest competition [stated the commission] with six to ten persons per place, is found, year after year, in the Seamen's Arctic and River Fleet *Uchilishcha*. [The reason for this is doubtless the prospect of a sailing career and foreign travel.] There are usually three to five applicants per place at the light industry *tekhnikum* (excluding the mechanics' speciality) and also for economic specialities in other *tekhnikumy*. Training in specialities linked with computer programming, radio and electronics is also popular, but the competition is not more than two candidates per place, as people know that preference is given to applicants living in Leningrad. Certain specialities in metallurgy, construction and machine-building are not popular enough. There is difficulty in recruiting young people for the metallurgical, industrial and land survey institutions; specialities in the housing construction, electro-technical and artificial limb *tekhnikumy* are not popular either.

Secondly, there was quite a high rate of failures during admission procedures. Thus in the machine-building and instrument-making sector (which took no less than 86 per cent of the full-timers) there were, to start with, 2·4 applicants per place, but after the examinations the figure dropped to 1·5, of whom only the most successful were admitted. Data available from a study conducted by D. I. Zyuzin in Gorki in 1972 suggested that the same rates obtained there. 'It is mainly candidates of the incomplete and complete Leningrad schools with inadequate grades who enter,' stated the Leningrad commission's report (p. 37). 'The majority have marks of 3 (that is, a bare pass). The expanding *SSUZ* network, the retention of the best pupils for the ninth classes of the general school and the growth of *VUZ* intakes make it harder each year to recruit the best pupils. Most candidates for the *SSUZ* entrance examinations do not justify the marks in their school-leaving certificates.' Preparatory courses, like those available at some *VUZy*, were set up to improve matters.

The need to increase applications for the least attractive specialisations probably explains a change that was made in *SSUZ* admission procedures in the mid-1970s. Candidates for places in mining, heavy construction, smelting and founding *SSUZy* were admitted, on an experimental basis, direct from the eight-year school without entry exams, if they had marks of 4 or 5 in their leaving certificates (*BMV*, no. 4, 1977, p. 4). The procedure was successful enough to be continued into the school year 1977–8.

The relative unattractiveness of the *SSUZy* inevitably affected the social composition of their pupils. Intakes into the Leningrad *SSUZy* at that time were given as 65 per cent 'workers' and 5·5 per cent 'peasants', leaving nearly a third to come from the 'employee' or white-collar social groups. This breakdown was distinctly more 'proletarian' than that of the local *VUZy*, where 52 per cent of the entrants were of employee origin (Tsarkov and Korolev, p. 39). We may doubt whether many of the employees who sent their children to *SSUZy* were *VUZ*-trained specialists anyway; and the weight of this group may have been increased by relatively high concentrations in a few of the best institutions. A further reason for their presence was suggested by the Gorki study, which showed that between 1964 and 1970 a quarter of all *SSUZ* pupils intended to go straight on to a *VUZ*, despite the legal restrictions, and that the majority of them managed to do so. Without this possibility the 'employee' component would no doubt have been even smaller. The career intentions of *SSUZ* inmates varied by social group in a familiar manner, members of employee and higher-income families being especially keen on pursuing this course (Zyuzin, p. 11).

Any account of the institutions providing training in manual and middle-grade technical skills in the USSR must necessarily be fraught with complexities. Both the low-grade vocational schools and the *SSUZy* produced, over the years, an impressive flow of manpower; but they both, in a sense, failed to develop fully as planned. The reorganisations to which the *PTU* system was subject, while erasing many negative features, did not allow the schools to achieve the dominance (*vis-à-vis* on-the-job training) which was so long desired. The secondary special educational institutions, on the other hand, retained their second-class image with regard to the *VUZy*. In social terms both the lower and secondary special establishments continued to serve the interests of the less favoured and possibly less talented children.

NOTES

1   The decree stated, for example, that trainees were put on accelerated courses and used for production work too soon; instruction was bad; textbooks, premises and

equipment (such as machine tools) were lacking; there was a great shortage of teachers; there were too many specialities; and newcomers were not assigned to suitable groups or were recruited at irregular intervals (Blinchevski and Zelenko, p. 82).

2 The available figures are taken from the unpublished Candidate theses of S. M. Lemelev and A. M. Butenko. Unfortunately the writers give no indication of how their percentages for 'voluntary' recruitment were arrived at. The voluntariness of an intake in any given year is presumably best measured by the number of applications over the number of recruits, expressed as a percentage. Probably this is what the authors did.

In spite of the difficulties of definition and the general unreliability of Soviet statistics, I think the information provided by these scholars provides a firm enough base for generalisation. The figures were, after all, intended only for a restricted readership, and since the data are disagreeable the compilers would hardly try to exaggerate them – on the contrary. The confidential local reports from which they were drawn would tend to be fairly objective. If the 'voluntary' category covered some 'partly voluntary' intakes, this would almost certainly have been mentioned.

It seems strange that Lemelev does not give any figures for 1947, 1948 or 1949, especially as he covers these years in his treatment of other questions. The omission leads one to suspect that there was a shamefully high level of involuntary recruitment, especially in *FZO* schools, at this time. If so, it would accord with the immense increase in the numbers recruited.

3 See decrees of 29 August 1945, 30 September 1946 and 30 June 1947.

4 *Reshenia*, vol. 4, p. 120. By the beginning of January 1957 about 17 per cent of all SLR pupils were said to be in institutions of this type, but this figure does not accord with subsequent data on the pupils' educational levels (see page 87) and seems highly inflated. A possible explanation is that the technical *uchilishcha* took many children who had more than seven years' general schooling but who had dropped out of senior classes before graduating.

5 Kiparenko also implied (although he did not say so directly) that SLR training was wasteful of financial resources. Indeed, the newspaper *Trud* (4 April 1957) showed that the cost of training young miners for underground work in various trades in the SLR was 5,000–6,000 roubles, as against 200–300 roubles directly on the job. State budget statistics yielded an average figure of about 1,500 roubles a year for every SLR trainee, whereas comparable outgoings on production training were, it seems, only a few roubles.

6 In 1959 the *FZU* schools trained 87,000 workers. No details are to hand on the institutions not brought into the *PTU* system.

7 It was now charged with the overall planning of vocational and technical education throughout the country, both in the *PTU* and on the job; organising the placement of *PTU* trainees and other school leavers; controlling lists of recognised skills; organising teaching programmes, pedagogical research and staff training. Financial control and the establishment of the state maintenance norms were also among its functions. The office structure which was set up to do all this work was still in existence in the late 1970s (Bulgakov, pp. 96, 99). In 1974 the State Committee for Professional and Technical Education was also charged with the administration of the new teaching production combines for general school pupils (see page 54).

8 Advanced skills specifically listed at this time were automation mechanics, radio and electrical work, agricultural mechanisation, typesetting and certain trades in the food-processing and light industries.

9 The older 'teachers' institutes' at this level were reorganised either as (secondary) pedagogical *uchilishcha* or pedagogical *VUZy*.

10 'On improving the training, distribution and use of specialists, with higher and secondary special education' (Karpov and Severtsev, p. 10).

11 'On measures for the further perfection of the administration of *SSUZy* and on the improvement of the quality of training specialists with secondary special education'

(*SPR*, 1975, p. 362). This paragraph should be considered together with pages 109–10.

12 By the mid-1970s, for example, eight-year school leavers with a certificate of merit, and officers and petty officers released from service, did not need to take the entrance examination at all, while many people – including those sent by enterprises and those with two years' practical work behind them – had only to pass the examination and were exempted from the ensuing competition (Mriga, p. 113).

4
Higher Education under Khrushchev and Brezhnev

The development of higher education in the USSR since the death of Stalin is very much a success story, though it was not without its frictions and failure. As with other sectors, our object here is to map the pattern of change, with reference, where possible, to social repercussions.

We shall adopt, in the main, the same approach as before. After a brief historical introduction, we shall review the overall growth rates and a few other major statistics. Next we shall consider administrative arrangements, both outside and within the *VUZ*, and the structure of the average *VUZ* course. The changes outlined in the December 1958 reform, including the development of part-time facilities, can conveniently be dealt with as a distinct topic. We shall then pass on to problems of research and staffing, and conclude with a summary of the main trends over the Khrushchev and Brezhnev years. Student problems are sufficiently well publicised and numerous to warrant a chapter of their own.

HISTORICAL BACKGROUND

The system of higher education which existed in Russia in 1914 was small but relatively prestigious. It comprised 105 universities and institutes, more than half of them private, with a total student body of 127,000. They were fed by a system of *gimnazii*, and were mostly humanistic in orientation.[1]

Higher education, by its very nature, presented the Bolsheviks with a number of awkward problems. In the first place the higher schools had enjoyed a measure of autonomy under the provisional government, and this had either to be married with the new state organisation or suppressed. Secondly, the schools admitted young adults rather than feckless children, so the political and professional content of their work could not but be of particular importance. Thirdly, higher and, to a lesser extent, secondary special education could only be offered to a minority, which called for some kind of selection. The social and political implications of this were to cause many headaches. Finally, the teaching and research staff, though mostly anti-Bolshevik, were highly specialised and not, in the short term, replaceable. The first decade of Soviet power witnessed many attempts, sometimes conflicting, to solve these difficulties in an acceptable manner.

War Communism and civil war reduced the *VUZy* (as they came to be called) almost to a state of chaos. In August 1918, shortly before they were due to start their first post-revolutionary year, Lenin, in a proudly egalitarian gesture, threw the doors open to all Soviet citizens aged 16 or over, regardless of whether they had adequate schooling. Academic ranks were abolished, and the so-called 'communist students' were encouraged to infiltrate every area of *VUZ* administration. On top of all this there were the appalling material shortages and political tensions of the day.

The years of the New Economic Policy saw a return to some kind of order and coherence. The first *VUZ* statute, promulgated in September 1921, 'reorganised the *VUZ* for the purposes of the social revolution' and reduced such autonomy as it had just enjoyed. The appointment of the rector, together with the confirmation of senior teachers, was handed over to the *Narkompros*. Deanships and more junior posts were to be filled at the discretion of *VUZ* learned councils. The communist students, who made up only a few per cent of the total but had laid claim to considerable power, were expected to accept the new order and assist by keeping an eye on the 'bourgeois' faculty. Palpable material privileges were soon given to the latter, particularly in the matter of rations and living space, and a commission was set up to safeguard their interests. It seems that in the relatively relaxed atmosphere of NEP a temporary *modus vivendi* was achieved.

The new regime clearly had to replace all courses containing un-Marxist or anti-Marxist features by others of an acceptable hue, and several steps were taken to this end. Teachers of an overtly anti-Bolshevik persuasion were dismissed: in February 1921 the Institute of Red Professors was set up to train communists for teaching approved versions of the social sciences. Marxism was made obligatory for all *VUZ* students in the same year (though implementation of this measure ran into great difficulties). Another Bolshevik principle was acknowledged in January 1925, when the 'link with production' was declared to be of primary importance, and production practice was made an integral part of the *VUZ* course. About the same time more emphasis was placed on the expansion of technical courses.

The problem of student selection was intimately linked with that of admission tests. The first result of the open admissions policy had been a flood of applications from persons totally unequipped for study. It was in order to control this situation that a system of preparatory faculties, or *rabfaki*, was started for workers and peasants in February 1919. The idea suited the circumstances of the day, and by 1932 the number of participants had grown to a third of a million. They were entitled to a modest state stipend while they studied. The *rabfak* system helped workers and peasants, but proved insufficient to counter *VUZ* teachers' preferences for well trained applicants from more cultured backgrounds. Open admission was therefore supplemented by a system of nomination through state organisations, on the understanding that the nominees would be of true worker or peasant extraction. Even so, by 1923 only about a third of the *VUZ* students were from these groups, the remainder being divided about equally between Soviet state employees and representatives of the former bourgeoisie.

As the decade progressed, however, the deleterious effects of proletarianisation and the neglect of proper entrance examinations became ever more apparent. In 1925, for instance, graduation rates in the *VUZy* of the RSFSR were running at well under 10 per cent of intakes (*Kulturnoe stroitelstvo SSSR*, 1956, p. 201; Fitzpatrick, p. 106). Fall-out was exacerbated by a purge of Trotskyists among the student body.

Concern with quality prompted the *VUZ* authorities, from 1926, to take the majority of applicants on an open (that is, unnominated) basis, nomination being reserved for national minorities, the children of the military and a few other groups. This shift involved greater reliance on admission examinations as a method of sieving out the most able. Yet, perhaps because it was backed by better *rabfak* preparation, the new policy did not cause any long-term drop in the proportion of students of worker or peasant origin; indeed, these contingents rose to about half of the total in 1927. Overall enrolments by this time recovered from setbacks earlier in the decade, and were running at nearly 170,000.

Stalinisation of the Soviet *VUZ* is clearly perceptible from the middle of 1928, when the Party passed the first of an important series of decrees on higher education, and a new statute came into operation. The process, like so much else that Stalin did, was proclaimed as a sharp departure from an existing unsatisfactory situation; but it can just as easily be interpreted as a genuinely Leninist development.

The change which received most publicity was the increase in full-time enrolments. These jumped overall to half a million by 1932, and by 1940 reached 812,000, in 817 *VUZy*. *VUZ* research activities were stepped up and enrolments in the post-graduate, or *aspirantura* system (which had been started in the middle of the decade) rose from 2,000 to 13,000. The contingents in secondary special educational institutions, incidentally, rose from 190,000 to 975,000 over the same period. The expansion was designed primarily to satisfy the needs of industry, transport and the teaching profession itself; the agricultural and health sectors gained least. At the same time there was an emphasis on narrowing specialisations, shortening courses (from over four to as little as three years) and increasing their production element.

As the 1930s progressed, however, the problems of hurried growth made themselves felt, and we again find emphasis being placed on quality. *VUZ* practice became more formalised. After 1932 the policy of proletarianisation was abandoned, and the decade saw a growing predominance of children from white-collar families in *VUZ* auditoria. The difference as against pre-revolutionary days lay in their Soviet rather than bourgeois provenance. An ever larger proportion of students was taken from the new tenth classes of the general school; completion of this, at one time, released candidates from *VUZ* entry examinations altogether.

Part-time courses had been common since the early 1920s, but they were often haphazard and not usually examined. After 1929 they were subjected to increasing standardisation; and finally, by a decree of August 1938, they were brought into alignment with full-time courses. The students taking them were by then said to number nearly a quarter of a million.

The increase in the number of *VUZy* (usually effected by splitting institutions) required considerable capital expenditure, and one way of meeting it was to extend dual control of *VUZy* between the *Narkompros* and the people's commissariats which received all, or the majority of, graduates. At one point the number of commissariats so charged grew to thirty-four, but it was cut back to seven or eight in the middle of the decade. Geographically, most of the new *VUZy* were established outside European Russia – in the Ukraine, the Caucasus and Central Asia. The emphasis on planning which characterised industrialisation after 1928 also expressed itself in the introduction of a strict system of placement and employment of graduates. This was still operative, with remarkably few changes, half a century later.

The technical *VUZy* acquired their own central administrative body, the All-Union Committee for Higher Technical Education, in 1932, which was transformed into a committee for handling all higher education in 1936. Internal *VUZ* organisation was covered in some detail by decrees of 19 September 1932 and 23 June 1936; here we find a formalisation of course structure (with 'electives', or optional subjects), regular examinations, provision for student discipline and the restrictions on admission to research which were enshrined in the final Stalin *VUZ* statute of September 1938.

VUZ staffs could not but be profoundly affected by all these developments. The 'bourgeois' specialists, in higher education as elsewhere, suffered in consequence of the Shakhty trials of 1928 and the purges of the late 1930s. It is doubtful whether Stalin's often quoted statement of June 1931, about the need to care for these people, offered much protection. The higher their status, the more likely they were to be arrested. Those who kept their jobs were, however, quickly swamped by an influx of politically reliable newcomers; the number of *VUZ* teachers, according to De Witt, rose from about 29,000 in 1927 to over 50,000 by 1940. Academics were encouraged, as the 1930s progressed, by the retention of earlier material benefits, the reintroduction of ranks, access to state honorifics and a growing differentiation in salaries.

The Second World War was as destructive for the *VUZy* as it was for other sectors of education. At its most desperate point only 300 institutions were functioning, while student numbers fell to 227,000. The later war, and post-war, years were devoted to rapid reconstruction, and by 1946 the former number of institutions and enrolments had been surpassed. The development bore, however, a quantitative rather than a qualitative character; and as we shall discover in the ensuing pages, when the Khrushchev leadership came to power, it was still confronted by a system bearing the hallmarks of the late 1930s.

GROWTH AND COVERAGE: A BIRD'S EYE VIEW

The main growth trends in the higher education sector can be easily summarised. Government policy after the death of Stalin consistently favoured an increase in student numbers, and the student body grew overall from about 1½ million in 1953 to just over 5 million in 1978. Intakes (arguably the best measure of official intentions) rose from 431,000 to 1,026,000 over the same period. By the late 1970s there were said to be over nineteen students per thousand of the population, and the USSR claimed to be among the world's leaders in this respect; the *VUZy* were by then said to be producing 93 per cent of the economy's requirement of graduates (*VVSh*, no. 9, 1976, p. 15).

Closer inspection reveals some interesting variations in the rates of growth (Figure 4.1). Both full and part-time intakes were rising steadily in the early 1950s, but between 1954 and 1958 the Khrushchev leadership allowed them to drop back. This was despite an obvious increase in the popular demand for *VUZ* places and the continuing need for specialists. No proper explanation for this failure has ever been offered, to my knowledge, but the most likely one, as reflected in the legislation, was official hesitancy over the *VUZ–SSUZ* ratios and the proper function of higher education. After 1959 intakes to full-time courses grew at an extraordinarily steady rate for two decades. The part-time sector also did extremely well, although correspondence courses suffered something of a set-back after 1966, as a consequence of policies which we shall need to consider. It is noteworthy that even so in 1978 part-time admissions made up some 40 per cent of the stream.

The total supply of *VUZ* graduates, year by year, needs to be considered together with that of graduates of the secondary special educational institutions. The decree on higher and secondary special education promulgated in August 1954 evinced concern about the over-production of *VUZ* (as opposed to *SSUZ*) graduates, especially for the spheres of material production, transport and communications. To judge from the data available, some quick improvements were made in consequence. The output of middle-grade specialists was increased very much faster than that of *VUZ* graduates until the peak year of

1958, the ratio changing from 1·4:1 to 1·9:1 in favour of the former. But afterwards it again receded, and in 1977, at 1·4:1 was still said to be unsatisfactory (*NONK*, 1971, p. 190; Ushakov and Shuruev, p. 63).

The 'mix' of *VUZ* graduates by specialisation is another matter which proved troublesome. Emphasis on the qualifications most useful

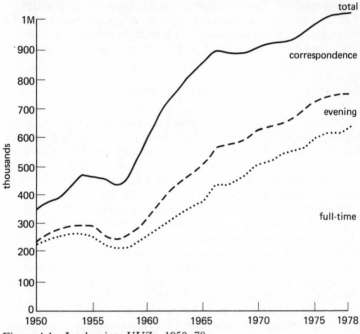

Figure 4.1   Intakes into *VUZy*, 1950–78.

Note: The types of study are vertically (cumulatively) arranged, with the top line of the graph showing the overall total.

Sources: NONK, 1977, p. 246; *Nar. khoz.*, relevant years.

for industry, construction, transport and communications was, of course, characteristic of higher education under Stalin, and suited the paramount policy of industrialising at the expense of the service sector. The years after his death saw intensification of the slew towards 'production' specialisations, and by 1978 over 317,000 graduates, or 40 per cent of the total, qualified in them (Table 4.1). In addition the 'university' specialisations had a significant scientific content, while the health sector, though not productive, was of course mostly serviced by scientists. Modern industrial specialisations, including electronics, radio, construction and machine-building, have registered the largest gains, matched in the humanities only by the Soviet version of economics.

Young people's chances of higher education were greatly improved by the overall expansion of facilities. Analysis is again bedevilled by a lack of statistics – the Soviet authorities being very secretive about this

Table 4.1   *Graduations from VUZy by Specialisation Group*
(*thousands*)

Production sciences	1950	1978	Factor of increase*
Energy	2·4	16·9	7·0
Machine-building	9·1	81·2	8·9
Electronics and automation	1·4	49·8	35·6
Radio and communications	1·4	21·0	15·0
Chemical technology	2·6	15·0	5·8
Construction	4·9	55·1	11·2
Agriculture	12·9	58·6	4·5
Transport	3·1	19·7	6·4
Pure sciences and humanities			
Economics	10·1	101·8	10·1
Law	5·7	15·6	2·7
Health	20·7	56·6	2·7
University specialities	12·3	60·0	4·9
Pedagogical specialisations	77·6	162·2	2·1
Art	2·4	7·6	3·2
Others	10·4	50·4	—
Totals/overall change	176·9	771·5	4·4

* That is, the multiplier required to arrive at the 1978 figures from those of 1950.
Source: Nar. khoz., 1978, p. 481, adapted.

matter – yet an impression of the change can be gained from comparing the number of people going into full-time *VUZy* with the estimated 18-year age cohort in selected years.[2] On this extremely approximate basis it seems that at the beginning of the Khrushchev period only one 18-year-old in every twenty had the opportunity of entering full-time higher education. Towards the end of the 1950s a rapid improvement set in, initially as a result of the 'war dent', and the ratio fell to perhaps one in nine. Thereafter full-time intakes kept a little ahead of the recovery in the age cohorts, so that by the late 1970s the figure was up to about one in eight – which was again very good by international standards. No official breakdown of the student body by age has ever, to my knowledge, been published, though it was recently stated that the great majority were between 19 and 24.[3] From the middle of the decade women comprised just over half of the total enrolment.

The growth of the student body has been accompanied by an increase in the number and size of *VUZy*, not to mention their staffs. In 1951, when 887 institutions were listed, the average enrolment was about 1,400 students: Khrushchev, partly in an effort to improve efficiency, reduced the number of *VUZy* to a low of 731, with an average of 3,600 students. Subsequently new institutions were founded, and by 1978 there were 866, with an average of 5,900 students. Universities seem to be the largest type, with 9,000 students or more, while agricultural and pedagogical institutes are the smallest, sometimes with less than 2,000. All *VUZy* are divided into three categories, according to size, economic importance and research activity. The teaching staff, overall, rose from about 87,000 to 380,000 over approximately the same period, maintaining a crude ratio of fourteen to sixteen students per teacher. By 1979 some 17,000 held the research degree of Doctor, and 160,000 that of Candidate of Science, which is some token of quality.

The cost of educating the average student (surely one of the least meaningful of all social statistics) has been the focus of much debate. State budget data show that it fell from 578 roubles per annum in 1950 to a low of about 400 in 1965, but rose again to 675 roubles by 1978. More full-time as opposed to part-time study, new buildings and more sophisticated classroom equipment were probably the main factors in the increase. It is, however, not entirely clear what these figures covered, and there were plenty of variations. V. P. Korchagin showed that 'direct' expenditures per full-time student in the early 1970s were running at 920 roubles per annum, as against 268 and 107 roubles for evening and correspondence students. Education appeared to cost most in universities and medical institutes, and least in polytechnical and pedagogical institutions.[4] One's scepticism about much of this arithmetic arises from its failure to allow for such things as production lost when young people become students rather than workers, the parental support which many of them needed, unregistered vacation earnings and, in all probability, state outgoings on military training.

The efficiency of the *VUZy*, taken as the relationship between intakes of students and subsequent graduations, also varied with time. Proper figures are, once more, lacking: but my own estimates suggest that the full-time institutions were graduating around 90 per cent of intakes in the mid 1950s, when they were taking fewer applicants, mostly straight from school, and before Khrushchev began his reorganisation. The rate dropped to just over 70 per cent a decade later, but the Brezhnev years, beginning with the 1965 intake, reversed the trend, and by the late 1970s graduation rates were up to over 80 per cent of intakes. The success of evening and correspondence courses is even more difficult to judge, but I suspect that the rate rose from about half in the 1950s to over two-thirds in the mid-1970s.[5]

A policy which became evident during the Brezhnev period involved a qualitative differentiation between the *VUZy*, particularly universities as against institutes (see page 140). It is significant that while, under Khrushchev, the number of universities grew by only nine (to forty-two), in the eleven years following his dismissal twenty-four were created. The July 1972 decree indicated the need to upgrade them and 'transform them into leading teaching and methodological centres . . .

for training teaching and research staff and for research in the fundamental sciences'. A more detailed enactment of June 1974, 'On improving the training of cadres with a university education and on raising the role of the universities in the system of higher schools', envisaged an expansion of their material facilities, priority financing and, indeed, specific improvements in all aspects of their work (Voilenko, Vol. 1, p. 212). Given the official aim of raising *VUZ* standards in general, reliance on the strongest units was quite understandable, but there is no doubt that it accorded ill with egalitarian ethics.

The location of *VUZy* could not but continue to raise problems in a country as large as the Soviet Union. Khrushchev was particularly worried by the concentration of institutions in the large towns of European Russia, if only because their graduates were unwilling to take jobs in less hospitable spots. The August 1954 decree proposed some relocation, so that more students would be trained near their future place of work. A further development of this idea was the August 1961 proposal to move thirty-two of the eighty or so agricultural *VUZy* out to state or experimental farms (*KPSS o kulture, prosveschenii i nauke*, 1963, p. 505). These and other plans do not, however, seem to have been implemented to any significant degree.

Khrushchev's main success in repositioning *VUZy* was the founding of five new universities in ethnic minority areas and a new academic complex at Novosibirsk. At least eighteen of the new universities founded by the Brezhnev leadership between 1965 and 1974 were also outside European Russia. It is noteworthy that student intakes in some of the border republics, particularly Kazakhstan, Kirgizia, Tadzhikistan, Armenia and Azerbaidzhan, rose at rates significantly above the national average.

Although principally concerned with the training of undergraduates, the *VUZy* have sizeable contingents of postgraduate researchers.

When Khrushchev came to power there were in all about 30,000 *aspiranty* (persons registered for the degree of Candidate of Science) of whom some 17,000 were in *VUZy*, including 14,000 on a full-time basis. Most of the remainder were in research institutes and are of less concern to us here. The *VUZ* registrations fell sharply for three successive years (matching the fall in other intakes) and then grew rapidly: a plateau of about 55,000 was reached in 1965 (Figure 4.2). The *VUZ* more or less held their own in the total of registrations, but there was – as might be expected under Khrushchev – a big shift towards part-time registrations. By 1964, in fact, no less than 37 per cent of the *VUZy aspiranty* were in the part-time sector, as opposed to 18 per cent a decade earlier. The Brezhnev leadership seems to have followed an altogether more cautious policy, and after 1973 the numbers of *aspiranty* actually began to fall, particularly in the full-time sector. The main inference to be drawn from this is that an optimum rate was thought to have been achieved or surpassed; there was no indication of a fall-off in the demand for places.

Enrolments, however, are only one aspect of the problem. Some *aspiranty* did not complete the course; many finished late; and not all of those who finished acquired a Candidate title. Despite the lack of proper statistics it is clear that completions were running at 4–5,000 a year in the mid-1950s, but fell to a low of 3,000 in 1960. Thereafter they improved steadily, passing 11,000 in 1970, after which they appear to have steadied; by that time the great majority of *aspiranty* must have been getting through. Part-timers then made up a third of the total. The resulting erratic pattern of Candidate awards through all channels may be appreciated from Figure 4.3.

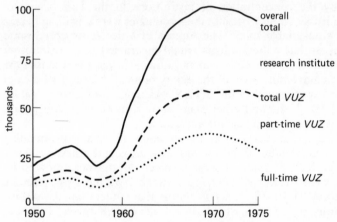

Figure 4.2   *Aspiranty* in *VUZy* and research institutes, 1950–75.
Source: NONK, 1977, p. 310. See *Note*, Figure 4.1.

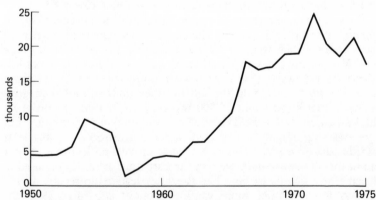

Figure 4.3   Candidate of Science degree awards, 1950–75.
Source: As for Figure 4.2, above.

We know much less about the training of Doctors of Science; by 1975 the number of degree-holders stood at 32,000 compared with 9,000 in 1954. Most postgraduate research, like undergraduate work, was concentrated in the sciences: in 1970 about 80 per cent of all *aspiranty* were working in such fields.

It is not inappropriate to conclude the section with a comment on the academic worth of Soviet degrees, or 'diplomas' as they are called. This is not something for facile judgement. The factors involved, such as course content, the quality of the teaching and variations in standards between establishments, quite preclude it. A full discussion would also have to allow for the incidence of exceptionally brilliant and weak students, which is unknown. All one can do is counter a few common misconceptions and state a point of view.

Protagonists of Soviet higher education, including many who admit its shortcomings, argue that a Soviet degree is of significantly higher standing than, for example, a British one. Taking the quality of teaching, the students' abilities and academic starting points as roughly comparable, they point to the facts that the content of Soviet courses is narrower and more concentrated, in line with the vocational character of Soviet higher education; that *VUZ* training lasts four to six years, compared with three or four in the United Kingdom; and that his work experience gives the Soviet student an extra advantage.

While concurring that teaching standards and average student ability may not in most cases be measurably different, I think that three factors largely invalidate the other claims. First, the concentrated nature of Soviet *VUZ* courses (if more concentrated they are) is counterbalanced by the narrower range of information generally available to the student in other respects. He cannot, after all, legally obtain any printed matter, Soviet or foreign, which has not had the specific approval of the censor. Courses of training for relatively neglected fields (such as the service industries, medicine) are distinctly inferior, while all the social sciences and many humanities are fettered by the exigencies of a particularly primitive form of Marxism. To move to a more general plane, the Soviet student is virtually denied the cultural advantages of foreign travel of a protracted or unorganised kind, whereas the overwhelming majority of Britishers, despite a common impecunity, enjoy them.

Secondly, the longer period of study in Soviet *VUZy* is not as convincing an argument as might seem. The obligatory extraneous elements, particularly the ideological and military content, make up at least a fifth of the work-load. The Soviet student's practical work experience is not always successful or directly relevant to the problem of academic standards. Thirdly, the starting level in the UK may well be somewhat higher because some pre-university specialisation is built into A-levels, and the UK 'general' school course is longer than the Soviet one. If only for these reasons, I believe that the Soviet diploma is roughly comparable to the British first degree, and no more.

The evaluation of Soviet research degrees is even more difficult. The candidature of science cannot readily be equated with British 'master' degrees on the one hand or doctorates on the other. Although the *aspirantura* is formally a three-year course, the first two years are preparatory and the actual dissertation is supposed to be written in one. I suspect that the degree of Candidate of Science falls somewhere between an MA or M.Sc and a Ph.D., except in the case of the social sciences or humanities, where ideological restraints may well reduce its value significantly. Soviet doctoral dissertations, however, usually take many years to complete, and may be very impressive pieces of work.

PROBLEMS OF CENTRAL CONTROL

Higher educational establishments, like all others in the USSR, are supervised by both state and party bodies. The state ministries, which handle the day-to-day administrative matters, may conveniently be treated first.

In 1946 the old state Committee for Higher Education was upgraded into a ministry of union–republican status. This body was fully responsible for all the universities and about a third of the institutes throughout the country; it shared control of the remainder, principally the pedagogical, transport, medical and artistic institutes, with the ministries which employed their graduates (Medynski, 1947, p. 178). In March 1953 the Ministry of Higher Education was merged with the Ministry of Culture, but it reappeared with its former name and status in December 1955. It had extensive control over most aspects of higher education throughout the country; and although subject to numerous minor modifications as the years went by, it underwent little change of substance.[6] The fact that the USSR minister, V. P. Elyutin, appointed in March 1954, was still at his post twenty-five years later, is itself indicative of stability.

Khrushchev intervened comparatively little in the ministerial set-up. In the autumn of 1954 he certainly made an attempt to strengthen educational planning through *Gosplan,* and he granted the regional economic councils, after their establishment in May 1957, some control over the *VUZy* in their areas. But this shift was of only temporary significance, for the old balance was largely restored when the councils were abolished in 1965. As for the ministry itself, it was renamed the Ministry of Higher and Secondary Special Education, sometimes abbreviated as *MinVUZ,* in June 1959. Its republican interests were soon afterwards strengthened by the establishment of ministerial offices in the RSFSR, the Ukraine and White Russia, while state committees for higher and secondary special education appeared in most of the other republics (Hodnett and Ogareff).

Khrushchev's evident caution with regard to these instruments of administration was perhaps a little strange. True, there was no reason why his love of reorganisation should have penetrated every corner of the state structure. But given his plans for revamping higher education, one might well have expected him to attempt a more vigorous restructuring of the bodies which administered it. What he did do was to rely more heavily on the party organs.

The Brezhnev leadership, by contrast, showed a lively interest in the state machinery. The policy, evidently, was to increase ministerial power while creating an appearance of democratisation through the establishment of consultative committees. The USSR *MinVUZ* was greatly strengthened by the first major Brezhnev decree on higher education, promulgated on 3 September 1966. This measure empowered it to take greater control of twenty-nine *VUZy* which it had formerly administered jointly with other ministries, so as to make them centres for 'elaborating and generalising materials on teaching methods, compiling textbooks and training or retraining research and teaching staff'. The inspection of all *VUZy*, apparently regardless of their administrative status, now came within its purview, and it was directed to draw up new statutes not only for *VUZy* and *SSUZy* but also for its own republican branches. The proclaimed object of the redrafting was to increase the powers of the heads of individual institutions and (albeit paradoxically) promote intra-*VUZ* democratisation, but this, as we shall see in a moment, is not what really happened. The second major enactment of these years, the decree of 18 July 1972, gave the *MinVUZ* the right to make recommendations on the nomination and dismissal of rectors of the 'shared' institutions – only the heads of those run by the Ministry of Defence, the Ministry of Internal Affairs and the KGB being exempted from this provision.

The ministries and administrations which ran the other higher educational establishments in 1974 are listed in Table 4.2. As may be seen, the *MinVUZ* and its union–republican counterparts had sole control of some 351 of them (including all the universities), while the Ministry of Enlightenment ran another 176. The ministries outside the educational sector which undertook this task evidently did so because their specialisation needs were rather specific, and they required closer control of their 'own' graduates.

The data in Table 4.2, drawn from a study by A. B. Dainovski, throw some light on two other intriguing problems of higher education in the Soviet Union. First, the number of institutions in Dainovski's listing is 828, though in a preceding paragraph he quotes the current official total as 842. The simplest explanation of the discrepancy is that the fourteen *VUZy* on which there was no comment were of the 'closed' or generally inaccessible variety, and belonged to the Ministries of Foreign and Internal Affairs, and the KGB. (Military *VUZy* were in a separate category, see p. 194). Establishments belonging to these organisations are only occasionally mentioned in published sources.

Table 4.2 *Distribution of* VUZy *by Ministerial Subordination, October 1974*

Ministry or administration	No. of VUZy
Higher and secondary special education, USSR and union republics (henceforth u.r.)	351
Enlightenment, u.r.	176
Agriculture, USSR	99
Health, USSR, u.r.	81
Culture, USSR, u.r.	51
Sports and physical culture committees, of USSR, u.r.	14
Highways, USSR	13
Communications, USSR	7
Fishing, USSR	5
Trade, u.r.	5
Consumer societies, USSR	6
Marine, USSR	5
Civil aviation, USSR	5
River fleet, RSFSR	3
Communal services, u.r.	3
Cinematography, State Committee for, USSR	2
Medical supplies, USSR	1
Writers, Union of, USSR	1

Source: Dainovski, p. 101.

They were, for example, stated to be entitled respectively to three, nine and six of the 1,216 Lenin scholarships available for distribution in 1977 (*BMV*, no. 3, 1977, p. 14). The number of students they contained must therefore have run into many thousands. Secondly, the fact that the closed *VUZy* are excluded from the listing suggests that they are also absent from other statistics as commonly represented.

The Brezhnev years saw the creation of three types of committee charged with assisting the *MinVUZ* in its work. Mention must be made in the first place of the permanent commissions for education, science and culture attached to the supreme soviets, which we have already considered in connection with the general school. Notices of their meetings published in official gazettes show that they devoted a little of their time to matters of higher education, particularly the implementation of existing laws and the investigation of specific problems. It seems most unlikely, however, that these bodies had a greater impact on *VUZ* policies than on other aspects of schooling.

Secondly, the July 1972 decree established within the USSR *MinVUZ* itself a 'higher school council', comprising leading officials of the union–republican ministries of higher and secondary special education, *Gosplan*, the State Committee for Science and Technology, the Academy of Sciences, the trades unions, the Central Committee of the *Komsomol* and the student representatives. The attentions of this august body were to be concentrated on 'working out scientifically based recommendations for improving teaching, educational, scientific and research work in the *VUZy*, long-term training plans, the direction and use of specialists, and raising the qualifications of research and training staff', that is, virtually all aspects of *VUZ* work (*SPR*, 1973, p. 204).

A meeting held in February 1974 which was also attended by 'responsible officials of the CPSU Central Committee' discussed plan fulfilment for 1973 and developments in 1974, and then adopted 'an extensive decree which was circulated to educational institutions, higher and secondary special schools' (*VVSh*, no. 4, 1974, p. 7). The council's terms of reference strongly suggest that such decrees could have been of a recommendatory character only.

Thirdly, the July decree set up 'councils of rectors' in large urban centres to 'co-ordinate *VUZ* activities and generalise their positive experience'. Local officialdom seems to have responded with some enthusiasm to this proposal, for by the middle of 1974 no less than sixty-eight such bodies were in existence, and they were still being created in the summer of 1977 (*VVSh*, no. 7, 1974, p. 7; *BMV*, no. 7, 1977, pp. 24–43; no. 6, pp. 6 ff.; no. 5, pp. 29 ff.). The Moscow Party Office (*Gorkom*) set a glowing example. The council here consisted of a hundred persons – including party, educational, trades union, *Komsomol* and student representatives – and spawned sixteen commissions with ten or fifteen members each, covering most, if not all, *VUZ* activities (*VVSh*, no. 4, 1974, p. 48). The commission organised programmes of lectures and seminars for senior *VUZ* personnel, monitored higher educational activities and publicised useful findings. The full council met only at the end of the academic year, to assess the results; day-to-day running of the plant was left in the hands of a presidium.

So much for state machinery. As was indicated earlier, effective control of education has been exercised, since soon after the Revolution, by the Central Committee apparatus. The party leadership used this apparatus not only for supervision of state bodies but also to direct the work of individual *VUZy*, acting through local party offices and the party members on *VUZ* staffs. Many instances of this practice have been discussed in print.

Senior officials – local secretaries for example – may intervene directly through a rector's or dean's office: in any case educational affairs are supposed to be discussed regularly by local party committees. At the town or district level such work is usually done by professional party 'instructors', who maintain contact with the primary party organisations inside the *VUZy*. Such organisations have for a long time involved themselves in virtually every aspect of the life of their institutions, with the ideological courses an object of special attention. The system of party control within the *VUZ* differs from that of other types of educational establishment mainly in that it is more detailed and intensive; the managment of young adults is politically more demanding than that of children.

Several changes took place in the system after the death of Stalin. With the passage of the December 1958 reform, there was undoubtedly great intensification of party work in higher education. The Departments of Science and Schools which were established in *oblast* and *krai* party offices of the RSFSR supervised the *VUZy* as well as other types of educational institution. Subordinate units for *VUZ* affairs were subsequently set up in some towns and districts: by 1973, for example, the party office of the important Sverdlovsk district in Moscow had its own Department of Science and Higher Educational Institutions, supported by supernumerary sectors for '*VUZy* and *SSUZy*' and 'science'. Elsewhere individual instructors did the job, as before.[7] Khrushchev did not alter the role of the primary party organisations inside the *VUZy*, but he did give party organisations in research institutes 'directly connected with production' what was called the 'right of supervision of the activities of the management' (October 1961).

The approach favoured by the Brezhnev leadership was in fact an extension of this. At the Twenty-Fourth Party Congress in April 1971, the same right was given to party organisations in 'educational, cultural, and health establishments' which were administratively self-contained. Brezhnev made a specific reference to it in his speech to a student gathering in October 1971; and an increase in party, *Komsomol* and trades union activity was called for in the July 1972 decree.

To judge from articles published subsequently, the new ruling was intended both to increase party intervention in *VUZ* affairs and to promote stricter control of appointments. Two short quotations will illustrate what sometimes happened as a result.

Since the Twenty-Fourth Congress of the CPSU [wrote V. N. Yagodkin, a Moscow party secretary, in 1973], the nomenclature controlled by the Moscow town and district committees has been made more exact. The town committee nomenclature now contains 304 persons – all the rectors, *VUZ* party committee secretaries and most of the heads of social science faculties. The secretaries of *VUZ* party bureaux at faculty level and all social science teachers are on the district committee nomenclature . . . Within the *VUZy* a nomenclature of leading members of staff whose appointments are confirmed at meetings of the party committees and bureaux has also been fixed.

Such 'nomenclature' status for positions meant, of course, that they could not be filled without party approval (*Iz opyta ideologicheskoi raboty partii*, 1973, pp. 304–5).

Each half year [wrote a member of the Moscow Ordzhonikidze Engineering and Economics Institute about the same time] the *VUZ* party committee draws up a list of the most important matters to be taken under party control . . . The party committee, together with the rector's office [*sic*], determines the reserve lists for promotion to responsible jobs, including those of pro-rector, dean, faculty heads and directors of research laboratories. The committee is now trying to ensure that each member of staff, regardless of age, has a possible replacement, and that teachers and scientific workers could replace one another . . . Transfer within faculties, research sections and other institute services, re-elections for further terms of office and also the award of scholarly titles, can take place only if there is a positive socio-political recommendation from the *VUZ* party committee or the bureaux of the faculties and research sections. (Samsonov, pp. 9–16)

The question arises as to how extensively these new powers were used. An authoritative article in the journal *Partiinaya zhizn* in 1978 warned that in exercising the right of control 'party organisations [should] not replace rectors' and deans' offices, or the heads of research sections. On the contrary, communists must make sure that all administrative organs in the *VUZ* exhibit independence and initiative in their work, fulfil their duties in a creative manner and bear full responsibility for the decisions they take' (no. 13, 1978, p. 69). Such changes of emphasis are a well recognised feature of party–state relations in the USSR; the suggestion is that the drive to extend this variety of party control was also, after a time, relaxed.

The post-Stalin period saw a considerable growth in party membership among academics and research staff. According to the few available data, CPSU members among Doctors and Candidates of Science in all kinds of institutions increased as follows (figures in percentages):

	Doctors of Science	Candidates of Science
1950	25	32
1957	40	46
1967	46	45
1977	65	51

One would not wish to underrate the significance of this trend, but it must be viewed against the massive increase in party membership overall (from 6·3 million in 1950 to 16 million in 1977) and against the growth of higher education itself. The absolute number of party members in higher and secondary special educational institutions increased from approximately 84,000 in 1957 to 314,000 in 1977, presumably matching the growth of employees. By 1973 42 per cent of all *VUZ* teaching staff were said to be in the Party, compared with an average party saturation rate of about 10 per cent among the adult public at large. Party membership amongst *VUZ* students must remain small, since the great majority of them are under age: but by 1978 no less than 95 per cent were said to be in the *Komsomol*, as against 54 per cent of all young people in age-groups eligible for membership (*NONK*, 1977, p. 301; *SPR*, 1978, p. 381; *PZh*, no. 7, 1973, p. 14).

PROBLEMS OF INTERNAL ADMINISTRATION

In the early 1950s the *VUZy* were still functioning under the terms of the September 1938 statute. More detailed and up-to-date versions were introduced in 1961 and 1969, representing, in some measure, different organisational ideals. The main contours of the institution, however, remained virtually unchanged, and may briefly be summarised as follows.[8]

In accordance with the pre-revolutionary tradition, Soviet *VUZy* are of two distinct types. On the one hand there are *universities*, which train all kinds of 'specialists', but with some emphasis on research workers and teachers in the main theoretical disciplines. Like universities in the West they embrace all the major branches of learning in both arts and sciences, and are rather prestigious. Their courses of study normally last five years, full-time. On the other hand there are *institutes* which specialise in a given field of learning and provide, as often as not, rather more practical training. The length of courses here varies between four and six years, according to the discipline involved (Medynski, 1947, p. 170; *SES*, pp. 499, 1,394). The academic year for both universities and institutes is divided into two semesters, lasting from early September until late January and from early February until late June. All establishments are subordinate to the state in every significant respect, and are financed from the national budget.

The declared aims of all Soviet *VUZy* include the training of highly qualified specialists devoted to their work; giving students and staff a good grasp of Marxism–Leninism; composing textbooks; conducting research which promotes socialist construction; raising the professional standards of academic staff; and popularising learning. Teaching takes the familiar forms of lectures, seminars, practicals, consultations, private study and production work; all such teaching and research is subject to ministerial approval.

The *VUZ* is headed by a rector who is nominally responsible for everything that goes on in the institution.* He is assisted by pro-rectors for teaching, research, part-time study and administration. The *VUZ*

---

* Formerly this title was bestowed only on the heads of universities. Institutes had 'directors'.

'learned council', comprising mainly senior staff members, may advise in some matters. All rectorial acts fall within ministerial purview. The basic internal units are the faculties headed by deans, and departments (*kafedry*) headed by senior professors. The *VUZ* may run other units such as annexe departments (*filialy*), laboratories and consultation points, as need by. It may or may not be permitted to have postgraduate students. Invariably there are standardised rules for staff and student conduct, and a cluster of approved socio-political organisations.

Detailed changes in *VUZ* organisation since the death of Stalin are the main concern of the pages that follow. Four rather general changes of emphasis may however be mentioned at this point.

The first involves the nature of the relationship between the *VUZ* head and his staff. In the 1938 statute the emotive term *edinonachalie*, or one-man control, was used to describe it. Although after 1961 the rector still retained formal overall responsibility for the work of the institution, this word disappeared. The deans, formerly 'promoted from among the professors', were now to be elected for terms of three years by secret ballot of the learned council. (The form of election in each *VUZ*, however, had to be approved by the Ministry of Higher and Secondary Special Education, and party influences certainly made themselves felt.) The *VUZ* learned council was itself slightly democratised, in that the subordinate 'faculty' councils acquired the right to elect to it staff members of their own for three years at a time.

Matters were not, however, to rest there. A decree on improving higher and secondary special education, promulgated in September 1966, called for more democracy in the *VUZy* and more independence for the rectors, but without saying how this was to be brought about. The 1969 statute consequently re-emphasised the responsibility of the rector for *all VUZ* work, while the other legislation we have just considered suggested he may have lost some power to the *MinVUZ*. The three-year limitation on office-holding by deans was now abandoned, so that they could now, once elected, decanate until retirement. All these points indicate that the Brezhnev leadership favoured some return to earlier rigidities.

The second shift was due to the impact of Khrushchev's 'link with life' policy. The text of the 1961 statute contained a great number of provisions for part-time study, extra-mural consultation centres and annexe departments. Collaboration with the enterprises which were to receive undergraduates for practice or permanent employment at a later date was also covered in great detail. Thirdly, allowance was made for closer relations with the non-Soviet world; under this rubric I would include the establishment of the post of pro-rector for foreign students, and certain provisions for international exchanges of technical information. (The year 1960 had, of course, seen the establishment of the Patrice Lumumba People's Friendship University in Moscow, designed to train young people from African, Asian and Latin American countries.[9] Foreign contacts were to receive much less prominence in the 1969 version of the statutes, when official priorities changed again.

Fourthly, the position of the students was reflected in various ways. The Khrushchev version contained a detailed list of rights and duties which had formerly been omitted. The Brezhnev statute appeared to allow for much greater student involvement in *VUZ* affairs, but without providing any effective means of ensuring it. Students were to be consulted on the learning process and ideological work; they were expected to monitor individual progress, the granting of stipends and the allocation of hostel accommodation; they could have a say, through their representatives, on the fate of those who failed their exams. Greater stress was laid on their ideological training, with specific mention of the need for patriotism and physical fitness. The real reasons for this change are not easy to fathom. It may have been part of a broader show of democratisation in the political sphere, or a cautious response to increased turbulence in student politics in the West.

VUZ COURSES – FORM AND CONTENT

Soviet higher educational establishments offer courses which are both highly standardised, in the Soviet manner, and complex, as befits a modern economy. My intention here is to illustrate the usual course structure and show how it has developed since the death of Stalin (that is, when development is perceptible). I shall start with the problem of the range of subjects offered, and then consider the general configuration of an arts specialisation (more extended analysis being impracticable in the confines of this study). The obligatory subjects which all or most students must take (the so-called social sciences, a foreign language, production practice, physical and military training) are our next port of call. I shall conclude the section with an account of the examinations and tests which buttress the whole programme.

(1)   *The Range of Subjects*

At the time of Stalin's death the subject matter taught in Soviet *VUZy* was divided into some 900 rather narrow specialisations (*spetsialnosti*), each of which had its own curriculum. Specialisations were vocational in orientation and rather narrow. All had to be approved by a ministry. In addition, individual *VUZy* offered a limited number of sub-specialisations (*spetsializatsii*) which students took on an obligatory or voluntary basis, according to circumstances. Excluded from the listing were topics unacceptable to the regime, including ideologically blighted areas of science, subjects of an anti-Marxist nature and a host of subjects irrelevant to state interests.

The decree of August 1954 voiced clear dissatisfaction, if not with the range of specialisations, then with their narrowness: 'specialists of a broad profile' were, it said, now needed. As a result, a tidying-up operation was inaugurated, and a new breakdown of 274 broader specialisations, grouped in five general branches and twenty-two categories, was published in September 1954 (Zinoviev, p. 25; Karpov and Severtsev, p. 55). Many of the formerly distinct specialisations were turned into sub-specialisations. As time went by, however, the volume of facts which students had to master grew apace, and this required more and narrower specialisations, rather than the contrary. The listings were changed at frequent intervals, and whole new sets were approved in December 1966 and September 1975. By 1979 the total was 449 (Ushakov and Shuruev, p. 58; *BMV*, no. 12, 1975, p. 2).

A comparison of the lists of 1954 and 1975, though a little precarious (given the role of sub-specialisations), is not without its fascination. The applied sciences registered considerable expansion; in fact, nearly all the new specialisations, numbering just under 100, were to be found in this sphere. They included gas and oil technology, energy systems, atomic engineering, plastics, transistors, communications, aviation and automation techniques (military and space technology must have been hidden amongst them somewhere). These were backed by an expansion of the pure sciences, though mainly at the sub-specialisation level. Genetics, the centre of so much controversy under Stalin, appeared as a *VUZ* sub-specialisation in the mid-1950s.

Among arts subjects the most noteworthy innovations were in the area of language-teaching. The number of Soviet languages taught as a native tongue rose from seventeen (which included the non-Russian union–republican languages, plus Finnish, Tatar and Buryat Mongolian) to twenty-nine. The main beneficiaries were, naturally enough, the Turkic and Caucasian tongues. True, this ran counter to the reduction of teaching in minority languages in the general school, but it may also be viewed as a sort of cultural recompense. As for languages of the European groups, Hungarian, Dutch, Icelandic, Slovene, Macedonian and Albanian made their appearance. The 1975 list contained no fewer than thirty-four African and South-East Asian tongues, nearly all, apparently, quite newly introduced and reflecting government interest in these areas. Structural and applied linguistics were also now registered. A few applied arts, such as decoration of various kinds, fashion design and industrial graphics, were brought in.

The political sensitivity of the social sciences had long put them in a category of their own. The core subjects – political economy and philosophy – were throughout available as two specialisations, constructed around such versions of Marxist thought, economic practice and historiography as were approved by prevailing leaderships. Economics and planning, on the other hand, were broken down into a large number of specialisations – thirty-one in 1954 and forty-three by

1975. Most of the new ones involved the 'organisation of administration', that is, management skills. International law, social and work psychology, scientific atheism and scientific communism also made their appearance.

The caution of the authorities in this sphere sometimes led to strange anomalies, of which sociology provides an interesting example. Soviet sociology, which had advanced with some success after the Revolution, was effectively suppressed by Stalin in the early 1930s on the pretext that it was adequately represented by historical materialism. In June 1958 as part of the destalinisation process, the Soviet Sociological Association was established. By 1967 the discipline had acquired its own research institute in Moscow and a veritable network of centres and laboratories throughout the country. Much of the work they produced was intended to improve planning procedures. Naturally enough, the practitioners began to demand the introduction of a proper sociology specialisation for undergraduates. The Ministry of Higher and Secondary Special Education, however, adamantly refused to concede this, and sociology was taught only in a few optional courses or at postgraduate level. At a public discussion in the summer of 1978 N. I. Mokhov, an official of the ministry, gave reasons for its opposition. Some elements of the discipline, he said, were already included in other courses, while all of it was sometimes available on an optional basis. As to practical difficulties, Mokhov innocently claimed that there was no 'sociology' entry in state labour plans, so the ministry could not know how many 'sociologists' were needed; that it was difficult enough to find jobs for philosophy students with some training in it; that neither textbooks nor teachers were available; and that graduates with other specialisations, like economics or law, were more effective at the workplace. 'In past years,' he added significantly, 'sociology has contained, alas, not a few erroneous propositions. All this must be borne in mind.' The propensity of the discipline to question ideological premises about harmony in Soviet social structure, or to reveal dismal realities, was clearly a major hindrance to its acceptance. And so it was that even in the late 1970s Soviet higher education still lacked a proper sociology degree (*SI*, no. 4, 1978, p. 183).

The list of *VUZ* specialisations contained, by and large, what was culturally, economically or politically useful to the state, and specifically excluded all that was ideologically suspect. Given the censorship restrictions on the books made available to the public, the absence of any given subject from the *VUZ* specialisations list usually marked an unfilled gap in popular culture.

(2) *The Structure of the Curriculum*

Soviet higher educational courses have always tended to be heavy in terms of workload, if not of intellectual content. Such curricula as are accessible (for they are not regularly published) show time inputs of from just under 4,000 instruction hours for the arts to 5,000 or more for the sciences, not counting several weeks of practical work. In addition all students have their private study, and most of the men have to undergo a course of military training as well. Attendance at all classes has been obligatory since the early 1940s.

Details from a curriculum used in the late 1970s at the Moscow Lenin State Pedagogical Institute to train teachers of English, French, German and Spanish are shown in Tables 4.3a, 4.3b and 4.3c. This curriculum exhibited most of the standard features of a Soviet humanities course. The students had to work through twenty basic specialisation subjects, six ideological subjects, a number of options and physical training (no military component being revealed). The non-basics, it will be noted, together made up over 15 per cent of the declared work-load. The course included two 'course' essays and seventy-nine examinations and tests. There were eighteen weeks of production practice in the form of teaching and Young Pioneer work.

The number of tabled hours came to thirty or thirty-two per week, depending on the semester; though still within the maximum of thirty-six fixed by a ministerial instruction of 8 December 1974, it meant an arduous working day. (A 1968 investigation of time-use among students of the Azerbaidzhan Oil and Chemistry Institute provided some detailed information on this. During the semesters the students, who had a similar load of contact hours, devoted between eight and eleven hours a day to classes and private study: Ibragimov, p. 139.) The question arises as to whether such onerous courses are really needed, particularly for the more straightforward skills.

A notable feature of the Soviet *VUZ* curriculum is its paucity of choices. Once they have chosen their specialisation, students have only two kinds of choice of course open to them: the sub-specialisation options (*spetskursy*), at least one of which is obligatory in the final year, and the electives (*fakultativy*), which are entirely voluntary and a matter of personal enthusiasm. Both the range of such subjects and the amount of time they absorb tend to be small; at the Moscow Pedagogical Institute there were thirteen subjects, but only sixty hours, or just over 1 per cent of all contact time, were set aside for them. The Azerbaidzhan Oil and Chemistry Institute in 1965 offered seven, with a total allocation of 168 hours. Some electives give students the right to take a test or exam, the results of which may be entered, as an additional recommendation, in the *VUZ* diploma (Zinoviev, p. 48). Both types of course may be important as a means of developing students' and teachers' personal interests. Some limitation of choice is justified if the specialisations are purposely narrow to begin with, but whether the existing restrictions are too severe is arguable. Extra-curricular interests can usually be developed only by going on to postgraduate research or by starting a second degree, which entails difficulties of its own (see page 132 below).

Table 4.3 (a) *Curriculum of the Moscow Lenin State Pedagogical Institute (MLSPI), Late 1970s* *
Specialisation 2103: Teacher of two foreign languages

	Lectures (hours)	Seminars (hours)	Labour, practicals (hours)	Totals (hours)	Percentages	Number of tests	Number of exams
Ideological subjects							
1 history of the CPSU	84	86		170	3·5	1	2
2 Marxist–Leninist philosophy	80	60		140	2·9		2
3 political economy	70	70		140	2·9		2
4 scientific communism	40	40		80	1·7	2	
5 scientific atheism	18	6		24	0·5		1
6 Soviet law	40			40	0·8	1	
Specialisation subjects							
7 introduction to the specialisation	36			36	0·7		
8 juvenile physiology, school hygiene	42		8	50	1·0	1	
9 psychology	74		26	100	2·1	1	1
10 pedagogics	100	20	30	150	3·1	1	2
11 foreign-language teaching	50		50	100	2·1	1	1
12 Russian language	60	80		140	2·9	2	2
13–19 basic foreign language (history, theory, practice, literature, etc.)	228	20	2,208	2,456	51·0	18	15
20 regional study	50	20		70	1·5	2	1
21 introduction to linguistics	50	20		70	1·5		1
22 Latin			70	70	1·5		1
23 comparative typology, Russian – foreign language	30			30	0·6	1	
24 second foreign language			710	710	14·7	3	3
25 learning machines		38		38	0·8	1	
26 options (see Table 4.3 (b))	20	40		60	1·2	2	
27 PT			140	140	2·9	4	
TOTALS	1,072	500	3,242	4,814	100·0	41	34

Table 4.3 (b) *MLSPI Curriculum (cont.): Options, Electives, Examinations*

Options (item 26)	Electives	Exams, etc.
1 methodology of communist education	1 Marxist–Leninist ethics	Tests–41
2 text analysis	2 Marxist–Leninist aesthetics	Exams–34
3 special pedagogics course	3 lyrics	Course essays–2
4 special psychology course	4 professional orientation	a) foreign-language teaching
	5 methodology of educative work	b) history and theory of language
	6 methodology of class supervision	State exams–4
	7 labour protection and law	(final)
	8 PT	a) scientific communism
	9 seminar on training for pioneer work	b) foreign language
		c) second foreign language
		d) pedagogics with foreign-language teaching

Course projects, diploma project–none. But capable students may be allowed to write a dissertation instead of state exam (b) or (d).

Table 4.3 (c)   *MSPLI Curriculum (cont.):*
               Work-Load Distribution by Semester

(Year and semester)	Length (weeks)	Average weekly work-load (hours)	Examination session (weeks)	Exams	Tests	Production Practice (teaching, Pioneer care) (weeks)
First year						
(1)	19	32	5	3	4	
(2)	18	32		4	5	
Second year						
(1)	19	30	6	3	5	
(2)	17	30		4	5	
Third year						
(1)	18	30	7	4	3	
(2)	17	30		5	3	4
Fourth year						
(1)	19	30	6	3	2	
(2)	12	30		4	4	6
Fifth year						
(1)	12	30	3	1	5	8
(2)	12	30		3	5	

Despite frequent complaints about the excessive work-load and the multiplicity of subjects, the main contours of the *VUZ* curriculum have changed little since the death of Stalin. Such changes as I can trace have involved, primarily, the revision of course content and the updating of textbooks. As in other sectors, the extreme centralisation of administration means that this is done by ministerial order rather than by individual initiative. The August 1954 decree called for a revision of courses 'so as to exclude superfluous material and repetition, and give the students more time for independent work' (Karpov and Severtsev, p. 64). Further reviews were made in the late 1950s and the mid-1960s, while the July 1972 law ordered yet another, lasting two years, and the *systematic* review of course material thereafter.

In the mid-1950s no less than 40 per cent of the technical subjects lacked up-to-date textbooks (Korol, p. 316). The August decree called for the writing, in the course of three or four years, of modern, high-quality volumes, and extra leave was granted for teachers who undertook it. There seems at first to have been a real improvement, in quantitative terms at least, for between 1950 and 1965 the output of textbooks and brochures rose from an average of seven to ten volumes per student. By 1978, however, it had fallen back to eight (*Pechat SSSR v 1978 godu*, p. 42).

The main language of instruction in Soviet *VUZy* has always, of course, been Russian. Non-Russian students have the right to be taught in their native tongue, though this is not always practicable, as the use of a minority language in the classroom may cause problems for mono-lingual Russians, not to mention other minorities. The degree to which it happens varies with the importance of the language involved and the availability of teachers and texts. It is also more likely in areas where there is intense nationalist feeling (Jacoby, p. 157).

In any case, the authorities have long encouraged the study of Russian among non-Russian students. Decrees passed in 1938, 1948, 1954 and May 1964 made Russian language classes obligatory wherever teaching was done in another tongue, and demoted the outside foreign language to optional status. The number of regulations on the matter indicates that it has remained something of a problem or, to put it another way, that this variety of russification has met significant resistance.

(3) *The Obligatory Subjects*

(a) *The 'Social Sciences'*. When Khrushchev came to power two basic ideological subjects – the fundamentals of Marxism–Leninism and political economy – were obligatory to all *VUZy*, regardless of specialisation, while a third – dialectical and historical materialism – was also taught at universities. The teaching was done by separate social science faculties and was a particular concern of *VUZ* primary party organisations. It took up some 400–500 hours, 8–11 per cent of the course time, according to institution, and was concentrated in the first years of study. Medicine appears to have been an exception in so far as the allotment was only 250 hours. The principal textbook used was the Stalin-oriented and thoroughly misleading *Short Course of the History of the VKP(b)*; Marxist–Leninist viewpoints permeated the material of many other courses.

Given the concern of the Soviet leaders with ideological rectitude, it is not surprising that successive change-overs in the Kremlin should have entailed delicate revisions. When Khrushchev came to power not only did Stalin's name have to be removed from the printed page and his role reassessed, but the admitted ineffectiveness of the courses as he authorised them had to be remedied. A decree of the Ministry of Higher Education of 3 July 1956 replaced the *Short Course* by a new Khrushchev-oriented tome called *The History of the CPSU*. Dialectical and historical materialism (later to be renamed 'Marxist–Leninist philosophy') was now made obligatory for all *VUZy*, so that the standard set became political economy, dialectical and historical materialism, and *The History of the CPSU*. These changes, to judge from curricula available, entailed no increase in the amount of instruction involved. Khrushchev authorised a revision of *The History of the CPSU* after ousting his opponents in the so-called 'anti-party group' of the late 1950s, and a new edition appeared in 1962.

In June 1963 a new course – the Fundamentals of Scientific Communism – was introduced into the last year of study. This involved an instruction load of twenty to seventy hours, depending on the *VUZ*, at the expense of the other social sciences (Voilenko, Vol. 1, p. 187). 'Scientific communism' was intended to give 'a cohesive picture of socialist and communist society, show the movement towards communism as an inevitable result of the struggle of the working class . . . and reveal the paths of struggle for a new social order'. It also had to 'show the social and political foundations of the ruin of capitalism and the triumph of socialism' (*BSE*, vol. 17, 1974, p. 347). Since the existing three courses were already filled with approved explanations of reality, the need for a fourth was, to say the least, questionable. 'With the introduction of this new course,' wrote one Soviet observer, 'the struggle with unnecessary duplication of material has acquired even greater importance' (*PZh*, no. 21, 1964, p. 54).

The students' poor understanding of Soviet economic organisation was another long-term worry. In July 1956 and again in April 1961, the *VUZy* were required to improve the teaching of political economy (Karpov and Severtsev, p. 84; Voilenko, Vol. 1, p. 194), and a stream of new textbooks bore witness to their efforts. A course called Scientific Atheism was proposed for historical and philosophical faculties in 1964 as part of one of Khrushchev's anti-religious campaigns (Abakumov *et al.*, p. 70). Though supposedly an elective requiring about eighty contact hours, it seems to have been made compulsory in some cases.

The fall of Khrushchev inevitably provoked another spasm. The first major Brezhnev pronouncement on ideological work (still regarded as authoritative in the late 1970s) was the August 1967 Central Committee decree 'On Measures for the Further Development of Social Sciences and Increasing their Role in Communist Construction'. This exceptionally tedious document envisaged a long-term revitalisation of the study of philosophy, economics, scientific communism, history (particularly of the CPSU) and law. As far as higher educational establishments were concerned, great emphasis was to be laid on improving the social science departments, especially by raising the quality of the teachers. Further training was to be introduced for them, and posts in ideological subjects were to be filled to more exacting standards. In 1969 a new, Brezhnev edition of *The History of the CPSU* was brought out; fourth and fifth editions followed in 1971 and 1974. Now it was Khrushchev's ideas and contributions which had to be downgraded.

The ineffectiveness of ideological courses was the subject of another burst of criticism in June 1974, when the authorities published reports on indoctrination in two highly respectable *VUZy* – the Bauman Technical *Uchilishche* in Moscow and the Saratov State University.

This was, of course, tantamount to criticising such instruction throughout the country, without actually saying so.[10] The main points made on this occasion have a certain timeless quality, and may be quoted to illustrate the genre:

> Important questions of theory and practice and of the history of the Communist Party and socialist state are sometimes set out in a superficial manner . . . criticism of contemporary bourgeois theories, reformism and revisionism is not sharp or convincing enough . . . many teachers do not create conditions for the creative discussion of topical questions of Marxist–Leninist theory . . . students sometimes do not get convincing answers to the questions which trouble them . . . many graduates are inadequately trained in contemporary philosophic and economic sciences . . . there are still instances of a negligent attitude to study and violations of social order among students . . . competitions for filling vacant teaching posts in ideological subjects and the attestation of research and teaching staff are often conducted in a formal manner . . . More than half of the teachers in the departments of political economy and philosophy of Saratov University do not have a basic higher education in these specialities. (*SPR*, 1975, p. 357)

The unacknowledged points at issue were the hopeless rigidity of the permitted philosophical interpretations and their absolute irrelevance to most students' practical needs. It was no accident that the ideological classes, though obligatory, were poorly attended (Jones, p. 434).

The decree went on to demand improvements in every conceivable direction. It included, however, two rather specific changes in the teaching and examination arrangements, which were quickly adopted (Voilenko, Vol. 1, pp. 188–94). First, the ideological courses were spread over all years of study instead of being concentrated in the first three, with the extension of Marxist–Leninist philosophy to two years. Secondly, a common state examination for scientific communism was now introduced everywhere, replacing single topics – CPSU history, political economy, dialectical and historical materialism – according to *VUZ* before (Karpov and Severtsev, p. 82). A separate but associated development was the introduction of a new thirty-hour course of Soviet law. This was prompted by a decree on the need for more legal education among students (May 1973) and was made obligatory in both *VUZy* and *SSUZy* (Voilenko, Vol. 1, p. 215). The 1976 curricula to hand suggest that these changes were effected without any significant increase in the instruction load.

Outside the curriculum, students' ideological activities were encouraged continuously. Without pursuing the matter in depth, one may note that the most common forms of involvement during these years were 'young lecturer' schools and 'social professions' faculties (providing training in such skills as public speaking and political agitation), together with essay competitions in the social sciences, *Komsomol* history and the international youth movement. The holiday work brigades (see page 166) were said to be enormously beneficial to the students' ideological development (*PZh*, 1973, no. 7, p. 13).

(b)   *Foreign Languages and Physical Training.* The subsidiary foreign language and physical training courses offered in Soviet *VUZy* share the distinction of being among the least disturbed elements in the curriculum for many years.

An ordinance of September 1940 stated that every *VUZ* graduate should be able to read specialist literature and conduct a conversation in a foreign language. In fact, he could not take his state examinations unless he had successfully completed a course in one (Movshovich and Khodzhaev, p. 124). The matter was, however, very subject to neglect. The languages themselves were often badly taught, many students were not interested in learning them, and the chances of using them (given Russia's isolation) were minimal. The Khrushchev leadership, intent on the development of foreign contacts, made two distinct efforts to improve the situation.

In September 1955 a decree of the Ministry of Higher Education re-emphasised the importance of knowing a foreign tongue (though, more realistically, only for purposes of specialist translation) and set out more specific rules for instruction. Universities and engineering and physics *VUZy* were to offer 240–70 hours on the first two courses, while other *VUZy* offered 140.[11] A further decree passed in May 1961 (Voilenko, Vol. 1, p. 206) made 240 hours of language teaching the common minimum for all non-linguistic *VUZy*, and provided extra, optional, lessons. It declared that another attempt should be made to bring students in the humanities faculties of universities up to good conversational standard. No important changes seem to have been recorded after that.

Physical education first became obligatory for medically fit students in 1929. Since then it has commonly been run by a separate department with trained instructors; some of the older curricula show that, when listed, it took up about 130 hours. The main emphasis has always been on athletics, which ties in with voluntary sporting activities. Instructions of December 1955 introduced a new set of fitness programmes and tests. Students were divided into three groups according to their athletic ability, and PT was co-ordinated with the para-military *GTO* ('ready for labour and defence') movement. The instructions were reissued, with some changes of detail, in February 1960, and have been retained in that form up to the present.

The mid and late 1950s saw a number of changes in the administration of public sport with the aim of improving Soviet performance in the international arena, and some of these affected the *VUZ*. In 1957 an all-union students' sports society, called the *Burevestnik* (or 'stormy petrel'), was set up for enthusiasts. It had branches in most *VUZy*, and its membership rose from about 400,000 in 1959 to 1,800,000 in 1976 (De Witt, p. 312; *SES*, 1979, p. 181). A trades union regulation of the same year promoted the establishment of student summer sports camps. Some idea of the overall development of interest in this sphere may be gained from the fact that the number of Master of Sport titles issued throughout the country rose from 3,300 in 1950 to 147,000 in 1978.

(c) *Production Practice.* The vocational pressures on Soviet *VUZ* courses have meant that large numbers of students, particularly in the more practical disciplines, spend much time, particularly in the vacations, observing and practising the skills of their future profession. According to regulations of 1938 which were evidently still in force when Khrushchev came to power, students were sent out to such places as enterprises, farms, offices and schools, for periods varying from six weeks to a full year.[12] The work they did was supposed to match their growing skills and end with direct supervised involvement at professional level. At first, the numbers involved were relatively small; but even by the late 1940s inadequate placement and supervision caused doubt to be expressed about the usefulness of the operation (Korol, pp. 343–5).

Nevertheless, Khrushchev could not fail to exploit so admirable a link with life. The August 1954 decree called for the drafting of new regulations for industrial training, and stated that *VUZy* should be provided with their own workshops and, where necessary, raw materials. The special responsibilities of the enterprises which received students for practice were also reaffirmed.

A new statute was not, in fact, approved until 18 January 1956; but together with ministerial instructions which followed in March, it covered all the administrative arrangements in great detail. There were to be three periods of production practice during the course of study, during which the student was supposed to go through all the basic 'production operations' connected with his specialisation. Time inputs were somewhat reduced and unified (twenty to thirty weeks for most technical and agricultural specialities, six to twenty weeks for history, mathematics, physics, law, medicine, teaching and sports). In addition to practice in their specialities, students were to be instructed in organisational and economic matters. The costs of training by and large devolved on the enterprise concerned, but the students themselves, except where they were actually replacing permanent personnel or performing production tasks, continued to be considered as outsiders and eligible for the usual *VUZ* maintenance grant. How far the new measures were implemented is not easy to discover; but complaints about continuing friction and abuse of student labour continued.

The December 1958 reform (or, more exactly, attempted reform) of higher education was much concerned with the problem of production practice, and aimed to blur the distinction between it and regular work. The reform could thus have reduced the need for production practice in the older sense; but such practice was probably intensified in cases where *VUZ* authorities postponed reorganisation and relied on familiar links. The answer to this puzzle lies buried in ministerial archives. In any case a new statute, designed to fit the post-reform situation, was approved in December 1959. This envisaged a dual system: production *work*, for students as learners, on the earlier courses, followed by production *practice* for those in their senior years. Students were to involve themselves in 'socially useful' labour and seriously learn workers' skills. Reports which appeared in official journals at first greatly praised the new arrangement; but it was not long before the familiar administrative and social difficulties came to the fore. Urgent calls for improvement were made in decrees promulgated in July 1962 for the RSFSR and in May 1963 for the country as a whole.

Under the Brezhnev leadership, production practice was modified twice. A statute approved on 30 May 1968 dropped the concept of production 'work' as such, and stated that the aim of the practice was to strengthen theoretical knowledge gained by the student during his *VUZ* course. A decree published in August of the same year ensured the payment of normal maintenance grants during the practice periods, such payments having evidently been suspended some time previously (*SZAT*, 1974, p. 240). All this amounted to an implicit rejection of the Khrushchev trend. Yet that was not the end of the matter, for a statute published in July 1974 again emphasised that the practice was not only a back-up for theoretical studies but also a means of acquiring *practical* skills (Voilenko, Vol. 1, p. 240). The responsibility of the *VUZ* authorities in ensuring satisfactory instruction was now set out in great detail: and renewed emphasis was laid on students' socio-political involvement at the workplace.

To judge from references in major pieces of legislation, the production component continued to be most troublesome. A comprehensive list of defects given (together with an array of successes) in a decree of December 1974 may be mentioned by way of conclusion. It complained that production practice was sometimes shortened or organised hastily, on the basis of unsatisfactory work programmes; students were in some cases given workers' jobs for the whole period of practice, thereby excluding the training programmed; there was sometimes a lack of contact between *VUZy* and enterprises; and there were instances of students ignoring enterprise rules, absenting themselves and not indulging in approved socio-political activities (Voilenko, Vol. 1, p. 246). The decree called for better control of production practice and forbade *VUZ* authorities to send students out to building sites, agricultural work or other activities 'at the expense of time set aside in *VUZ* study plans for production practice'.

(d) *Military Training*. In the early 1950s, under the terms of the 1939 conscription law, military training was in principle obligatory for all male students. Exemption could be requested on family or medical grounds only, since there was no conscientious objection. Such training has remained a regular feature of *VUZ* life up to the present, the legal basis for it being updated in October 1967. Unfortunately, apart from these general provisions I have not been able to trace much official documentation, perhaps because the matter lies primarily in the competence of the Ministry of Defence. I have therefore relied on reports provided by a few students who were at one time or another personally involved.[13]

Training seems to be in all cases run by a separate military department and confined to the senior years of study. In the mid 1970s, for example, students of the Moscow Institute of Engineering Transport had no military commitments at all during their first two years, but from the third until graduation they spent one day a week (three two-hour periods) in a special block attached to the institute. Here they were systematically instructed in basic military skills, drill and marksmanship, and in military specialities close to their studies. Students of the Novorossiisk Polytechnical Institute in the late 1960s did two four-hour stints weekly, also from the third course onwards, and acquired skills in aerial navigation. The training in this case was said to be particularly onerous, sometimes entailing access to classified material, with all the attendant rigmarole of state clearance and verification. At the Leningrad Kalinin Polytechnical Institute students studied rocketry in a specially converted church which was kept under armed guard. Prowess in military training is checked, like ordinary subjects, by regular tests and examinations, and failure can mean loss of a maintenance grant.

Field training is fitted into the summer vacations. At the Leningrad Institute, for example, male students had to undergo two twenty-day periods of training as sergeants in their second and fourth vacations. When the normal state examinations were over, the graduates went off for a lengthier period in the field (seven weeks in the case of the Moscow Institute) and then, after some days of revision, took a full state examination in military subjects. Failure at this point could entail a difficult period of military service in the ranks, and for this reason was said to be extremely rare. Successful students went into the reserve as junior lieutenants.

I have not been able to determine the kinds of *VUZy* in which no military training is imposed. Such establishments are few in number and mostly artistic or humanitarian in orientation. They include the conservatories and theatrical, bibliographic and some pedagogical institutes. Other *VUZy* which have a large percentage of women in the student body may also be assigned to this category, since the maintenance of a military department for a very few men might not be worthwhile. But the unpopularity of such *VUZy* among men may then be sealed for ever, as male graduates would normally be required to do an unpleasant period of service in the ranks.

The extent to which women are involved cannot be determined, either. All female students in medical institutes have to do military training, and those at other *VUZy* may be called on to learn such skills as nursing, radio communications and translation, for military uses. Sometimes, however, this is voluntary. When not engaged in these activities, female students have extra free time.

(4)   *The Examination System*

As we have already noted, an elaborate examination system became characteristic of the Soviet *VUZ* (as, indeed, of the general school and *SSUZ*) in the 1930s. Since then all the work that a Soviet student does – with the possible exception of the electives – is subject to some kind of assessment. Five types of hurdle can be distinguished: (1) the *VUZ* entrance examinations, (2) course tests, (3) course examinations, (4) the diploma project or its equivalent and (5) the final, or 'state' examinations leading to the issue of a *VUZ* 'diploma'. There has been little significant change in this system since Stalin died, so I shall begin by describing the most recent sets of rules, leaving until last brief comment on such development as has been publicised.

A general school-leaving certificate has been obligatory for admission to an institution of higher education since June 1936. To join a full-time course the applicant must be under 35: otherwise there is no age limit. This statement of principle covers a web of rules regarding privileges for those who were exceptionally successful in their earlier schooling or who acquired particular types of work experience.

Most applicants begin by choosing their *VUZ* and specialisation from the detailed handbooks published annually by the Ministry of Higher and Secondary Special Education. They are then required to submit an application to the rector of that *VUZ*, appending certification of complete secondary (or other advanced) education, a recommendation of suitability (usually provided by their school) or confirmation of satisfactory employment, a medical certificate and photographs. The entrance examinations are normally held in August and are, of course, competitive.

The actual level of demand for *VUZ* places is not revealed consistently, and it is difficult to judge change over time. However, a few ministerial reports have shown that in the late 1970s there were usually about 1½ million applications for some 600,000 full-time places, which gave a ratio of about 1:2·5 (*BMV*, no. 2, 1977, p. 7; no.

2, 1978, p. 8). There were, as might be expected, great variations according to such factors as which *VUZ*, subject and locality were involved. Within Leningrad University, for example, applications in the years 1968–74 ranged from 1·6 to 12 per place, the differences between faculties remaining on the whole fairly stable over time (Table 4.4).

Table 4.4   *Applications per Place at Leningrad University, by Faculty, 1968–74*

Faculty	1968	1970	1972	1974
Applied				
mathematics	—	3·7	2·3	1·6
Physics	2·1	2·0	2·4	2·2
Chemistry	2·3	2·1	1·9	1·9
Geography	3·7	5·7	4·6	5·0
Economics	3·0	3·0	3·5	3·7
History	9·4	8·5	10·0	12·0
Law	7·0	10·3	11·2	7·5
Philosophy	4·5	4·8	4·9	5·3
Philology	7·5	6·5	6·7	7·0
Journalism	5·3	4·0	2·6	2·7

Source: Lisovski and Dmitriev, p. 44, selected items.

The subjects required for the *VUZ* entrance examination comprise Russian (or other native language), both written and oral, plus two others, according to specialisation; mathematics, with physics, chemistry or biology must be offered on the science side, and history, geography or a foreign language in the humanities. The examination questions are based on the general school programme, but require some extra work. Most of them are answered orally before a *VUZ* selection commission. The 'ticket' system is commonly used, with marking on the five-point scale, as described earlier. The results of orals are made known immediately, and those of written exams within a few days. A single 'unsatisfactory' mark means that the applicant has failed and is precluded from proceeding further.

Given the competition for *VUZ* places, bare passes are usually insufficient to ensure admission. The points gained by each applicant must be totted up, and those with the highest scores are offered places. Several possibilities are open in 'tied' and 'borderline' cases. The examiners may admit the applicant with the higher mark in the most relevant examination or (alternatively) a better performance at school. Sometimes a borderline applicant may be offered a place, but in a specialisation which is less popular and requires a lower overall score. In some cases he may gain admission to another *VUZ* which has unfilled places and is prepared to accept his marks without further verification. Unfortunately, the time restriction on the application procedure usually precludes this, and there is no more than one chance of a *VUZ* place in any given year. One suspects that some of the less popular *VUZy* would in fact welcome a 'clearing house' arrangement.

The admission rules also discourage applications for second degrees. According to an instruction of 9 February 1961 which remained valid at least into the mid-1970s, a person could be admitted full-time for a second specialisation only if he needed it at his place of employment, if his existing work became impracticable for medical reasons, or if he was obliged to move to an area where his original specialisation was not required (*SZAT*, 1974, p. 261). Part-time study was allowed on approximately the same terms, though there is evidence that they were not always strictly observed. In all cases credits for courses completed earlier at another *VUZ* were a matter for individual arrangement. It may be that most second degrees are acquired through the party channels (page 184).

Aggregated results of the entrance examinations are not usually published, but standards have been the subject of complaint from time to time. A ministerial instruction of December 1976, for example, stated that only one-third of applicants to the *VUZy* of Central Asia and the Caucasus had passed all the entrance exams. In 1977 the RSFSR Ministry of Enlightenment conducted an experiment in five *oblasts* of European Russia, to verify the standards of 1,000 applicants to pedagogical *VUZy* who had 'good' and 'excellent' marks in the general school. Of these only 237 performed as well at the *VUZ* portals; 424 were admitted, but on average marks only, while 219 failed altogether.[14]

Entrance examinations at *VUZy* offering particularly desirable training have long been subject to abuse from over-zealous candidates (or their parents). The most common deviations mentioned in ministerial reports involve direct infringements of the rules, falsification of documents and alteration of mark sheets (*BMV*, no. 2, 1977, p. 7; no. 2, 1978, p. 8). Parental interference is occasionally castigated in the newspapers. It varies, some people assert, from political or administrative influence in the European areas to cash payments in the Soviet Orient.[15]

Several safeguards have been devised against abuse of the system. No application can be examined by a single *VUZ* teacher; written work is supposed to carry a number, rather than a name, so as to conceal the writer's identity; outsiders can be allowed to act as examiners only with the proper authorisation; the sittings of selection commissions are of restricted length, so as to obviate the need for replacement examiners; the composition of the commissions has to be changed by at least half every year; and the re-examination of failed candidates is categorically forbidden. After the admissions have been decided, the examination results on which they were based have no further significance for course performance.

During his years of study the *VUZ* student has to pass around seventy tests and course examinations, covering all the obligatory subjects (Tables 4.3a, 4.3b) and military skills. The *tests* are intended to serve as a continuing check on his progress. They may be done as written papers, essays, laboratory work or production practice; in ideological subjects they may also take the form of open question periods. Only in the case of electives does the student, in theory at least, have the choice of taking them or not. In most cases they are either passed or failed, though the *VUZ* sometimes has the right to introduce graded marking. All of the student's results are entered into his personal mark book, and success is normally essential for passing up. A student who fails a test may be allowed to take his course exams and proceed to the next year of study, on the understanding that the failure is retrieved.

Course *examinations*, as the name implies, are more formal. They are usually held at the end of the semester, during the 'examination session'; three or four days are allowed for preparation. The exams may be oral or written, and are usually done by ticket; all carry a graded mark. Passes are entered into the student's mark book but failure may not be, so as to give a chance of retrieval.

In fact failure in three or more examinations entails exclusion from the *VUZ*. If the student pips one or two he may, with the rector's permission, proceed, but only on condition that he successfully resits them in the first subsequent month of study. Such failure cannot, as a rule, be retrieved during the same session, although the dean of the faculty has the right to order a resit, with the services of the same examiner, if there is adequate reason. A student may repeat up to two years of his course if his work has been disrupted by illness, family circumstances or involvement in officially authorised business.

The third type of hurdle is the *diploma project* or *diploma work;* most of the last semester is usually devoted to it. It offers the student his third type of choice within the framework of the course, in so far as he can either select a topic from an approved faculty list or suggest something himself. The length of the work is stipulated by the faculty, and supervision is usually provided by a senior member of staff. The project or work is supposed not only to serve as an index of its author's academic prowess, but also to complete the learning process in 'systematising, fixing and broadening' his knowledge and developing his work and research techniques. Of the two types, the diploma work is more recent and is used primarily for courses in the humanities. The seriousness with which this stage is regarded is evident from the fact that the text is forwarded for perusal and discussion in the final examination.

The tests and exams which the student undergoes during his training have more than an academic significance: eligibility for a maintenance grant, which has to be applied for twice annually, depends entirely on passing them. Teachers presumably offer as much help as they are able, but cessation of the grant is automatic in the event of failure.

The *state examination,* based on the March 1974 statute, marks the culmination of the *VUZ* course. It is conducted by a commission (or commissions, if the *VUZ* is a large one) consisting of the rector (or pro-rector), the dean of the faculty (or his deputy), senior teachers and a representative of the faculty of social sciences. Outside specialists may be brought in as needed; the chairman of the commission must be approved by the ministry or administration to which the *VUZ* is subordinate. The tasks of the commission are to check 'the scientific, theoretical, ideological, political and practical training' of the student, to give him a qualification and diploma (with or without distinction), and to suggest course improvements for the future.

A student is allowed to appear before the commission only if he has fulfilled all course requirements. He must present (1) confirmation of this fact, together with the set of marks achieved, and (2) a recommendation from a party, *Komsomol* or other social organisation based on his social and political activity. Both of these documents are read out before the formal questioning, or 'defence' and form part of the final assessment. The other documents needed are (3) a supervisor's report and (4) an assessment of the diploma project or work. The defence is public, but the discussion among commission members which follows it is closed.

The three or four subjects actively examined at this point must include the diploma project (work) and scientific communism. The ticket system, with five-point marking, is used again; there is a provisional upper limit of forty-five minutes for testing each subject. A diploma 'with exellence' is issued to students who have at least (1) an 'excellent' mark in 75 per cent of their courses and 'good' in the remainder, and (2) an 'excellent' mark in all of their state exams. The results of the examination are made known the same day.

Failure in any part of the state examination is treated with surprising liberalism. If it is a question of the diploma project, the commission may allow the student to rewrite, or to start another. Other subjects may be retaken within a term of three years. In the meantime the student is given an academic certificate and directed into a job, as though he were a successful graduate. Special arrangements are, of course, made for persons who were not able to take the state examination for reasons beyond their control. Regulations are identical for full- and part-time students, except that, for those on correspondence courses, the times of the examination sessions need not fit the normal *VUZ* semesters. The state examination commission, on completing its task, submits a detailed report on its work to the *MinVUZ* (*BMV*, no. 5, 1974, p. 27).

The question of the development of the *VUZ* examination system since the early 1950s may, as we suggested, be dealt with in a few words. The entrance exams were subject to a considerable amount of change of detail, but not of principle; as this was of social rather than educational significance, it can best be dealt with in Chapter 5. A comparison of the May 1951 and June 1973 statutes on internal examinations and tests reveals comparative quiescence. Regulations merely became more comprehensive so as to cover part-time courses, and contained a few new restrictions on resits. At the same time references appeared, Brezhnev-fashion, to the need to consult 'public opinion' when deciding the fate of marginal failures.

The state examination hardly changed, either. The May 1938 statute was slightly modified in the early 1960s, and then replaced by a more detailed version in March 1974. Under the terms of this the composition of the commission was loosened, so that outside specialists could be more easily brought in; the fixed dates for its sessions were dropped; and (echoing the terms of the August 1954 decree) the rules for issuing diplomas with excellence were made somewhat more stringent.[16]

VUZ REFORM AND THE PART-TIME SECTOR

In higher education, as in the general school, Khrushchev wished to lessen the distinctions between student and worker and between full- and part-time education. The December 1958 reform was, amongst other things, an attempt to adapt *VUZy* to this end: its provisions are thus best treated together with the policies for combining study and work. The matter of improving higher educational opportunity for the less privileged children, to which the reform was also strongly directed, can be best considered as a student problem.

(1) *Pre-Reform Work – Study Arrangements*

By the early 1950s part-time study was, as we have seen, well established. It could be undertaken on an evening or correspondence basis, either through special part-time institutions or at extra-mural faculties attached to full-time ones. In 1955 there were eight evening and twenty-two correspondence *VUZy*: in addition, 205 full-time institutions (out of the total of 765) had evening, and 412 correspondence facilities (De Witt, p. 231).

Part-time students followed courses which were closely modelled on the full-time variants, with some restriction in the choice of specialisations. Such courses lasted an extra year or more: applicants were supposed to be already employed in jobs which matched their proposed subject of study. Evening students usually attended classes on the premises of a local *VUZ*, while correspondence students studied at home. The reading and essay assignments of the latter could be supplemented by individual or group consultations at a local annexe or consultation point. All part-time students were required to attend designated *VUZy* for a full set of tests and examinations.

Despite help with work release schemes, the disadvantages of both kinds of part-time study were daunting. Participants were expected to shoulder an exceptionally heavy work-load, while getting much less help than full-time students. Correspondence courses were particularly difficult to pursue. The part-time sector tended to be poorly financed and staffed; it was also, as we have noted, very inefficient in terms of graduation rates.

Despite these long-standing drawbacks, the August 1954 decree emphasised the need to double the number of part-time students (at the secondary special and higher levels) by 1960, while trebling part-time enrolments in agricultural and technical specialities. Complete figures are again not available, but it seems that these targets were in fact surpassed. At the same time attempts were made to ease the outstanding difficulties of study, by improving material facilities on the one hand and extending work–release provisions on the other. In September 1954 the Ministry of Higher Education acquired the right to open consultation points for smaller numbers of students, and the statutes approved for annexes and consultation points in February 1956 permitted improvements in the services offered. There were new rules – too detailed for us to consider here – on the supply of teachers, textbooks and equipment.

The provisions for work–release were still based on older legislation passed in 1939 and 1941. Supplements to the September 1954 decree extended these significantly; would-be evening students now became entitled to ten days' unpaid leave for *VUZ* entrance exams (a benefit formerly limited to correspondence students), while up to thirty days of paid leave were made available annually for tests or examinations. All part-timers on the last course of technical *VUZy* became eligible for no less than four months' leave for their diploma projects, with pay or stipend, and arts students, who at that time did not normally undertake projects, were given one month. Extra time was also to be allowed for any travelling involved. These not ungenerous provisions, however, were limited to students who successfully passed all their exams (Karpov and Severtsev, pp. 117, 121; *SZAT*, 1956, p. 459).

(2)   *The December 1958 Reform Proposals*

Sadly, there is no evidence that these changes brought about any improvement in quality or significantly eased the difficulties of study over the next few years. Perhaps, given the nature of the problems involved, only slow amelioration could be hoped for. But Khrushchev seemed intent on expanding the part-time sector nevertheless, and the December 1958 reform included provisions for a considerable strengthening of its role.

The clearest description of what was proposed came in the decree of the USSR Council of Ministers of 4 August 1959, which stated that there were to be three channels for part-time, and no less than seven for full-time study; all of the 'full-time' variants were, however, to have strong part-time or production admixtures.[17] A new type of joint *VUZ*–enterprise establishment, called the *Zavod-VTUZ*, was to be promoted to facilitate combinations of work and study in technical fields.[18] The reform as a whole was to embrace all specialisations but to add not more than six months to any. It was to be started, for first-year students, in September 1959. The August decree did not set a deadline for its completion, but ministerial comment made it clear that the reorganisation would proceed only on a year-by-year basis, thus extending over the length of a full *VUZ* course.

We have already discussed the changes in the nature of production practice which ensued. The proposed system, it will be noted, demanded some complicated financing. Students were to be paid first as learners, money being passed for the purpose from the *VUZ* stipend fund to the enterprise; next as regular workers; and finally as specialists on the enterprise payroll. The workers who taught them in the early stages were to receive the normal rate for instructors. Presumably the enterprises and organisations themselves had to bear production or other losses due to these arrangements. In the interests of smooth running, the *VUZy* were to be linked with selected enterprises and organisations by ministerial order.

The emphasis on part-time study prompted another round of improvements in work–release benefits. New rules published for both *VUZ* and *SSUZ* students in July 1959 contained further important concessions, in particular the right to days off over long periods.[19] Collective farm administrations were recommended to introduce similar provisions for their members. In November 1961 the authorities relaxed regulations for the timing of examinations, so as to alleviate the difficulties which arose when a lot of young people presented themselves simultaneously. These provisions were still valid in the late 1970s.

So much for the letter of the reform. The arrangements proposed were, I think, too far-reaching and complex to be successful. Many of the reform's central aspects – including the planning, financing and work–study proposals – bristled with difficulty. The best exposition of the practical problems I have come across was provided by a party secretary of the Tomsk Engineering and Construction Institute who was personally involved in them. Appearing as it did in one of the most authoritative party journals, it deserves quoting at length:

This year [he wrote, in the summer of 1960] first-year students in the mechanical and construction faculties, like students in other institutes, have been signed on as workers at building sites, where for two years they will learn a trade . . .combined with evening classes at the institute . . . From the third year onwards they will study full-time . . .

Some building managers and permanent staff at first adopted an incorrect attitude towards them, used them on subsidiary jobs and did not give them building materials . . . The students lost interest and often left the site . . . The party bureau of the institute invited the managers, together with party, trades union and *Komsomol* representatives, to discuss . . . all the difficulties, the mutual complaints and demands. We agreed to create student work brigades under the control of experienced instructors, give them work and clothing, arrange proper payment for them and find ways of establishing discipline on both sides . . . After that the students' production instruction improved noticeably and many shortcomings were corrected . . .

Before he came to the institute as a *dotsent* [senior lecturer], Comrade Oblonin was a civil engineer . . . and he often visits the sites where the students work . . . Once he saw they were not setting bricks properly, so he immediately asked the foreman over and together with him showed them how to do it. He found out from talking to the students that they were being paid less than they should have been, so he intervened and the matter was soon put right . . .

The problem of discipline among the students has certainly not been solved. Some of them have not yet got used to observing the strict building-site rules or doing their work neatly. Others take advantage of laxity on the part of the foremen, come late, leave early or miss work . . .

And what about their studies? It must be admitted that we were quite concerned as to whether yesterday's schoolchildren could cope with the heavy and unfamiliar burden of combined study and production work. The results of the first semester have shown that *VUZ* study can be combined with productive labour . . . Obviously it is difficult to study and work. A strong will, determination, orderliness and patience are essential . . . But it would be wrong to ignore a certain overburdening of students on the evening and full-time courses . . . In order to spare students unnecessary and tiring journeys [between the site and the institute] the party bureau suggested that consultations [with teachers] be held in the site hostels and that a subsidiary library be opened there with a study room and drawing-boards. That was done . . . We concerned ourselves with improving living conditions . . . All these measures, however, have only partially solved the problem. We should evidently think about shortening the students' working day. (*PZh*, no. 6, 1960, p. 36)

Considerable malaise about the general progress of the reform was expressed in legal enactments, and we can do no better, for purposes of analysis, than summarise them.

(3) *Failure – and a New Approach*

According to a decree promulgated in the RSFSR on 9 August 1962, the re-organisation of courses had only been 'started', while the relocation of *VUZy* and the enlargement of them which the reform entailed were still 'being carried out'. True, five *Zavody-VTUZy* and over 200 new production-based faculties had been established, but since there were at least 2,000 faculties throughout the republic this was not very impressive. The USSR decrees of 9 May 1963 on the development of higher and secondary special education, and of 9 April 1964 on the part-time sector, confirmed the presence of virtually all the old evils but made no constructive proposals for removing them. Since the latter document contains one of the most authoritative critiques of work–study arrangements ever made under Khrushchev, it, too, deserves quotation. Despite all the successes registered, it said:

> a significant number of students do not finish their courses on time; many drop out, particularly from the first courses . . . the quality of theoretical training . . . in some cases does not match up to requirements . . . Persons are admitted to *VUZy* without sufficient regard to their practical work experience . . . the provision of textbooks is unsatisfactory . . . few professors, qualified teachers or production specialists are involved in the teaching. Some managers and social organisations overload part-time students with production and social tasks . . . do not promote them as their qualifications improve, nor help them master new technology . . . Existing premises and equipment are inadequate to ensure normal conditions of study . . . New annexes, and particularly consultation points, are often organised without proper premises being available. (*SZAT*, 1965, p. 210; *SPR*, 1964, p. 240)

Revelations of the damage which the reform had actually caused to Soviet higher education were contained in an unusually poignant article by T. D. Samilova in the September 1965 number of the journal *Vestnik vysshei shkoly*. All types of part-time higher education, she claimed, gave considerably worse results than full-time courses. Nearly 60 per cent of the students on evening courses and 70 per cent of those on correspondence courses failed to complete their studies on time, while their fall-out rates were nearly 30 and 40 per cent respectively. Part-time students had only a quarter as much time available for study as full-time students, and the great majority of them had to use their free days and holidays for this purpose. They had two and a half times less sleep than was required to meet physiological norms, and as a result fell ill more often or at least took a lot of time off on medical grounds.

The fall-out rate between the full-time *VUZ* intakes of 1953–4 and

1959–60 (which, significantly, spanned these years) had risen from about 20 to 40 per cent; the number of persons repeating a course increased 2·4 times, and the number switching courses, or *VUZy*, rose by 70 per cent. These facts were not readily explicable in terms of an increase in the size of the student body; Samilova implied that most of the blame should be placed on the method of selecting students – in other words, the privileges accorded to candidates who had spent time on production. Up to 60 per cent of these, she said, tended to drop out in the first year. In 1964–5, moreover, 61 per cent were in jobs which had no relation to the subjects they wished to study at a *VUZ*. A third of them had studied in part-time general schools, where standards were known to be lower. Also, they were much more heterogeneous in age and experience than young people straight from school, and thus more difficult to teach. Their presence had caused the average age of the student body in full-time institutions to go up by two years. All in all, Samilova left no doubt that from the academic point of view the *VUZ* 'reform' had been a disaster.[20]

A return to the status quo ante required no far-reaching organisational innovations. The new official policy, as reflected in the key decrees of September 1966 and July 1972, involved some quiet abandonment, downgrading mixed work and study schemes, and laying greater emphasis on academic quality. To judge from his few speeches on the subject, Brezhnev was not much interested in higher education and was prepared to leave matters to anti-reformist officials. Khrushchev's proposed sandwich schemes were mentioned no more in major enactments. The proportion of part-time students, as we have already noted, was allowed to fall away markedly, though the numbers tended to creep up again later. A debate published in *Vestnik vysshei shkoly* in the summer of 1966, while again recognising the grievous shortcomings of the sector, emphasised that it could be improved.[21] Production practice for *VUZ* students, as we have seen, reverted to a more subordinate and pedagogical activity.

The new emphasis on distinctiveness and quality was expressed principally in upgrading the strongest *VUZy*, improving facilities, and raising the qualifications of teaching staff. The September 1966 decree allowed the USSR *MinVUZ* to authorise major *VUZy* to develop their own publishing facilities, and twenty-five leading institutions were given extra staff and funds to do so. Several decrees dealt specifically with the role of the universities; one published in June 1974 stipulated that they were to be the main source of teachers for other *VUZy* and the leading methodological centres for all higher education. They were to concentrate more on research, receive better equipment and enjoy preferential treatment in matters of finance (Voilenko, Vol. 1, p. 212; *VVSh*, no. 8, 1974, p. 45).

The efforts made to improve staff ratings were in fact quite extraordinary. 'Faculties for raising the qualifications of *VUZ* teachers', offering four-month courses, were started at selected *VUZy*. Other courses of similar length were instituted under the aegis of the USSR Academy of Sciences for teachers of pedagogical institutes, while three-month practice periods at leading industrial and agricultural enterprises, *VUZy* and research institutes were stipulated for teachers of 'special' disciplines. By the mid 1970s 50,000 teachers were apparently being trained under such schemes annually.

POSTGRADUATE RESEARCH

The system of postgraduate research, leading to the degrees of Candidate and Doctor of Sciences, had been formalised by the mid 1930s. Despite a great deal of minor amendment it remained basically unchanged into the late 1970s. Let us begin with the rules for Candidates.[22]

Under the terms of the November 1950 statute people under 40 who possessed a *VUZ* diploma and an aptitude for research could apply for admission to the *aspirantura,* which led to the degree of Candidate of Sciences. The entrance examinations included the fundamentals of Marxism–Leninism, the chosen specialisation and a foreign language. Applicants were expected to provide the admission board with proof of teaching or production experience, but this stipulation could be waived for promising individuals.

The *aspirantura* lasted three or four years (depending on whether it was full- or part-time), and was divided into two parts. In the first, which normally lasted two years, the *aspirant* prepared himself for a qualifying examination called the 'candidate's minimum'. The remaining year was devoted to writing a dissertation on a theme approved by the rector and the learned council. Although, to judge from the statutes, this approval was entirely within the competence of the *VUZ,* some control must have been exercised at ministerial level, if only in the form of subsequent confirmation. Dissertation work was an individual matter between the *aspirant* and his supervisor, who was supposed to be a competent senior member of staff, approved by the Ministry of Higher Education. The *aspirant* worked to an agreed plan, and could attend any lectures or classes relevant to his work. He might be expected to do some tutoring himself, and be nominated to the junior post of *assistent* for the purpose. The statute contained provisions for the *aspirant* to be tested regularly on his progress.

After successfully passing his candidate's minimum, comprising dialectical and historical materialism, a foreign language and a topic basic to the field of study, he could work on his dissertation. A number of formalities, including the printing and distribution of an outline (*avtoreferat*), would follow completion; suitably qualified opponents would then be named, and a date set for the defence. We have no means of knowing what proportion of dissertations was rejected or referred back for academic (or indeed political) reasons; but defences have on occasion been observed to be superficial, and learned councils have been sharply criticised for laxity of judgement.

If successfully defended, the candidate dissertation would be sent on to experts in the Supreme Attestation Commission attached to the *MinVUZ*; and if it was approved, the *aspirant* would be granted a Candidate of Sciences degree in one of the nineteen recognised fields of endeavour.[23] The commission had the right not only to query the decisions of the *VUZ* learned councils but also to annul degrees issued – a curious practice indeed from a Western point of view. *Aspiranty* with or without a candidate's degree were subject to state posting for three years, just like ordinary graduates. Failure to fulfil this obligation likewise made them liable to prosecution 'as established by the law'.

The rules for Doctors of Sciences – who were far less numerous – contained no 'minimum' and allowed much more flexibility in research arrangements. The applicants normally had to be Candidates of Science under 45, with research experience and a knowledge of more than one foreign language. Whereas the candidate dissertation had only to 'reveal the candidate's general theoretical and specialist knowledge of matters dealt with in the dissertation, and his ability to conduct independent research, which must express itself in the achievement of a new scientific or learned result', the doctorate had to 'present the solution to, or theoretical generalisation of, scientific problems which were of significant scientific interest' (Movshovich and Khodzhaev, p. 318; Karpov and Severtsev, p. 321).

The number of places available for postgraduate research was, as might be expected, a matter within ministerial competence. All the universities and the majority of the institutes were authorised to take *aspiranty*, though not all had the right to conduct defences. The number of *VUZy* allowed doctoral candidates was much more restricted. Full-time *aspiranty* were entitled to a stipend of 600–700 roubles a month, depending on the *VUZ* they attended, compared with 140–315 roubles for ordinary students (see page 164 below). Part-timers could claim an extra thirty days' holiday a year with maintenance payments for examinations and study purposes.

The state has always shown a readiness to encourage postgraduate research by less formal means. A decree of May 1954 allowed suitably qualified outsiders – persons who had taught for three years or more in schools or other educational institutions, for example – to be 'attached' to *VUZy* for this purpose and admitted to the candidate's minimum examinations without formal inscription as *aspiranty* (Karpov and Severtsev, p. 296). If they were successful they could be granted *aspirant* status for one year, so as to write their dissertation. This could in turn be replaced by published or unpublished work, or authorship of a high-quality *VUZ* textbook. Senior *VUZ* staff, moreover, could be permitted to start a dissertation without the candidate's minimum. A decree of the Ministry of Higher Education of January 1953 allowed learned councils to apply for degrees on behalf of people who had made particularly outstanding contributions to science, technology and the humanities, even if they had no higher education at all (Karpov and Severtsev, p. 321).

From the point of view of the state, full-time *aspiranty* have always been expensive trainees. In a recent set of cost coefficients for different types of *VUZ* study, they had a rating of 2·5, as against 1·0 for full-time undergraduates, 0·4 for correspondence students, 0·5 for evening students and 0·3 for part-time *aspiranty*.[24] These figures may or may not have been realistic, but taken at their face value they go a long way towards explaining the authorities' efforts to find outside sources of funds. In fact much postgraduate work – particularly that pertaining most to the productive branches of the economy – has long been financed on a contract basis by production ministries or large enterprises.

(1) *Developments under Khrushchev*

The years 1955–7 witnessed, as we have noted, a disturbing drop in the number of people registered for the *aspirantura*. Since, to judge from subsequent trends, there was a continuing demand for places, the fall must have been caused by deliberate restriction. Despite their potential usefulness, *aspiranty* were considered to be too 'divorced from life', and it may be that Khrushchev's prejudices affected intake policies. In any case a decree passed on 30 August 1956 listed numerous weaknesses in the system. There was a gap between the subjects researched, particularly in the more advanced branches of science, and the real needs of the economy; supervisors were often insufficiently qualified; many *aspiranty* had no personal experience of practical work; the quality of the dissertations was poor; there was an unhealthy tendency to classify them as being within the orbit of state secrecy so as to reduce the possibility of public discussion; and so on.

The first change stipulated by this decree was typically Khrushchevian in character, and involved restricting admissions, for the most part, to people with at least two years' work experience. Only mathematicians, theoretical physicists and a few others could proceed directly after obtaining their diploma.

Regulations covering the planning, supervision, and award of degrees were tightened up. The Supreme Attestation Commission was given the power to deprive learned councils which passed substandard dissertations of the right to conduct defences for up to two years. Most astounding, however, was the abolition of the formal provisions for writing doctoral dissertations: this was now to be done through 'active participation in the research work of scientific institutions, *VUZy* and industrial and agricultural enterprises'.

People who had worked, or were working, on production, were given extra encouragement. The existing stipend scales were retained for *aspiranty* fresh from their diploma examinations, but those who had spent two years in a job could now claim a stipend to equal their former wages, up to a limit of 1,000 roubles a month: the average wage was then about 700 roubles, so some must have benefited considerably from this provision. Secondly, the work–release provisions were extended to include three months of paid leave for persons completing a candidate dissertation and six months for those writing a doctorate. The clear intent of the authorities to make the *aspirantura* system more flexible boded well for the future, at least in terms of numbers. A new statute, embracing these provisions and lowering the upper age-limit for full-time applicants to 35, was introduced in June 1957 (De Witt, p. 378).

Official interest in research, especially that of real national significance, certainly intensified as the 1960s progressed. A decree of June 1961 granted enterprises the right to direct suitable people into full-time *aspirantura* (in the same way that they could direct workers to become students under the September 1959 decree), on the understanding that those chosen would return to their home ground after qualifying. At this point it was revealed that the abolition of the *doktorantura* five years before had had deleterious effects on advanced research, and steps were to be taken to remedy it. Up to 1,000 *VUZ* posts were to be set aside every year for those who wished to write doctoral dissertations, and provisions were made to release them from teaching duties. Published work on advanced themes was acceptable, instead of a formal dissertation.

Improvement in the quality of the training was a key issue of the weighty decree of May 1962. Academic supervisors were to be made more responsible for aspirants' work, dissertations were to be made more topical and examined with greater strictness. Interestingly, the formula for originality was also modified: candidate theses now had to 'contain new scientific [or learned, the Russian term – *nauchny* – means both], practical conclusions and recommendations', and reveal the candidate's 'deep' theoretical knowledge. The doctorate had to offer the solution to a 'major scientific problem' and make 'a major contribution to learning and practice'. Changes were made in *VUZ* staffing arrangements so as to improve the continuity of research work in progress.[25] Yet another statute on the *aspirantura*, introduced in July 1962, reflected this change of emphasis, and remained the basis of the system into the late 1970s.

(2)   *The Brezhnev Modifications*

The shift in educational policy under the Brezhnev leadership affected not only growth rates but also research arrangements.

In November 1967 the earlier requirement that *aspiranty* should, in general, have spent a period of time 'on production' was bypassed, in that the decision with regard to admissions was transferred to the learned council. Many good graduates no doubt gained as a result, though, in the spirit of the day, they were now expected to take a more active part in the political and social life of the institution where they worked. Postgraduate study by people not formally registered was also further encouraged, and in June 1968 they obtained their own statute. Although research was to be concentrated in the largest and most suitable *VUZy*, the staffing of establishments in distant parts of the country was also designated for improvement in research opportunities.

The planned placement of people who had completed their *aspirantura* was brought under more detailed control in February 1970, and the post of probationary teacher was introduced in March 1973 with the aim of helping postgraduates to acquire lecturing skills. A letter of instruction issued by the *MinVUZ* in October 1974 called for *aspiranty* to be relieved of the many extraneous duties which were showered upon them, a major reason, it was said, for only half of them finishing their research on time.

The last change I wish to comment on during these years was also connected with the problem of quality. A decree of 18 October 1974 stated that the network of learned councils awarding research degrees and positions had 'expanded to such an extent that the Supreme Attestation Commission is not in a position to exercise active influence on their work', and that as a result 'many councils lowered their requirements' (Voilenko, Vol. 2, p. 51). The solution proposed was to improve the commission's internal organisation and transfer it bodily from the Ministry of Higher and Secondary Special Education to the USSR Council of Ministers, thus giving it better leverage over the ministries it dealt with.

TEACHING AND RESEARCH STAFF

The system of ranks for *VUZ* staff, established in January 1937 as part of Stalin's more general hierarchisation, was retained in its essentials throughout the period under review. The principal posts were those of rector, pro-rector and dean; professor (head of department) and ordinary professor: *dotsent* and *assistent*. Subjects less central to a given course of study (for example, ideology, foreign language) were taught by senior teachers and ordinary teachers (*prepodavateli*), four grades of research post were available for postgraduates, and there were several varieties of laboratory technician. The only detectable change was the introduction, in 1962 and 1973 respectively, of 'probationary' researchers and teachers (Voilenko, Vol. 2, pp. 25, 47). The scheme was, however, reinforced by provisions for hiring outside specialists as consultants and allowing permanent *VUZ* staff to take on additional part-time work. By and large, the parallel with Western practice needs no elaboration.

The method of appointment and removal of staff varied according to seniority and government policy. Most rectors and pro-rectors were appointed, as we have noted, at a ministerial level; heads of department could be nominated by the *VUZ*, but still required ministerial confirmation. Appointments to less senior posts were formally within the competence of rectors and learned councils, and the *MinVUZ* could intervene only when the rules were violated. However, detailed party supervision was ensured through the nomenclature system, and *VUZy* belonging to the Ministries of Defence, Internal Affairs and the KGB had their own rules (Voilenko, Vol. 1, pp. 5, 17).

Under regulations approved in February 1953, appointments in 'other' *VUZy*, from professorships down, were made via an openly announced competition, adjudicated by a suitable *VUZ* selection board. This practice was still current a quarter of a century later. In May 1973 extra rules were introduced for employing highly skilled specialists from production; a one-year contract for probationary teachers appeared; and refresher courses were set up for ideology teachers, traditionally the weakest brethren in the academic community (Voilenko, Vol. 2, p. 4).

The question of tenure was subject to some tinkering. The 1953 rules envisaged, alas, no permanence, and provided for teaching and research staff to face reselection every five years. To condense· a complicated matter into a few words, open competitions were to be organised for the majority of posts and suitably qualified persons chosen by a majority decision of the learned council. The appointment, or re-appointment, had then to be approved by the rector and/or the ministry, depending on the degree of seniority (Karpov and Severtsev, p. 300). The aim of this was presumably to make staffing arrangements more flexible and improve the career prospects of the young. However, it soon became obvious that realistic competition for a job which already 'belonged' to someone was quite impracticable: as one writer indicated, subordinates in a given institution would be unwilling for all sorts of ethical reasons to compete against a senior colleague, while the periodic removal of good men by putatively better could cause considerable disruption. A 1961 survey of re-attestation results in eighty-four institutes showed that over four years only one or two people per institute had lost their post or been demoted by such means (Lebin, p. 220).

This was doubtless why competitive reselection was abandoned in May 1962; afterwards, on completing their five-year contracts, *VUZ* staff were subject only to 're-election'. This rather formal procedure involved a review of individual records, and became a recognised point for promotion. The competition mechanism was restricted to new appointments, while dismissal had to be authorised by a majority of the learned council, on a secret vote, which also favoured stability. No figures are to hand on the working of these arrangements (*Reshenia*, vol. 5, p. 84; Voilenko, Vol. 1, p. 67).

The salary scales for academic staff anywhere are necessarily somewhat complex. Basic rates usually vary with qualifications, length of tenure and category of institution; many people may earn additional sums by extra duties, consultancy or publication.

The rates listed in Table 4.5 give a fair idea of the situation in Soviet *VUZy* in the early 1970s. Academics did not benefit from the 1972 wage increases for other teachers (see page 62), and some of the *VUZ* rates introduced in 1962 were still operative in the late 1970s (Chernenko and Smirtyukov, p. 603). Thus the average salaries for a maximum working day of six hours were quite modest; but the range in any given institution could be remarkably broad, and senior *VUZ* staff enjoyed what I have elsewhere described as élite incomes. Candidates and Doctors of Sciences were, in addition, entitled to extra living space and certain other material benefits.[26]

The 1964 Leningrad survey of occupational ratings referred to earlier showed *VUZ* teaching and research to be socially desirable (Osipov and Shchepanski, p. 48). Nevertheless, *VUZ* staff benefited fully from the

Table 4.5   VUZ *Salaries, 1978*
(*basic rates for selected administrative, teaching and research posts, in roubles*)

Rector	250–600
Pro-rector	300–550
Head of department	300–500
Professor	280–450
Dotsent	200–320
Senior teacher	145–320
Assistent or } Teacher }	125–270
Senior researcher	210–250
Junior researcher	150–175
Probationary teacher } Researcher }	100
(Average state wage	160)

Notes: Variations by rank: for rector and pro-rector, up to 150 roubles could be added according to category of *VUZ*; Doctor of Sciences degrees increased rates by up to 100 roubles, Candidate of Sciences degrees by 50 roubles; for heads of departments downwards ten years' service increased rates by up to 100 roubles. For possible royalty earnings, see Matthews, 1975, p. 8.

Sources: Kostanyan, 1979, p. 147; Voilenko, Vol. 2, p. 51; *Nar. khoz.*, 1978, p. 372.

upsurge of honorifics which took place after Brezhnev came to power.[27] No detailed breakdown of *VUZ* staff by rank seems to have appeared in the usual statistical sources since 1960, but at that time over 60 per cent were of senior status (that is, *dotsent*, senior teacher or higher). Such top-heaviness seems to have been a long-term problem in the Soviet *VUZ*, for A. B. Dainovski, writing in 1975, was still suggesting that it militated against efficient functioning (p. 147).

During the Khrushchev and Brezhnev years, higher education has been subject to some measure of change. After a pause in the mid 1950s it developed, like most other sectors of education, a strong growth pattern. Khrushchev was anxious to subject it to his theories of polytechnisation, even though the dangers of falling standards were, if anything, greater here than elsewhere. The *VUZy*, however, proved more resilient than the general school, and such reorganisation as took place was relatively restricted.

The Brezhnev leadership seems to have relied less on active intervention from the summit and more on the wisdom of the professional administrators. As a result one can trace a much more cautious approach, with less pressure for part-time study and, at a certain point, a halt in the growth of postgraduate research. Greater attention was paid to quality, and some types of *VUZy* were differentiated to a degree unthinkable under Khrushchev. The subject matter of the courses was, naturally enough, modified to suit changing economic and political needs.

From an academic point of view this switch in emphasis is probably to be welcomed. Other aspects of it, however, are less gratifying. In the sphere of administration Khrushchev was content to leave the ministerial structure more or less intact, relying on local party offices to push through unpopular change. The Brezhnev leadership appears to have increased ministerial centralisation and intensified party interference within the *VUZ* itself. There was a great wave of detailed codification, much of which may have been unnecessary. The establishment of rather powerless committees and the encouragement of approved socio-political activities among the students were offered as examples of true democratisation. All in all, the Soviet higher educational system, despite some institutional change under both leaderships, retained most of the characteristics imposed upon it in earlier days.

NOTES

1   Official Soviet figures. The material used in this section was drawn from the works listed in Chapter 1, note 1, with the addition of Chutkerashvili, Elyutin, Shumilin and Veselov.
2   This 'opportunity ratio' bears an obvious imperfection in that *VUZ* entrants are drawn from several age-cohorts; what we really need is an aggregate of ratios, at least for the 18 to 24-year-olds.

The absence of Soviet data on annual age-cohorts can be partly overcome, at least for our purpose, by use of the American estimates (prepared by Dr M. Feshbach and others). But this still leaves the 'age mix' of school leavers and, more dauntingly, that of successful *VUZ* applicants unknown.

A further complication is introduced if higher educational opportunity is thought of in terms of *graduations*, as opposed to *admissions*, since the drop-out variables then come into play. Three indices that have been used for Western studies – the proportion of age-groups 17–22 in higher education, school leavers 'qualified' for university entrance as a portion of the relevant age-group, and the 'transfer ratio' of qualified students to higher educational institutions – cannot here be meaningfully applied. (See Neave, p. 27.)

3 Zhiltsov and Lyalyaev, p. 46. A breakdown for first-year students at Gorki University in 1967 was 16–18 years – 71·2 per cent; 19–20 years – 22·2 per cent; 21–22 years – 3·0 per cent; over 22 years – 3·6 per cent (residue). Minkina *et al.*, p. 25.

4 The crude budget figures are calculated from state expenditure and student numbers in relevant issues of *Narodnoe khozyaistvo SSSR*. Other points based on Korchagin, p. 96; see Appendix C, page 208; Dainovski, p. 28; Ushakov and Shuruev, p. 97. Dainovski gives overall figures of 1,100–1,300 roubles for a full-time student in the early and mid-1970s, depending on type of *VUZ*, including hostel maintenance expenses.

5 In the article quoted on page 139, the Soviet writer T. D. Samilova suggests that inefficiency under Khrushchev was even more serious. Dainovski (p. 16) gives figures which are somewhat lower than ours, but admits they should be higher. The confusion over this issue in Soviet sources is further illustrated by its treatment in Ushakov and Shuruev. In the years of the ninth Five-Year Plan (1971–5), they state, 'fall-out' from the *VUZy* dropped from 5·9 to 4·7 per cent (p. 60). Yet in the following paragraph they give an undefined 'absolute fall-out' from full-time *VUZ* courses over the same period as 418,000 (discounting returnees), which works out at about 17 per cent of the average full-time contingent. The part-time fall-out was 802,000, or 36 per cent. The authors said that *SSUZ* rates were similar.

The inadequacies of the crude intake/graduation ratio, on which non-Soviet estimates have to be based, are obvious and only need listing. The first methodological difficulty lies in our ignorance of the exact length of courses, which varies mostly from four to five and a half years for full-timers, with a year extra for part-timers. Apart from this, any graduation figure *includes* (1) students who finish their course on time, (2) students who finish early (admittedly a tiny number), (3) repeaters from previous years and (4) students who have switched from other courses. It *excludes* repeaters who will graduate later, students who have left to join other courses, and drop-outs. Any generalisation on trends rests on the assumption that some unknowns are constant or cancel one another out.

6 The structure of the Ministry of Higher Education, as of 6 June 1956, was as follows:

(1) *main administrations for* (a) universities, economic and law *VUZy*, (b) polytechnical and machine-building *VUZy*, (c) mining and construction *VUZy*, (d) technological *VUZy*, (e) *VUZ* supplies and equipment, (f) capital construction;

(2) *administrations for* (a) social science teaching (that is, Marxist–Leninist ideology), (b) secondary special educational institutions, (c) methodology, (d) staffing;

(3) *departments of* (a) physical training, (b) planning of intakes and graduate placement, (c) foreign relations;

(4) 'First' and 'Second' Departments (unnamed, possibly military and KGB), (5) *central accounts office*, (6) *inspectorate*, (7) *main office*, (8) *equipment and Technical Services Office*.

The *bodies attached to the ministry* included (1) Supreme Attestation Commission, (2) Scientific and Technical Council, (3) Soviet Science publishing house, (4) State

Scientific Library, (5) State Institute for *VUZ* planning, (6) *High School Herald (Vestnik vysshei shkoly)* and *Secondary Special Education (Srednee spetsialnoe obrazovanie)* editorial offices.

No later listing of such detail is to hand, but the USSR and RSFSR Ministries of Higher Education were shown in the Moscow handbook of 1977 as together possessing all the important sections existing in 1956, or their equivalents. The USSR *MinVUZ* had by then also acquired administrations for foreign relations; for the instruction of foreign students and *aspirants;* and for managerial, research and teaching staff (Karpov and Severtsev, p. 18; *Moskva – Kratkaya adressno-spravochnaya kniga*, 1977, pp. 24, 64).

7   D. M. Stepnov *et al.*, pp. 124–7; Khaldeev and Krivoshein, p. 154; *PZh*, no. 17, 1962, p. 10.

8   Compare the standard *Ustav* of 5 September 1938; the two *Polozhenia o VUZakh* of 21 March 1961 and 22 January 1969, together with the *Ustav* of 23 June 1969.

9   The Lumumba Friendship University seems to have changed little since its establishment. The students are, as far as I know, selected by Soviet cultural agencies abroad (particularly through language classes). By 1980 the institution had 6,700 students from 103 countries, studying in seven faculties – preparatory, history and philosophy, physics and mathematics, medicine, engineering, economics and law, agriculture (*World of Learning*, 1980–1, Vol. 2, p. 1342, London 1980). It seems that a few thousand more were placed in ordinary *VUZy*; hence the change in the regulations.

10 The relevance of this to the official struggle against dissidence did not go unnoticed in the West.

A similar Central Committee decree was issued on ideological work in the Leningrad Kalinin Polytechnical Institute in 1973 (*PZh*, no. 16, p. 60) but this lacked recommendations for more general change.

11 Evening students had a lighter load, while there was no stipulated minimum for correspondence *VUZy* (Karpov and Severtsev, 1957, p. 89).

12 The breakdown provided by Medynski (1947, p. 183) was as follows: agricultural *VUZy* – 40–52 weeks; technical *VUZy* – 16–38 weeks; medical *VUZy* – 16 weeks; pedagogical *VUZy* – 12 weeks; universities – 6–16 weeks.

13 Accounts of military training by three people who studied at the Novorossiisk Polytechnical Institute, the Moscow Institute of Engineering Transport and the Leningrad Kalinin Polytechnical Institute in the late 1960s and 1970s are the main sources used. For purposes of comparison, I also consulted three older people who graduated from Leningrad and Moscow institutes in the early 1950s.

14 *BMV*, no. 2, 1977, p. 7; *PMP RSFSR*, no. 294, 28 November 1977.

15 See for instance *The Times*, 23 September 1969; Jacoby, p. 141; Jones, p. 175. One of several instances known to me personally illustrates the point. 'I felt so ashamed,' said a young girl without technical aptitude who was admitted to a prestigious technical institute. 'All the candidates, who had worked so hard, were waiting in the corridor, worrying about their forthcoming oral. My father [a prominent official] had arranged it with an examiner so that I would just pass.'

16 Formerly, an 'excellent' mark in the state examination had to be backed by an unspecified mix of 'good' or 'excellent' marks for courses. Now the proportion of 'excellent' course marks was set at a minimum of three-quarters (Voilenko, Vol. 1, p. 254).

17 The proposed reorganisation of *VUZ* courses was as follows:

(1) *Part-time study 'without work–release'*

(a) correspondence courses, supplemented by intra-mural work (laboratory activities, examinations and meetings at students' request)

(b) evening classes at a recognised *VUZ* or centre

(c) alternating full- and part-time study in the so-called *Zavody-VTUZy* – higher technical educational institutions directly integrated in large enterprises (see note 18).

(2) *Study 'with work–release'*

   (a) in technical and engineering economics *VUZy*: combined day- and part-time study for the first two years, with up to six months' part-time study included in the remaining courses

   (b) in *VUZ* disciplines demanding a great deal of laboratory, calculating and graphic work, and also in industrial economics, trade economics, statistics, history and other specialities: a mixture of full- and part-time study for one year on the junior courses and one year more on the senior courses

   (c) in *VUZ* disciplines such as agriculture, geology, highway construction and other occupations with a seasonal work pattern: theoretical and practical study alternating with production work throughout

   (d) for students who worked for at least two years in their chosen specialisation, or one close to it: full-time study, with obligatory production practice or work at an enterprise or organisation for at least one year on the senior courses of study

   (e) in medical *VUZy*: combined study and work for the first two years of the course, and then regular full-time study (restricted to people with secondary special medical education and a two-year work stage)

   (f) in technical *VUZy* and universities, for specialities like physics, chemistry and biology demanding a great deal of theoretical and laboratory work: full-time study on the first three courses, followed by a year's work, according to specialisation, at an enterprise or organisation

   (g) in pedagogical, medical, law, literary and art *VUZy* and in university specialities for which only candidates with a two-year work period are accepted: day study with one year's production practice at an enterprise or organisation (Kalinychev, p. 36)

18   Khrushchev was particularly anxious to develop the *Zavody-VTUZy* as a foremost element in the 'reform'. These would be *VUZy* specially integrated with industrial enterprises and modern workshops, or faculties (annexes) established by technical *VUZy* directly at industrial enterprises. Institutions of a similar kind had existed in the 1930s.

   They were described in some detail in a decree of the USSR Council of Ministers of 30 December 1959 (Kalinychev, p. 51). The idea was that *Zavody-VTUZy* should give training in the specialisations needed at the enterprises with which they were associated. Much of the instruction was to be part-time; indeed, classes could not take up more than five months in any year of the course, which was extended as a result to five and a half or six years. The students were to be released from work for attendance. Intakes and the direction of graduates were to be covered by the decree of the USSR Council of Ministers of 18 September 1959 (see page 156). The *Zavody-VTUZy* were to be financed by the ministries of higher and secondary special education and staffed by the same ratios as ordinary *VUZy*. The production enterprises involved were obliged to give them every possible material assistance. In addition the republican councils of ministers were enjoined, in the course of six months, to organise industrial enterprises *within* existing *VUZy*, using existing workshops or adding new ones.

   Subsequently, *Zavody-VTUZy* were established at five major production enterprises – the Moscow Likhachev Automobile Factory, the Leningrad Stalin Metallurgical Works, the Penza Calculating Machine Factory, the Rostov Agricultural Machinery Works and the Dneprodzerzhinsk Metallurgical Works – with the help of certain established *VUZy*, and a number of existing faculties were given a special production status.

   The agricultural equivalent of the *Zavod-VTUZ* was to be based directly on a large state farm, where the students would also labour. It was as part of this policy that the RSFSR Council of Ministers was required to remove agricultural *VUZy* from large towns to suitable farms and share research laboratories with them, so as to form massive scientific centres in the countryside. There is no doubt that a fairly extensive operation was envisaged. The aim was not only to teach students but also to produce goods, as the payment envisaged for the students' efforts showed. The collapse of the reform, however, brought the quiet abandonment of these intentions.

19 Candidates for places on part-time *VUZ* courses could now ask for fifteen days off, unpaid, for admission procedures, instead of ten as before. Paid leave for tests and course exams was increased to between twenty and forty days (as against thirty previously). All part-timers got thirty days' paid leave for their finals; and all of them, not merely those in technical disciplines, became entitled to four months' release on full pay (up to a maximum of 100 roubles a month) for their diploma project or work. Presumably as a kind of additional guarantee, they could ask for a day off every week, on half-pay, during the ten months immediately preceding their diploma project or state exams, and an extra one or two unpaid days' leave weekly on top of that, if they so desired (Voilenko, Vol. 1, pp. 315, 316).

20 I have listed these points elsewhere (Matthews, 1972, p. 300).

21 *VVSh*, no. 6, 1966, p. 27. The decree of 3 September 1966 stipulated that the salaries of rectors of the existing part-time *VUZy* should in general be equated with those of their full-time colleagues, evidently with the aim of raising their status. Minor regulations for improving the supervision of correspondence students' written work came out in June 1973 and September 1975 (Voilenko, vol. 1, pp. 320, 321). By 1978 there were two evening and fourteen correspondence institutes; and according to my count, 351 full-time *VUZy* had evening, and 614 correspondence, divisions.

22 The ensuing account deals specifically with research arrangements in *VUZy*, but those followed in research institutes were similar (Karpov and Severtsev, p. 280).

23 The 'fields of endeavour' were physics and mathematics, chemistry, biology, geology and minerology, technology, agriculture, history, economics, philosophy, philology, geography, law, pedagogy, medicine, pharmaceuticals, veterinary science, art, architecture and military science (Vidavski *et al.*, p. 320).

24 G. V. Kologreev, in Zhamin, p. 128. The ratios for undergraduate study are, it will be noted, fairly close to the figures given by Korchagin, Appendix C.

25 *Reshenia*, vol. 5, p. 79. The decree also indicated concern with the training and promotion prospects of research staff, and criticised well-known shortcomings, including dissertation themes which 'did not have any real scientific or practical value', the award of degrees for poor work, and late submissions by a majority of *aspiranty*. Provision was made for further expansion: a new appointment system was introduced under which promising young people could be accepted at *VUZy* or research institutes for two years (at the modest monthly salary of 100 roubles) as 'short-term researchers', before being directed to jobs like ordinary *VUZ* graduates. Learned councils were to be stricter in their consideration of proposed research topics, while the Supreme Attestation Commission was similarly ordered to raise its sights. A list of research specialities and a register of researchers were to be brought into being, so as to tidy up planning procedures. These now became primarily a matter for the State Committee for the Co-ordination of Scientific and Research Work (attached to the Council of Ministers) and part of the state plan at a national level. See also the decree of 20 February (*Reshenia*, vol. 5, p. 447).

26 Matthews, 1978. Note in this connection that the average wage was about 160 roubles. Income tax, running at a maximum of 13 per cent for all state earnings over 100 roubles, was not significantly redistributive.

27 By 1975 no less than thirty-one union–republican titles had been established, under the rubrics of Honoured Worker in Higher Learning, Honoured Worker in Science and Technology, Honoured *VUZ* Teacher and Honoured *VUZ* Worker (Zhaleiko, p. 134).

5
Some Student Problems

Like young people everywhere, Soviet students have their problems, and a fairly rich assortment at that. Here we shall consider a few of the more important and publicised of them.

The first is getting into a *VUZ* at all, for despite the impressive growth in facilities only a minority of young people can do so. Planned access to the intelligentsia is considered essential in a 'socialist' society, so *VUZ* selection procedures have received much attention from the authorities. The social composition of the student body and the attempts which have been made to render it more representative of society as a whole must be viewed from this angle. Students' attitudes to certain aspects of higher education, their living conditions and the question of drop-outs are our next topics. We conclude with a review of the mechanism for placing graduates in suitable employment, since this is regarded as an integral part of *VUZ* work.

All of these matters have been discussed or touched upon by Western observers, including myself, in the past.[1] In the account which follows I shall restate only what needs restating, and then in an abridged form. Material from fresher sources will be added when it is available. Reasons of space oblige me to confine the discussion to students registered at institutions of higher learning, but some of my generalisations will be relevant to others, particularly the pupils of *SSUZy*.

VUZ SELECTION POLICIES

In the immediate postwar years the problem of who should go to college was, in a sense, solved before it arose. The output of the general school was often less than the admission rate to full-time *VUZy*, so the overwhelming majority of children who got their school-leaving certificates had little difficulty in continuing their education in this manner. Needless to say, these children tended to come from the better-educated and more privileged Soviet families.

The rapid growth of contingents in the upper classes of the general school which took place in the early 1950s, combined with the relatively slow growth of *VUZ* admissions, led to an increasing discrepancy between the demand for, and supply of, *VUZ* places. By 1953 graduations from the full-time school were already up to the 579,000 mark, while intakes to full-time *VUZy* were only 265,000, with an extra 166,000 for the less desirable part-time courses. We cannot, of course, simply equate the number of school leavers with the demand for a higher education: some of these youngsters may not have wanted to continue their studies, while there were certainly older people who did. Nevertheless it is clear that the authorities were faced with a sharp increase in the public demand for higher education which could not be met, and that the discrepancy in the planned growth of the two sectors would only, in the short term, increase.

It also became evident that the growing demand for *VUZ* places would lead to an increase in the predominance of 'upper-class' children in *VUZ* intakes. The admission rules, containing as they did only stipulations about age and level of study, worked in their favour. Special advantages for candidates of proletarian or peasant origin had been abandoned in accordance with the 'egalitarian' constitution of 1936. Though he encouraged the expansion of most educational facilities, Stalin ensured that the new professional groups were the first to benefit at the *VUZ* portals.

As we noted above, in October 1940 fees were introduced for the last classes of the general school and (at a considerably higher rate) for secondary special and higher educational institutions. It is true that these were offset by reductions and grants for the poorest students, and eventually by rising wage rates; but they must have remained a problem for many less opulent families. Certificates of maturity (an old tsarist institution) were reintroduced for school leavers in June 1944, and admission to a *VUZ* without one became impossible. The system of gold and silver medals, which came a few months later, ensured preferential treatment for the most successful school leavers. Part-time study was but poor compensation for those who could not clear the full-time hurdles. The political relaxation which followed the death of Stalin meant that the public dissatisfaction engendered by this imbalance could not be so easily ignored.

The polytechnisation of the general school which began at that time was in part intended to promote a healthier balance in the student selection process. Orienting school leavers towards manual jobs would, it was hoped, reduce the demand for full-time *VUZ* places, particularly amongst those who would formerly have considered nothing else. After 1955, moreover, the full-time *VUZ* admission rules underwent progressive modification to encourage the less privileged to study.[2] People who had been employed for two years or more in factory, office or farm – the so-called 'production candidates' – were to have fixed and generous quotas of places set aside for them, and thus be sheltered from direct competition with applicants fresh from school. The medallists, who had been exempted from the strains of the *VUZ* admissions examinations altogether, were now required to sit them (though their performance in the general school still left them in a strong position). The 1956 abolition of fees, the new emphasis on part-time *VUZ* facilities and the improvements in day–release provisions were moves in the same direction.

The new approach, while reflecting social need, owed much to Khrushchev's personal proclivities. The Soviet leader made no secret of his disdain for the so-called 'white-handed' school leavers who, he thought, were squeamish about manual labour, and potential trouble-makers into the bargain.[3] The fact that most of them were in the *Komsomol* was no guarantee of compliance. Being himself of humble origin and a former part-time student, Khrushchev was quite convinced that society had much to gain from drawing more young workers and peasants into the *VUZy*, and thereby into the intelligentsia. At the same time he gave no sign that he was prepared to undermine preferential access for the élite to a small number of exclusive institutions. To this extent it may be argued that he was guilty of maintaining a double standard.

By 1958 it was clear that the new measures had not solved the problem of socially equitable admission to the *VUZy*, nor eased the tensions involved. Khrushchev publicly admitted in September that the proportion of workers' and peasants' children in the student body had not risen as he had hoped, and he gave the first official figures on students' social origins to appear since 1938:

> It is impossible not to see that there are still few children of workers and peasants in institutions of higher education. In the Moscow *VUZy*, for example, only 30–40 per cent of the students are the children of workers and collective farmers. The others are children of white-collar workers and the intelligentsia. This situation is, of course, clearly abnormal. Not to mention the fact that workers and collective farmers who are themselves studying at full-time *VUZy* can be numbered literally in ones and twos.

Although Khrushchev did not say so, there is no doubt that the situation was the same in other large towns.

The solutions now proposed were contained in the December 1958 reform and elsewhere. First, there were the measures designed to make the full-time *VUZ* less directly accessible from the ordinary general school. The proposed retreat to an eight-year norm in general education meant, in the short term at least, a reduction in the number of pupils obtaining the school-leaving certificate still required for *VUZ* entrance. Those who went on to a *PTU* or *SSUZ* (a trend increasingly encouraged) were ineligible for admission to full-time courses without a lengthy period on production. The anticipated switch to earlier employment, coupled with attendance at a part-time general school, would, it was thought, bring young people to the *VUZy* not as school leavers but as workers and peasants. The minority of children completing full-time ten-year school might still come from the more privileged social groups, but they would now have to face the extension of their course by a year and receive more manual instruction in the senior classes.

Secondly, the leadership strengthened the policy of protected quotas for 'production candidates' in *VUZ* entrance procedures. The result was that by the autumn of 1964, when Khrushchev was dismissed, no less than 62 per cent of all *VUZ* entrants were in this category.

A law passed on 18 September 1959 was another step in the same direction. It permitted state enterprises and collective farms to propose deserving young workers for places in universities and institutes, and pay them subsistence grants on the understanding that they would return after graduation (*SZAT*, 1965, p. 146). By 1964 about 14 per cent of the *VUZ* entrants were of this type. Candidates from working-class milieux and from collective farms stood to gain most from these innovations, though it seems that many young people from white-collar families took temporary jobs just so as to benefit. The participation of *Komsomol* organisations in the scheme may have meant that it favoured also more politically orthodox youngsters.

The third component of the policy was the expansion of evening and correspondence courses, accompanied by improvements in work–release provisions; it is worth noting that 1·1 of the 1·4 million increase in the student body between 1958 and 1964 comprised part-timers. All this was obviously to the advantage of young people who had to work to keep themselves. Lastly, the provisions of the December 1958 law which attempted to turn many full-time *VUZ* courses into sandwich courses meant that students would in any case be obliged to spend a great deal of their time at work and be temporarily equated with working folk.

The results of all these measures, in terms both of equalising admission chances and of reducing the distinction between student and honest toiler, were nevertheless disappointing. Although many studies showed a drop in the overall proportion of students of white-collar origin in the *VUZy*, the change was relatively modest.[4] At the same time the turmoil caused by Khrushchev's policies was considerable, and it evoked the same sort of opposition from those involved as had the polytechnisation of the general school. Enterprise managers disliked the stream of part-time students and bogus 'workers'. The academic community lamented falling standards, particularly in the more theoretical subjects, and the part-time sector had to absorb many young people who regarded it only as a *pis aller*.

The abandonment of the December 1958 reform had its impact on student selection. The return to a ten-year general school course and the downgrading of polytechnisation obviously favoured those who dreamed of direct passage to a *VUZ*. Some advantage was restored to medal-holders, in the form of a partial exemption from entrance exams. As for production candidates, a decree passed on 18 March 1965 authorised the heads of *VUZy* to share the available places between them and applicants straight from school in proportion to the size of each category. The numbers of production candidates fell dramatically as a result, and by 1973 were down to 23 per cent of full-time intakes (Lisovski and Dmitriev, p. 47). Part-time admissions fell relative to full-time ones. White-collar representation in the student body, as we shall see, rose again.

At the same time the Brezhnev leadership cannot be accused of completely abandoning Khrushchev's egalitarianism, for efforts to assist genuine workers and peasants (or their children) continued. The rules for production candidates were left on the books and still helped some people, as did the decree of September 1959. Small numbers of *PTU* and *SSUZ* leavers were allowed to proceed to a *VUZ* immediately after finishing their training. In January 1967 M. A. Prokofiev called upon the rectors of pedagogical institutes to reserve 60–70 per cent of their places for young people from the villages: in fact, 50 per cent of the student body of such institutes in the RSFSR were of rural background at that time. In January 1968 V. P. Elyutin called for increased representation of the working-class and rural youth in the *VUZy*, and over the next two years this theme was taken up by several prominent sociologists and journalists.

Specific arrangements were instituted to coach the weakest candidates. On 6 September 1969 *Pravda* published a decree 'On Organising Preparatory Sections attached to *VUZy*'. This envisaged the creation of eight- to ten-month courses in which instruction would be organised on a full-time, part-time or correspondence basis. Admittance was to be restricted to the best workers, collective farmers and demobilised soldiers; the scheme was similar to one run for ex-servicemen in 1945, and indeed recalled the *rabfaki* of earlier years. 'Young people starting these courses,' the decree stated, 'must have at least one year of work on production behind them. The selection of candidates and the running of preparatory sections will be done by industrial enterprises, etc., on the recommendation of party, *Komsomol* and trades union organisations.'

According to subsequent reports, the preparatory sections acquired some popularity. In the 1975–6 academic year, for instance, they existed at 621 *VUZy* and accepted 96,700 of the 170,700 people who applied to them: of these, 46·1 per cent were industrial workers, 8·9 per cent state farm workers, 11·4 per cent collective farmers and the remainder demobilised soldiers. The exclusion of representatives of the white-collar social groups may have been more apparent than real, for there were complaints about 'workers' not having done the required year on production. At the same time, some 94 per cent of the students who completed full-time courses and 78 per cent of those from correspondence courses got *VUZ* places (*BMV*, no. 3, 1977, p. 8). These high rates are not surprising, given the reportedly heavy fall-out from the courses themselves. The students who hung on must have been highly motivated, but even so they tended to drop out of the *VUZ* more readily later on.

Naturally, many of them were directed to study by their enterprises, under the terms of the September 1959 decree. Such sponsorship became increasingly important as the years went by, and in 1975–6 embraced 145,000 students, or about a quarter of the full-time intake. Although I have no precise information, I suspect these made up the bulk of the production candidates just discussed. At the same time many *VUZy*, particularly the military establishments, ran their own *ad hoc* courses for potential applicants, on a regular or occasional basis; by 1977 no less than 700,000 people were said to be engaged in them (*BMV*, nos. 2, 3, 1977; no. 2, 1978; *NONK*, 1977, p. 247).

STUDENTS' SOCIAL ORIGINS

Although publishing restrictions have prevented the appearance of regular data on this problem, a number of individual studies throw light on it. The social composition of the student body in the long term may be appraised from the crude percentages in Table 5.1(a). Since these figures are more meaningful when compared with the proportions of similar groups in society, I have supplemented them with what I term 'access ratios' (Table 5.1(b)).[5]

These ratios show that in 1938 people of 'employee' or white-collar origin had more than twice as much of a chance of getting a *VUZ* place as those of worker origin, and seven times as much as those of collective farmer origin. The small group of uncollectivised peasants and craftsmen were surprisingly favoured. These relationships presumably persisted into the early 1950s, at least for the first three groups. The columns of figures for the 1960s show the rather mixed effect of Khrushchev's intervention; but the continuing advantage enjoyed by the employees, despite all that had been done to remove it, is clear. The improvement in the representation of the peasants compared with 1938 must be set against a marked deterioration in that of the workers. The 1971 figures seem to reflect the retreat from Khrushchev's crude egalitarianism, and marked gains for the employees. The data for 1973 and 1977 (which covered only first-year students) may by contrast indicate some real reduction in the admission chances of the employees, to the benefit of others. One would not wish to generalise too confidently on such flimsy evidence, but it does seem that government policy in this sphere proved relatively ineffective for many years. The apparent rigidity of the social patterns, despite all the administrative pressures for change, may serve as a warning against facile belief in social engineering.

Table 5.1(a)   *Social Composition of Full-Time* VUZ *Students*
              (selected years; percentages)

	1938	1960	1964	1971	1973	1977
Employees	42·2	46·1	41·1	53·1	44·8	38·4
Workers	33·9	34·6	39·4	36·2	31·2	
Collective farmers	16·1	19·3	19·5	10·7	8·4	61·6
Others*	(5·6)	—	—	—	(15·6)	

* The figures given for 1938 and 1973 are not comparable; see *Notes and Sources* for these years.

Notes and Sources
   1938 All students in all years, no part-time courses operative. The 'Others' category here comprised uncollectivised peasantry and craftsmen; percentage discrepancy unexplained (Matthews, 1972, p. 291).
   1960 Students in all years (derived from Samilova, p. 119; data kindly supplied by Dr R. Dobson).
   1964 Students in all years (Matthews, 1972, p. 297).
   1971 Evidently students in all years (quoted by V. Elyutin in *The Times*, 23 November 1972).
   1973 Students in their first year (F. R. Fillipov, in *SI*, no. 2, 1977, p. 49). The 'Others' category, containing 15·6% of respondents to the survey, was not defined, but may have had a large 'parent–pensioner' component.
   1977 First year intake, from official summary (*BMV*, no. 2, 1978; *Instruktivnoe pismo* of 9 December 1977).

Table 5.1(b)   *Social Group Access Ratios to Full-Time* VUZy
              (selected years)

	1938	1960	1964	1971	1973	1977
Employees	2·38	2·50	1·95	2·12	1·95	1·69
Workers	1·04	0·70	0·73	0·66	0·78	
Collective farmers	0·34	0·61	0·79	0·54	0·64	0·80
Others	3·00	—	—	—	—	

Sources: Derived from Table 5.1(a) with help of 'class structure of the population' data from relevant numbers of *Nar. khoz.*

   The part-time sector seemed to present an obvious means for redressing the balance, which explained much of Khrushchev's interest in it. However, this was hardly so. Figures provided by E. L. Manevich for the country as a whole showed that by 1964 between a half and two-thirds of all part-time students were still of 'employee' background. A set of data for Kharkov *VUZy* over the ten years 1965–75 revealed but a tiny fall, from 41 to 39 per cent, in their representation overall, despite a great increase in the proportion of workers accepted for the first course. There is evidence that in some areas the part-time courses took large numbers of fresh school leavers rather than the mature workers and farmers for whom they were primarily intended.[6]
   There are, furthermore, good reasons for believing that higher educational opportunity was even less equally shared between social

groups than the figures we have so far considered suggest. First, the distribution of *graduations* is evidently more skewed (in favour of employees) than are the overall or admission figures. A number of studies, which I have discussed elsewhere, have shown an apparently strong correlation between the educational levels, the material well-being and the urban/rural location of a student's family on the one hand, and his chances of finishing a *VUZ* course on the other.[7] The ratios for graduations per social group, as yielded by an extensive Moscow Sociological Institute survey of 1973–5 and expressed in the terms of Table 5.1(b), were: employees – 1:2·8, workers – 1:0·43, and peasants – 1:0·56 (*SI*, no. 2, 1977, p. 42).

Another factor to be taken into account is the variation in the composition of the student body between institutions: for a diploma from a prestigious *VUZ* brings brighter career prospects. Figures published for a number of Latvian *VUZy* in 1968 showed that children of 'employee' families tended to predominate in better *VUZy* – the medical and polytechnical institutes and Riga University —whereas the collective farmers were most strongly represented in the (least attractive) pedagogical and agricultural institutes. The workers tended to be rather more evenly distributed (see notes 5 and 7 at the end of this chapter). Data available for Kharkov *VUZy* by area of study in 1974 were more mixed, but nevertheless revealed a high proportion of employees' children in the prestigious creative arts and relatively few in agriculture, where the collective farmers and workers were again most concentrated (Table 5.2). (Their weight in medicine was due to local, and for us unexplained, factors.) There is certainly further variation by department. A few *VUZy* which enjoy nation-wide prestige – and cannot (like the Ministry of Foreign Affairs' Institute for International Relations) be entered without special recommendation – are, I suspect, completely filled by the children of the élite (Matthews, 1978, p. 48).

Table 5.2 *Social Composition of First-Year Students in Kharkov* VUZy, *by Area of Study, 1974 (percentages)*

Area of study	Employees	Workers	Collective farmers
Creative arts	64·4	32·2	3·4
Medicine	34·5	44·5	21·0
Construction	33·2	58·8	8·0
Transport	31·0	62·1	6·9
Agriculture	16·1	49·6	34·3

Source: SI, no. 2, 1977, p. 76.

A third reason for believing that this kind of inequality has been understated lies in the possible misuse of social categories by *VUZ* applicants themselves. Although 'social position' must be entered in the

VUZ admission form, there appears to be no verification of the entry, and applicants may in some cases find it advantageous to put themselves down as belonging to a manual group.

Last, the social categorisation used is far too broad for proper analysis, and actually conceals inequalities within itself. Thus the group of 'employees' covers a broad range of non-manual occupations, from unskilled service workers to highly skilled specialists. A 1968 survey of Moscow students discussed by E. S. Samilova, for example, showed that the admission rate among 'employee' candidates varied from 28 per cent of those whose parents had five to seven years of schooling, to 67·5 per cent of the children of Candidates and Doctors of Sciences (1978, p. 103). It seems likely that most applicants from collective farms are from the skilled rather than the unskilled and truly peasant categories, and one has little doubt that there are comparable distinctions among workers. In a word, were a proper breakdown of the Soviet student body by major social indices available, I believe it would reveal a continuing and close resemblance to the inequalities familiar in capitalists lands.

ATTITUDES TOWARDS STUDY AND POLITICAL ACTIVITIES

The importance of higher education in the USSR has prompted many investigations of what the students think about it, and some results show a surprising degree of unorthodox motivation.

A fairly detailed retrospective analysis of some 4,000 Leningrad engineering students, undertaken by S. A. Kugel and O. M. Nikan-drov in the mid-1960s (p. 90), showed that while 45 per cent said they were moved primarily by an interest in the speciality chosen, 62·2 per cent of the respondents entered a *VUZ* just to obtain higher education – presumably *any* higher education – and 11·4 per cent were prompted by the desire to improve their material position (the totals did not produce unity because respondents could enter several options). Further analysis revealed that the configuration of answers was similar for full- and part-time students and had not changed much between 1950 and 1964. To take another case, three-quarters of a large group of Ukrainian students investigated by V. Rubin and Yu. Kolesnikov in 1966 said they had made up their minds about going to a *VUZ* between the seventh and ninth classes of the general school, that is, at a time when they could not have had a very clear idea about the subjects of study (p. 76).

There also seems to have been a measurable tendency for the more purposeful students to attend the more attractive *VUZy*. Kugel and Nikandrov demonstrated that the proportion of students who entered a *VUZ* out of interest for the subjects offered ran at about half in Leningrad University and the famous Bronch-Bruevich Electro-techni-cal Institute, but dropped steadily through varieties of technology, construction, mining and light industry to a fifth in the Leningrad Refrigeration Institute, and certain economics institutes (p. 93). There is also evidence that choices were more considered among students of white-collar background (Kogan, p. 273).

Having obtained a *VUZ* place, Soviet students' attitudes to their chosen subjects were by no means uniformly positive. The Rubin–Kolesnikov survey purported to show that on average over 12 per cent of a sample of 1,812 students at three *VUZy* in Rostov-on-Don had a negative opinion of their specialisation and of the *VUZ* itself. There was a rising incidence of dissatisfaction during the earlier years of the course, a peak in the fourth or penultimate year and some reduction afterwards.

The Kugel–Nikandrov study threw light on the question of how useful the participants thought their courses had been for practical purposes, after they had actually started work. Nearly 90 per cent said that the training helped them use scientific literature, and two-thirds that it helped them understand the most recent technology. About half said it had been of use for their managerial, administrative and research duties. Only 17–18 per cent, however, found it useful in organising the ideological and propaganda tasks with which they were charged.

It would, again, be rash to draw any far-reaching conclusions from the figures presented in these paragraphs. The survey data cannot be verified, and students' attitudes are notoriously volatile. But from the maximalist viewpoint of the Soviet authorities the pattern which emerges is disappointing. The *VUZ* is supposed to attract youngsters eager for involvement in communist construction, and to produce specialists who are well-trained and willing to do a precise kind of job. Yet the surveys suggest that Soviet students are frequently egotistical in their attitudes to learning and have doubts about the value of their studies, both before and after they graduate. A fair measure of disenchantment is not specific to the youth of Western societies.

Given the fact that by 1978 some 95 per cent of *VUZ* students were in the *Komsomol*, the extent of their involvement in, and reaction to, approved socio-political activities is another matter of moment. Several sociological investigations have purported to show, on the basis of large samples, that the overwhelming majority of students participate, though the proportion at any given point in the course seems to have been about half. Such activities have been loosely listed as 'educative work, giving public lectures, running circles and groups, membership of voluntary societies, work with adolescents and active involvement in external assistance projects'; but there has been a curious reluctance to define 'participation'. Several sets of figures reveal variations by year of study, including a sharp drop as compared with school years and a further steady fall over the *VUZ* course as the pressure of academic work built up. It has been claimed, on the other hand, that there were no significant differences in involvement rates between social groups.[8]

The primary reasons which, according to the Rubin–Kolesnikov study, prompted 600 students of Rostov University to engage in 'social activities' were, in descending order of political acceptability, (1) moral and ideological motives – 15·4 per cent, (2) a desire to adapt to the collective – 30·0 per cent, (3) a desire to promote personal cultural development and growth – 11·0 per cent, (4) personality limitations, habit – 8·0 per cent, (5) obligations imposed – 23·4 per cent, (6) other motives – 12·7 per cent. This breakdown reveals a remarkably low level of 'orthodox' motivation, and even some compulsion. No information was given on how the students rated social activities (as opposed to other ways of spending their time), though data were apparently collected. According to a sample of 1,500 fourth- and fifth-year students investigated by N. M. Morozov at a technological institute in the Moscow *oblast* in the mid-1960s, only 5–9 per cent felt the urge to do what was called 'social work' (p. 114). A large study of student attitudes at four Belorussian *VUZy* in the early 1970s also showed a considerable degree of indifference (Table 5.3). The low attendance levels registered for classes in ideological subjects, which I have already mentioned, were part of the same pattern.

Table 5.3 *Students' Attitudes to Specific Social Tasks*

Type of task	Undertaken by present incumbent	
	willingly	*rather unwillingly*
Elected member of *VUZ* social organisation (CPSU)	71·3	24·5
Member of student hostel council	63·2	36·8
Public lecturer, propagandist	58·4	32·5
Member of student wall newspaper committee	64·6	21·5
Komsomol group leader, Bureau member	64·2	31·2
Head of school circle, club, kindergarten club	58·6	34·5
Political lecturer, agitator	50·0	41·8
Member of people's vigilante group	46·6	43·1

Typical items selected; shortfalls to 100% unexplained. See also comment in note 8 of this chapter.
The survey covered 3,355 students of four Belorussian *VUZy* in 1971–3.
Source: Davidyuk, p. 73.

The attitudes of Soviet students to politics in the narrower sense of government policies have not, as far as I know, been objectively discussed in published Soviet sources. The official position is that the student body is solidly behind the CPSU in all important respects, and data are invariably offered as proof of this. The surveys mentioned here, however, and many others, provide massive if indirect evidence that enthusiasm is rather less pervasive than the authorities would desire.

STUDENTS' WELL-BEING

When Khrushchev came to power most students' grants were still governed by instructions issued in September 1943. As we have seen, applicants had to pass all their tests and examinations to become eligible for help, and about three-quarters of them obtained it. They were usually considered by order of academic record until the *VUZ* stipend fund ran out.

The size of the grant varied by type of establishment and year of study. It ranged from 140 roubles a month for first-year students in agricultural, pedagogical, medical and the lesser technical *VUZy* to 315 roubles for fifth-year students of universities and institutes serving favoured branches of the economy. Students achieving excellent marks in all subjects were entitled to 25 per cent on top of their basic rate. In addition, a few thousand special awards, named after public figures and worth up to 1,000 roubles each, were issued to outstanding students. Such 'named' awards were prestigious, and brought improved career chances.

The average wage in the mid-1940s was about 480 roubles a month, so ordinary grants, despite nominal accommodation and meals charges, betokened an exceedingly modest standard of living. The gap between what a student received from the state and what he needed for subsistence had to be bridged by parental help, earnings from production practice or outside work.

Khrushchev was much concerned about benefits for part-timers; he was less interested in the well-being of full-time students. The question must, however, have been causing concern when he came to power, because the August 1954 decree on higher and secondary special education drew attention to the needless complexity of grant regulations, and called for an early review of the awards procedure. Some help for the poorest students was envisaged by the August 1954 decree itself, in that it empowered the heads of *VUZy* and *SSUZy* to set aside the equivalent of 0·2 per cent of the institutional stipend fund for use in cases of 'extreme necessity'. It appears that one-time payments, not exceeding a month's grant, were occasionally made on this basis. The financial burden on some students was eased by the June 1956 abolition of tuition fees running at 300–500 roubles a year.

In August 1956 the old rules for issuing grants were at last modified (Karpov and Severtsev, p. 432). The new ones envisaged the establishment of *VUZ* commissions to make the awards, and introduced a means test principle. The student's family situation and income were now to be taken into account, so as to give preference not only to the most able but also to the needy. (This may have been done before, certainly, but without statutory backing.) The actual rates of payment, alas, were left at the 1943 level, even though the average wage had gone up to about 760 roubles in the meantime. And although inflation was not officially admitted, it was considered by some foreign observers to be significant enough to affect the rouble in people's pockets. So Soviet students without doubt got relatively poorer. The system of named stipends was retained, and indeed in March 1960, 2,200 'Lenin' awards were announced, with the same value as the old and apparently discarded 'Stalin' variety.

Brezhnev seems to have taken a more benign interest in student well-being than did his predecessor. In his speech to an all-union gathering of students on 19 October 1971 he announced that, in accordance with the directives of the Twenty-Fourth Party Congress, the Party and government had decided upon a 'significant improvement in the material and living conditions' of students of higher and secondary special educational institutions. A decree approved on the previous day in fact raised *VUZ* students' grants by 25 per cent, which meant that they were now to get between 40 and 60 new roubles a month, that is, 400–600 roubles in pre-1961 money (*SPR*, 1972, p. 170). Those who did exceptionally well and led an active social (or socio-political) existence were entitled to supplements of 15 or 25 per cent. The rise, incidentally, was planned only from 1 September 1972, by which time the average wage had risen to about 170 roubles and the state minimum to 70.

The new grants continued to be made on the same conditions as before, and over 70 per cent of the students still enjoyed them. The October decree called for more student accommodation, and better catering facilities and medical care. It is difficult to judge the results achieved, though it is known that the number of students in *VUZ* hostels rose by 192,000 (to 1·2 million) between 1970 and 1975 (*NONK*, 1977, p. 283). There was renewed interest in special awards, reflected in the creation of 100 'Karl Marx' stipends for students in the humanities (May 1968) and 1,700 additional 'Lenin' stipends (March 1970), all at the princely sum of 100 roubles a month (Voilenko, Vol. 2, p. 273).

So much for the grant regulations. More detail about the material standards enjoyed (or endured) by Soviet students can be gleaned from sociological investigations and from interviews with people who recently experienced it. Let us now look at the matter from that angle.

In the Russia of the 1970s a monthly income of 40–60 roubles, even with subsidised food and hostel accommodation, was hardly enough to live on. In the old Russian tradition, many students still got help from their families, in the form of parcels, clothes and money. Others found paid vacation work, with the active encouragement of the *Komsomol*. For many years this took the form of participation in regional development campaigns or harvesting (though the latter was not very lucrative and could be obligatory). In 1959'a regular system of vacation 'construction brigades' was started. It seems to have been quite popular, and provided the sturdier students with incomes of 200–400 roubles a month. By the mid-1970s over half a million students were said to be so employed annually.[9]

Outside jobs done during term have been shown, as might be expected, to have an adverse effect on study. A survey conducted at the Moscow *Oblast* Pedagogical Institute in the mid-1960s indicated that those who took such jobs devoted only about six hours a week to independent study, compared with a norm of fifteen to eighteen hours. Another survey at the same institute suggested that they missed many lectures; the time needed for employment obviously had to come from somewhere. There also seemed to be a correlation between outside jobs and bad examination results. An excellent, if brief, analysis of student health in one of the Gorki University studies of the late 1960s suggested that students who combined work and study were more subject to nervous strain. In any case, 25 per cent of all students did not normally get enough sleep, and only 60 per cent took care to eat regularly.[10]

Accommodation could be a major problem for students who had to live away from home. The acute shortage of living space which has long been a central feature of Soviet reality is aggravated by the strict system of residence permits operative in all towns. Militia offices may be instructed not to register newcomers on a permanent basis unless they already have both an occupation – which for students means a *VUZ* place – and somewhere to live.

In the mid-1970s the *VUZy* had hostel accommodation for about 45 per cent of the (full-time) student body; naturally, it was offered to 'outside' students first. A sample of just under 1,500 students at four Gorki *VUZy* in the late 1960s showed that 46·1 per cent lived in hostels, 21·4 per cent were at home with their families and 32·5 per cent were in private lodgings. Hostel accommodation, when available, is nominal in cost: rates of 70 kopeks and 1 rouble 5 kopeks a month were recorded in the provinces and Leningrad in the mid-1970s.

When the hostels are full, the *VUZ* authorities may grant a place to a candidate on condition that he finds his own lodging. Although Soviet law certainly permits private renting (provided other regulations are not infringed), the income it yields is heavily taxed and many landladies seek ways of concealing it. The beginning of the academic year, therefore, sees young people from other localities chasing around for private 'digs', which tend to be both scarce and expensive. In Leningrad in 1972 a simple room cost 40 roubles a month (this equalling the minimum grant), though in the small town of Sambor,

Lvovskaya *oblast*, the rate was down to 10 roubles. It is probable that many of the students registered as being in 'private accommodation' in the Gorky study were actually living with relatives, or were renting not a whole room but a 'corner', which is another hallowed Russian tradition. Though lodgings officers are unknown in Soviet *VUZy*, there is often an informal system whereby the service staff rent corners or beds to unaccommodated students.

The average Soviet hostel-dweller shares a room with two to ten other students, the norm being about four. Foreigners and research students are usually lodged two per room; the Moscow University hostel on Lenin Hills, where most students have a room to themselves, is untypical. According to V. P. Elyutin, the space norm for students in new hostels in 1971 was 5·7 sq. m., which is modest by any standards (*Vsesoyuzny slet studentov*, p. 43). Hostel furnishings are, to say the least, sparse: under the last regulations available (1967), each student was entitled to an iron bedstead, bedclothes, a bedside table, a chair, a workplace at a solid table and a share in a communal cupboard (Vidavski *et al.*, p. 271). There is normally a communal kitchen, a washroom and a cafeteria. Hostels I have visited created an impression of noisy and dilapidated adequacy. The food, though cheap, was generally poor, and sometimes gave rise to complaint.

Most students no doubt regard such conditions as normal and believe that things are no better in capitalist countries. Of 525 hostel students questioned in nine Gorki *VUZy* (but apparently not guaranteed anonymity) no less than 97 per cent declared themselves to be in general satisfied with their quarters. Perhaps part of the explanation for this extraordinarily high figure lay in the fact that nearly all of them were living in hostels by choice. Students who disliked doing so would probably have chosen a *VUZ* in their home town or found themselves a corner, and thus not figured in the sample. The proportion of hostel-dwellers who were not satisfied with the conditions for *study*, however, varied from 13 per cent at the Gorki Conservatory to 69 per cent at the Construction Institute. The fact that hostel accommodation is so cheap disarms criticism. Despite all the hardships, most Soviet students probably believe they are getting a reasonable deal from the state.

THE PROBLEM OF DROP-OUT

The loss of students from *VUZ* courses has always been a problem in Soviet higher education. We have already noted that by the late 1970s the drop-out rate overall was running at something like one in seven in the full-time sector and about a third in the part-time one (see page 104). These proportions, naturally, contained great 'internal' varia-tions. The loss was said to be higher in technical subjects than in the humanities, while some part-time courses had drop-out rates of 50–70 per cent (Dainovski, p. 16). Most of it probably occurred in the earlier years of study. The production candidates, the academically weak and the students from the less favoured social groups had most difficulty in staying the course. The cost of failure in national terms was undoubtedly great.

Some interesting revelations of a social character were made by S. L. Kostanyan in a study of fall-out at the Moscow Lenin State Pedagogical Institute (whose curriculum we have already studied). The author attempted to elucidate the real, as opposed to formal, reasons why 325 students left full-time courses in the year 1966–7. The MLSPI was arguably among the more prestigious Moscow *VUZy* and had a large proportion of female students, so it may not have been entirely typical of others throughout the country. But Kostanyan, at least, believed the results he obtained to be of general significance (Table 5.4).

Table 5.4   *Real Reasons for Student Drop-Out from Full-Time MLSPI Courses, 1966–7*

Reasons	Percentages	Totals*
Academic failure	25·5	82
Academic difficulties	1·8	6
Unwillingness to study	3·1	11
Family reasons†	14·7	48
Material difficulties	5·5	18
Transfer to another *VUZ*	13·9	45
Transfer to evening course	5·9	19
Health failure	9·9	32
Bad conduct	3·7	12
Other known reasons	0·5	2
Reasons unknown	15·4	50
	100	325

* Reconstituted from percentages.
† Including moving to another town, pregnancy, childcare, illness of adult family members.
Source: Kostanyan, 1973, p. 176, rearranged.

It seems he made no allowance for students who were influenced by more than one factor, but the figures as they stand show academic reasons to have been relevant in only about a third of the cases. An assortment of family circumstances explained about one departure in seven, and poverty (euphemistically entered as 'material difficulties') one in eighteen. Some students who gave no explanation may also have been obliged to leave for this reason, and I suspect it prompted most of the movement on to evening courses. Transfers to other *VUZy* were not, incidentally, insignificant. Unfortunately, no data were given for another 180 students who dropped out of the part-time division, but the difficulties of study doubtless figured large.

THE PLACEMENT OF GRADUATES IN THE 1960S AND 1970S

The Soviet authorities attempt nothing less than the placement of all graduates of higher and secondary special institutions throughout the country. This is possible because the educational sector is, in theory at least, closely planned, and because the authorities have since the early 1930s possessed legal instruments for holding graduates at their first job for a regulated period. Administrative order thus transcends not only such market forces as exist but also, often enough, the wishes and desires of the graduates themselves.

In practice planned placement sets a massive administrative problem for both central and local authorities. In 1978, for example, some 1,284,000 young people graduated from full-time, and 715,000 from part-time, courses of *VUZy* and *SSUZy*. All of the full-time graduates and, since 1968, many part-timers have to be directed into suitable jobs: a task of this magnitude, undertaken annually, is daunting. The broader social implications are also profound, for the government is virtually attempting to establish the occupational pattern of all newcomers to the intelligentsia.

In this brief survey we shall review the procedures for graduate placement since the death of Stalin, and consider the main problems which have arisen in implementing them. We shall also examine the response of the young specialists themselves. In order to make the topic a little more manageable, we shall concentrate exclusively on ordinary *VUZ* placements: the procedures for placing army, militia or KGB officers, defence and certain other personnel are not made public anyway.

(1) *Long- and Short-Term Planning*

Graduate placement procedures are necessarily linked with the system of planned admissions, and the two operations have changed little since they were introduced in the late 1920s. The level of admissions in each field of study must be fixed several years before graduation, with respect to both the length of the *VUZ* course and the exigencies of the five-year plans. It is clear that such long-term projections can only be approximate, and require refinement as time goes by.

As to intakes, estimates of future demands for specialists are worked out within each administrative hierarchy separately and transmitted to *Gosplan*, where they are co-ordinated and trimmed to fit the overall number of student places which it is practicable to provide. This last piece of information must come from the Ministry of Higher and Secondary Special Education, and be based on reports from individual *VUZy*; educational facilities cannot, of course, be expanded or contracted instantly to suit the demands of all potential employers. *Gosplan* then passes the revised estimates to the *MinVUZ* Department for Planning the Training and Distribution of Young Specialists, which determines how many students each institution should absorb.

The second step in the process takes place about a year before the students are due to graduate. *Gosplan* assembles, through the same channels, firm orders for the specialists needed throughout the country. At the same time the Ministry of Higher and Secondary Special Education requires all educational institutions to submit data on imminent graduations (as the numbers may, for obvious reasons, differ somewhat from those of the original admissions). The orders for specialists are finally approved by *Gosplan* according to 'gross' availability, and forwarded to the *MinVUZ*, which shares them between *VUZy* throughout the country as rationally as circumstances permit. Obviously, more direct arrangements may be made for ministries which administer their 'own' *VUZy*.

The 'personal' distribution of graduates is decided within the *VUZ* itself.[11] When the list of job vacancies comes through, the *VUZ* learned council sets up one or more Commissions for Personal Distribution, depending on the number of students to be dealt with. The average commission is composed of the rector or pro-rector, the dean of the faculty or faculties concerned, and representatives of the *MinVUZ*, the recipient ministries and administrations, the *Komsomol* and trades union organisations. Individual enterprises and organisations may also send someone to keep an eye on the proceedings on their behalf.

When it meets, a few months before graduation, the commission examines the academic progress, social activities, family circumstances and health of all final-year students, so as to come to a provisional decision on who should be offered what. It then interviews each of them in turn, preferably, as the statutes put it, in a 'solemn and businesslike atmosphere', and proposes one or more of the jobs on its list. The commission may examine any request which the student makes, and grant it; some people are released from obligatory placement for family, health or other reasons. But the fulfilment of the state plan is held to be of paramount importance, and the failure of a student to agree with the commission's decision does not free him or her from the obligation to accept the post allotted. The whole operation is supposed to conclude with the registration of the young specialist at his new place of work, after the month's holiday to which he is legally entitled.

(2)   Plan and Reality

A bare outline of the steps involved in graduate placement may give the impression that the system has been working smoothly. In fact it has always been plagued by difficulties. To begin with, the planning itself may vary in accuracy at any point. The authorities can make reasonable estimates of the number of specialists required in fields like education, health and administration, since these needs are dependent on more or less calculable factors or deliberate government policy. Demand in the field of material production, however, has always presented a knotty problem. For instance, efforts by planners to develop a methodology for determining an enterprise's requirement of production specialists on the basis of its output and labour force have not been very successful. Managers have shown themselves strongly inclined to over-state their requirements for specialist labour in the expectation that they will get only part of what they request. Prognostication has been further complicated by irregularities in the growth of the economy and sharp, unheralded changes in government priorities.

Furthermore, the actual placement of students may well raise problems of a personal character. On the administrative side, discrepancies between immediate economic needs and the numbers of students available may come to light only at this juncture. Figures which I have quoted elsewhere showed surpluses of up to 116 per cent and shortfalls of up to 66 per cent in several important fields (Matthews, 1972, p. 339). These instances cover the years 1946–50 and 1962 and are now rather dated, but proof of improvement is lacking. If such discrepancies emerge early enough the *VUZ* authorities may when practicable transfer students to a more appropriate course; otherwise the commissions have to direct them into the jobs that seem least unsuited to their skills or (in exceptional cases) release them from posting altogether. The Ministry of Higher and Secondary Special Education does not, it seems, include many spare places in the distribution plans it sends out, for 'planned' placement must mean a close correspondence between the profile of jobs and graduates.

For the students, placement is of necessity a somewhat stressful matter. The fact that many are not really interested in their topic of study implies that just as many may not be over-enthusiastic about the professional obligations which follow. Large surveys conducted in four Leningrad and nine RSFSR *VUZy* in 1969 and 1971 showed that only about 16 per cent of the respondents firmly planned to take production work. About 20 per cent had not decided and nearly all of the remainder hoped to do some kind of research, a pattern which differed considerably from their employment prospects (Lisovski and Dmitriev, p. 147). Over and above this, the problem of assigning places of varying quality among individuals of varying ability is not one which lends itself to easy solution. The more desirable jobs have thus tended to become the focus of all kinds of unofficial pressures. Further difficulties arise because the Commission for Personal Distribution has to make its decisions on the basis of course marks, before the final exams have been taken.

A student who has reason to believe that he will be landed with an unsatisfactory job, or who wishes to get out of official posting anyway, can approach a potential employer beforehand and request him to make a personal order for his, the student's, services. Some graduates try to take advantage of the release provisions covering personal circumstances. It is not uncommon for girls to find conveniently located husbands just before they graduate, since the hymeneal bond automatically frees them from placement in another town. According to occasional press reports, some students actually refuse their postings in the presence of the commission, but since by doing so they lay themselves open to pressures from the *Komsomol* and *VUZ* authorities they are few in number.

Difficulties do not end when the commission completes its work, for many students fail to turn up at the jobs allotted to them, even after agreeing to do so. The ministries which have suffered most from this in the past – Agriculture, Enlightenment and Health – are those which offer less well-paid jobs in rural or remote areas. Other graduates may arrive at their designated post but, on finding they do not like it, invent a pretext to leave. Outright desertion can cause some trouble with work documentation, but it is by no means rare. On the other hand, the employers may act improperly. There is a tendency, often criticised, for them to give young specialists jobs in offices rather than on production, or release them from their posting without proper verification.

The employer organisations sometimes refuse to take the planned numbers of graduates; in the RSFSR the proportion of such refusals rose, according to one source, from 4·2 per cent in 1965 to 7·17 per cent in 1970 (Ushakov and Shuruev, p. 144). The categories used in official handbooks are mostly too vague to allow proper calculation of the overall success rates in transferring *VUZ* graduates to long-term employment according to specialisation, but it is possible to form a few impressions. Between 1970 and 1975, for example, the agricultural *VUZy* turned out about 269,000 graduates, and the pedagogical *VUZy* about 725,000. Yet the numbers of agricultural specialists and teachers with degrees rose, over the same period, by only 124,000 and 299,000 respectively. Even allowing for retirements and other unknowns, the figures suggest that a very large proportion of the graduates opted out.

The numerous possibilities of failure in the placement mechanism make it inevitable that the end result should diverge markedly from the ideal. Some problems, of course, may be solved by timely modification of plans and directives and by switching undergraduates to other courses. Sometimes graduates may not like their posting but accept it with as much grace as they can muster. Occasionally, discrepancies may cancel one another out. Nevertheless, the faults of the system tend to be strongly cumulative.

One may ask, in view of this, whether it would not be better for state and students alike if obligatory placement were abandoned altogether. In terms of cost-saving and efficiency it well might. But abandonment would mean the withdrawal of the state from a vital sector of the labour market, introducing realistic salaries for less attractive jobs, and allowing directors and managers freedom to do their own hiring. There has never, since the collapse of the NEP, been any suggestion that this could happen. And given the authorities' sensitivity about political control, there is little prospect of it coming to pass in the foreseeable future.

(3) *Legal Control of Graduates*

The weaknesses of the placement system have been an object of concern since the mid-1930s, and many efforts have been made to correct them, either by modifying the procedures or by exhorting graduates to do their patriotic duty. Although these changes have been limited and of little avail, brief consideration needs to be given to those which have most impinged on student life.

The commissions for personal distribution, like so many governmental organs, suffered from Stalinist centralisation, and by 1953 they had lost virtually all power to depart from the placement plans received from on high. One of the lesser benefits of the post-Stalin thaw in labour relations was some increase in their authority. In December 1955 they were given the right to grant 'free diplomas', which allowed the holders to find their own work if there were no suitable vacancies. At the same time the health and family grounds on which graduates could refuse a posting were extended. Statutes introduced for the commissions in November 1957 and October 1963 were progressively more liberal. Graduates were to be supplied with much more information on their rights, responsibilities and future working conditions. The commissions were given a freer hand in re-directing them if it transpired that proper employment was not available. On the other hand, the receiving organisations were granted the right to re-direct young specialists to more suitable jobs internally if necessary.

The next version of the statutes, approved in April 1968, went even further in the same direction. The commissions could now examine orders for specialists 'critically', and depart from the plan if these orders did not correspond with the graduates' specialisations or carried no guarantee of living space (which had always been a major cause of desertion). Young specialists acquired the right to request the head office of the organisation in which they were employed to move them if their particular manager could not give them suitable work. Stronger links were to be encouraged between *VUZ* and enterprise, and managers were expressly forbidden to employ young specialists on office duties.

A new clause made the graduates of part-time and evening courses subject to placement for the first time, and granted them the right to change their jobs before the end of the three-year term if they could not obtain a responsible post in the enterprise where they had worked as students. How far these changes were implemented we do not know: but they were evidently designed to make placement practices a little more reasonable and humane, thereby improving their efficiency.

The post-Stalin period also saw a relaxation of penalties for erring graduates. A law introduced in February 1934, when Stalin was tightening control of the labour market, made people who refused to accept their posting liable to a minimum of six months' imprisonment, with partial or complete confiscation of property. This sanction was subsequently changed a number of times, but omitted from the 1957 statutes. The graduate then, it seems, had to face only socio-political pressures if he refused to go to his job, or normal loss of social security benefits if he deserted it. Managers, incidentally, were still forbidden to employ graduates who did not have the necessary documentation, but this was now apparently defined as an administrative, not a criminal, misdemeanour.

Perhaps it was the failure of this relaxation which prompted Khrushchev to impose new restrictions. Under the terms of the 1963 statute, graduates were to be handed their diplomas not when they graduated but a year later, *if* they were still ensconced in the jobs to which the commission had directed them. On 5 November 1964, just after Khrushchev's removal, the *MinVUZ* acquired the right to deprive graduates of their diplomas if they did not take up their posts, a policy which had been actively canvassed by the *Komsomol*.

The Brezhnev leadership adopted a milder policy in this respect. A law of 3 September 1966 stated that graduates were to get their diplomas immediately on graduation as before, and the deprivation rules were repealed. Tinkering with the regulations at this level then stopped, perhaps because the authorities came to the conclusion, for a time at any rate, that administrative imperfections could not be remedied by this means. But the question of the overall viability of the system remained, in my view, far from decided.

NOTES

1   See, for a good survey, Dobson, in *Annual Review of Sociology*, 1977. Also Matthews, 1972, chs 10 and 12; in *Soviet Studies*, vol. 27, 1975, pp. 86–108; and in M. G. Field, 1976, ch. 5.
2   The various provisions discussed here and below are buried in the relevant versions of the *VUZ* applicants' handbooks (see page 130), mostly entitled *Spravochnik dlya postupayushchikh v vysshie uchebnye zavedenia SSSR*. Particular reference has been made to the 1945, 1959, 1963, 1969 and 1971 editions.
3   The Russian term *beloruchka* is usually applied to people afraid of getting their hands dirty. For other comments by Khrushchev, see his speeches before youthful audiences on 11 April 1956 and 18 April 1958, and his notes to the Presidium of the

Central Committee of the CPSU of 21 September 1958, in Khrushchev, pp. 8, 40, 46.
4   See the references in note 1 to this chapter and the tables discussed in the next section.
5   This ratio simply measures the discrepancy between the size of a given group – employees, workers or peasants – in society and in the student body. Thus perfect equivalence would give a ratio of 1:1, while a social group which comprised, say, 50 per cent of society, but provided only 25 per cent of the students, would register 1:0·5.
6   I. I. Sheremet, in *SI*, no. 2, 1977, p. 76; V. A. Podtorak in Fillipov, 1976b, p. 96. An analysis of admissions to Tartu University evening courses (one of the most detailed available) showed that by 1973 71 per cent were women, of whom 74 per cent had also been able to register within two years of leaving school. Half of the young men were in the same situation (despite the complication of military service). Over half of all the students in the survey were not working in their field of study specialisation anyway (article by L. Yakobsoo, in Kyaembre *et al.*, p. 63).
7   Certain items of information are considered in *Soviet Studies*, vol. 27, no. 1, January 1975, p. 86. Further convincing if indirect indications are to be found in Vasilyeva, pp. 126 ff.); Khairullin, p. 128; Balabanov, p. 16.
8   Rubin and Kolesnikov devoted particular attention to this problem (pp. 131 ff., 176). Surprisingly analogous results were obtained from a survey of 3,355 students in four *VUZy* in White Russia in 1971 and 1973 (Davidyuk *et al.*, pp. 62, 66, 69). It is regrettable that the wealth of information which both of these investigations produced was, presumably for reasons of censorship, so inadequately presented.
9   *BSE*, Vol. 25, 1976, p. 7; Davidyuk *et al.*, p. 79.
10 The Gorki study mentioned here and below was entitled 'Sotsiologia i vysshaya shkola' and appeared in *Uchenye zapiski Gorkovskogo Gosudarstvennogo Universiteta*, vyp. 100, seria sotsiologicheskaya, tom II, Gorki, 1970. This and the MOPI items were discussed further in Matthews, January 1975, p. 94. See also T. D. Samilova, quoted on page 139.
11 This rather complex system has been subject to a great deal of minor modification over the years, and there is a body of legislation on it. The functions of the commissions during the late 1960s and 1970s are described in the statutes of the USSR Ministry of Higher Education of 2 November 1955, the decree 'On Measures for Improving the Training of Specialists and Perfecting the Management of Higher and Secondary Special Education in the Country' of 3 September 1966, and the version of the statutes for the personal distribution of young specialists approved on 18 March 1968.

6
Supplementary Educational Services

The institutions for what might be called 'formal' education do not, of course, provide all the training available in the USSR. Important 'supplementary' services exist as well, and it is to these that we now turn. They may be classified for our purposes under the following general headings: facilities for children from about the age of 3 until they start the general school (not counting nursery facilities for toddlers); training for young people 'on the job'; 'special' schools for the handicapped and (separately) delinquents; courses in ideology, politics and administration for party members, officials and the public at large; professional military training; and finally the tiny, though not insignificant, non-state sector. Considerations of space limit us to an overview of each topic, with particular reference to the situation in the late 1970s. As noted in the preface, the main purpose of the chapter is to improve our perspective of the educational system proper, rather than investigate in detail organisations which lie outside it.

PRE-SCHOOL FACILITIES

Soviet women have always been expected to work outside the home, not only to suit the demands of the economy but also to supplement the family income. In recent years, according to certain American estimates, up to 90 per cent of women in the working age-groups have actually been employed (Feshbach and Rapawy, p. 152). As might be anticipated, facilities for the care and education of young children appeared early. They were, in fact, first established by the People's Commissariat for Enlightenment in December 1917; and from the beginning of the 1930s, when industrialisation was proceeding in earnest, increasing attention was devoted to them.

During the Khrushchev years the number of permanent (as opposed to seasonal) places for 3- to 7-year-olds rose from 1·6 to 5·2 million, providing coverage of about one child in four. The distribution was, however, very uneven: by 1965 there were places for nearly half the children in the towns but for only one out of eleven in the countryside. The Brezhnev years saw further strong growth, and by 1976, with nearly 9 million children inducted, coverage must have approached totality in the towns and a quarter in the countryside. The number of pre-school institutions often lagged behind plan. For instance, the levels stipulated by the directives of the Twenty-third Party Congress for 1970 were not reached until some five years later. The satisfaction of rural needs, particularly those of collective farm families, was particularly difficult. No data are to hand on the regularity of the children's attendance or turn-over in existing places. However, in the summer of 1978 a supplementary network of seasonal camps and playgroups supported nearly 2 million children of pre-school age, while Young Pioneer holiday camps provided vacations for 11 million older ones (*Nar. khoz.*, 1978, pp. 417, 471).

In institutional terms pre-school education has not changed greatly since the early 1950s. Children aged 3–7 attend a kindergarten or a combined nursery and kindergarten (introduced for administrative convenience in May 1959). Both nurseries and kindergartens take children on a weekly, daily or shift basis, and charge fees for their services (a matter to which we shall return in a moment).

Kindergartens may be run by enterprises or by local education authorities, though the enterprise-based ones may be obliged to set aside places for the children whose parents work elsewhere. Registration is done on parental initiative (Abakumov *et al.*, p. 330). In all cases the children's activities must be approved by the educational authorities, while standards of accommodation and hygiene are the concern of the ministries of health. Private kindergartens are specifically banned, but there are occasional reports of informal child-minding groups run by individuals at home.

The growth of general education has had important implications for what children are taught at this stage. A decree passed in May 1959 criticised the pre-school teaching materials as lacking in unity and consistency, and called for a new programme. This was devised and implemented in the RSFSR and other union republics by the late 1960s (Prokofiev *et al.*, p. 51). It involved for older children a start in reading, writing and arithmetic, and contained, in accordance with the current trend, a section on 'labour'. By the late 1970s many kindergartens were running groups for 6-year-olds as preparation for the general school, and even allowing children not registered earlier to join for this purpose.

The effectiveness of this work has been investigated by Soviet sociologists, and the results of a 1973 survey of the first classes of schools in Moscow and Moscow *oblast* are not without interest (Zyuzin *et al.*, p. 102). Over 66 per cent of the 3,175 children investigated had come straight from a kindergarten, while another 8·5 per cent had attended one, but not in the year before starting school. Most of the remainder (a few were not accounted for) had not enjoyed this benefit at all.

The authors found that, on the whole, the kindergarten children were better prepared for primary instruction, though the matter is not quite as clear-cut as it might seem. For one thing, kindergartens vary in quality, mainly according to the institution they are attached to. Thus a kindergarten for employees of, say, the USSR Council of Ministers, would probably be superior to one run by a small-town soviet. Secondly, it was the children from more favoured backgrounds who were the most likely to be sent to kindergartens. Of all the parents covered by the survey, 76·9 per cent of the employees, 62·6 per cent of the workers and 22·6 per cent of the peasants used the service. The sociologist F. R. Filippov, in his discussion of the same problem, quoted investigations which purported to show that readiness to send a child to a kindergarten also rose with parents' educational and skill levels (1976a, p. 55). It looks, therefore, as though there have been marked social differences in the use of services. The less favoured children, who, to judge from some evidence, most needed help and stood to gain most, tended to go to the poorer kindergartens or none at all.

We noted in passing that fees are payable for the use of the facilities. This practice was inaugurated in August 1948. The fees (designed partly to recover costs and partly, no doubt, as a disincentive to irregular use) were originally set at between 3 and 18 roubles per month for each child, depending on the length of the day, parental income and the degree to which facilities were used. At that time the average wage (outside the peasant sector) was about 48 roubles a month, so that the sums involved could have been quite significant. Poor parents, large families, war widows and single mothers got reductions of up to half, so as to ease the burden. The same rates were, however, still in force in the early 1970s, when the average wage was around 130 roubles, so payment must have come to serve as little more than a token of earnest (Altschuler, p. 3). One of the surveys referred to by Filippov showed that whereas 13 per cent of the families questioned did not wish to use the child care facilities, only 0·2 per cent were put off by the cost (p. 56).

TRAINING NEW LABOUR ON THE JOB

Leaving school usually presents more problems than entering it. The majority of young work-seekers in the Soviet Union have always, as we observed in Chapter 3, received such specialised training as they got directly at work. In fact, of the 6,500 skills listed in a recent handbook only a thousand or so were regularly taught in the *PTU* system (Batyshev and Shaporinski, pp. 19, 434). We shall now consider what training on the job has meant in practice.

Unfortunately, the term as used in Soviet statistical compilations covers at least three categories of persons, who should, ideally, be treated separately: trainees who formerly worked elsewhere; young persons who were hired but were in fact given very little appreciable instruction; and people, numbering over 30 million in 1978, who were involved in raising their skill level. This last, as a work-associated process, is not particularly meaningful in an educational context and we shall not pursue it further. Table 6.1 contains the undifferentiated data as usually presented, and illustrates the claimed steady growth over the years.

Table 6.1   *Trainees in Manual and Non-Specialist Skills* (*millions*)

| | Acquiring a new skill on the job | | | SLR–PTU leavers |
	Manual (except collective farmers)	Non-manual	Manual (collective farmers)	
1955	(2·5)	(0·3)	+NA	0·65
1960	2·8	0·2	+NA	0·74
1965	3·4	0·3	0·25	1·1
1970	4·8	0·2	0·22	1·6
1975	5·5	0·2	0·35	2·1
1978	5·8	0·2	0·43	2·3

( ) average 1951–5.
NA – not available.
Sources: Trud v SSSR, 1968, p. 320; *Nar. khoz.*, 1978, pp. 380, 382.

Our earlier discussions have implied that training young people on the job has always been a troublesome matter. The fact that trainees are included in the enterprise 'labour plan' and are entered in the unions' 'labour agreement' has never eliminated the difficulties. The locally operated *bronya* system of September 1957 was an attempt to ease matters by direct state intervention. This was followed, as we have seen, by the strengthening of planning provisions for hiring and stricter administrative controls. Nevertheless, enterprise managements always seemed to retain some power of manipulation, and their willingness to train young workers varied with current needs and pressures. So from the point of view of the individual, getting accepted for one of the training schemes about to be described was not always easy.

(1)   *The Main Training Schemes*

The main types of training have traditionally been organised on an 'individual', 'brigade' or 'course' basis. In the mid-1960s – no later data are to hand – at least half of all learners (outside the collective farm sector) were taught individually. About a fifth were organised into brigades, or work-groups, either attached to ordinary production brigades or functioning independently with their own instructors (*Trud v SSSR*, 1968, p. 320). The remainder were taught on permanent courses run by organisations or enterprises, this method being the most formal.

Individual training was said to have been common in machine-building, metallurgy, rubber and asbestos production, transport and light industry; brigades were most used in construction enterprises. The course system, on the other hand, was the predominant method of teaching young people who were going on to acquire more advanced skills or had to learn the use of farm machinery. It was apparently much encouraged during the 1970s, with the collaboration of local *PTU*. The length of the training periods has for many years been fixed at between three and six months, depending on the complexity of the trade, with an average close to three. This might seem less than adequate from the standpoint of Western practice; yet in the USSR longer terms required special authorisation.[1]

Individual and brigade learners are allotted to experienced artisans, and are supposed to acquire their skills as the work proceeds. However, certain minimum standards of achievement were introduced in 1932, and elaborated thereafter. That there is no clear division between learning and producing is evident from the rules for payment. The December 1959 statutes, which covered learners as well as schoolchildren, stated that learners' guaranteed pay should start at 75 per cent of the lowest step in the relevant scale and fall to 20 per cent in the fourth and subsequent months. Clearly, the intention was to make up the difference by earnings for production of acceptable quality. An obligatory theoretical element, comprising an introduction to technology, safety techniques and simple production economics, which took up about thirty-six hours a month, was introduced in July 1969 (Novikov and Grechanik, p. 119). On completing their training, young workers have to appear before a 'qualification commission' which tests their theoretical knowledge and their manual skill. If they pass satisfactorily they obtain a regular skill rating.

Instructors are chosen from among such people as qualified workers, foremen and brigadeers, and approved by the chief engineer of the enterprise. Ideally, they should have full general schooling and have taken a 'pedagogical minimum' course. According to the 1959 rules, most instructors got from 7 roubles a month for teaching one learner to 3½ roubles per head for four or more. Those who took on a minimum of twelve to fifteen learners were released from their production jobs at their average rate of pay. The money was, however, payable as a lump sum only when the young worker qualified, so that instructors were expected to shoulder very specific responsibilities without immediate return. These conditions, which were not at all conducive to enthusiastic teaching, were still valid in the mid-1970s (Terebilov, pp. 254, 594).

(2) *Changes under Khrushchev and Brezhnev*

Concern about the poor quality of on-the-job training was, as we have noted, expressed in the 1950s, when the future of the state labour reserves was under discussion. Despite his interest in work schemes, Khrushchev did not at first pay much attention to the situation: he hoped, no doubt, that the expansion of the SLR/*PTU* schools and polytechnisation would ease the situation. He may also have wished to avoid yet another tussle with enterprise managements.

But by the early 1960s prospects of a spontaneous improvement had apparently faded, and the decree of 20 December 1962, which was devoted principally to enterprise training, revealed a dismal picture. 'There are serious shortcomings,' it said, 'in vocational training on production . . . the training of workers and the development of their skills at many enterprises and construction sites is of a low standard . . . existing courses are not provided with classrooms, teaching aids or technical literature . . . teaching programmes are out of date.' The decree did not change the forms or methods of training, but called for detailed improvements in planning, shifted the onus of this on to *Gosplan*, and ordered more training premises to be built (*Reshenia*, vol. 5, p. 256). It was followed by the publication in May 1963 of statutes which codified in some detail all the permissible training procedures (Mishutkin, 1965, p. 430); Aleksandrov *et al.*, p. 254). This was in effect the first comprehensive set of regulations to be approved since the RSFSR labour code of 1922.

The Brezhnev leadership was concerned to make the system more tightly knit. The organisation of 'instruction course combines, teaching workshops, practice areas, study rooms and laboratories' was required in March 1968, and improved arrangements for theoretical training followed in October. The spring of 1969 saw a flurry of detailed instructions on the new units and the training methods they were to adopt. Methodological cabinets, or centres, were to be set up under the aegis of the *PTU* administration and production ministries (Novikov and Grechanik, pp. 48, 56, 113).

This new drive, however, was also less successful than had been hoped. The economist V. M. Moskovich, writing in 1970, still found on-the-job training very unsatisfactory. His exposition of its shortcomings was, indeed, one of the most authoritative to come to my notice; and since it was being repeated in substance at the end of the decade it may aptly be used for a final assessment here.[2]

Such training, according to Moskovich, suffered from bad planning, which reflected only the immediate needs of a given enterprise or the capabilities of existing staff and equipment. As a result there was often a gap between numbers of trainees and the longer-term needs of industry. Such discrepancies could be made worse by some enterprises over-fulfilling their training plans, while others fell behind. Next, there was a tendency for training to be reduced to instruction in a narrow speciality, involving only a few simple operations. This meant that young people became dissatisfied and changed their jobs quickly, and that any modifications of the production process required extensive re-training. Young workers acquired only a bare grounding in theory; new techniques and technology were neglected; training periods were pared down. Many enterprises lacked basic instruction facilities, and learners were often taught practical operations in the course of the production process.

Moskovich singled out the regulations covering instructors as another source of trouble. Many lacked a general education and were not trained to teach. Learners took up their time and reduced their earnings, yet the sums paid for this imposition were totally inadequate. The basic rate of 7 roubles per learner had apparently been operative since the early 1950s, when the average wage was around 65 roubles (*Zakonodatelstvo o trude*, 1954, p. 113). It was still the same in the early 1970s, when the average had risen to about 125 roubles. It was also a flat rate, regardless of the instructor's skill level. The teaching of theoretical courses, moreover, was paid at only 1 rouble an hour, and rarely yielded more than 20–25 roubles a month. In consequence enterprise personnel were by and large unwilling to take on learners. Instruction became a matter of social duty, imposition and, inevitably, neglect. Moskovich quoted a survey which showed that 70 per cent of the cases of spoiled production and 30 per cent of breakdowns resulted from a lack of skill on the part of people trained mainly on production (p. 290). The retention of the 7-rouble rate in the course of the 1968 reform was, I think, a clear indicator that the authorities, though anxious for improvement, were not really prepared to pay for it.

It is noteworthy that this problem, like so many others of an educational character, has always had important social implications. Early employment is the obvious course for less advantaged children, and any inadequacies in the training they receive can only exacerbate any deprivation already experienced.

SCHOOLS FOR SPECIAL CATEGORIES OF PUPILS

The Soviet authorities frequently express great pride in the provision made for children with physical and mental disabilities. The education of the four main categories – the blind, deaf and dumb, physically disabled and mentally deficient – was the subject of official discussion as early as August 1918; and special services, including schools with boarding facilities, lengthened days and protracted courses, were developed as time went by. Such schools attracted particular attention in 1960 and 1961, when efforts were made to align them as far as possible with the December 1958 reform. Special schools were at this time also established for children suffering from poliomyelitis (Deineko, p. 463). By and large handicapped children are taught as many general school subjects and skills as they can manage. Teachers have extra training and receive higher rates of pay for this work (Medynski, 1955, p. 127).

It is difficult to judge the adequacy of the network available, but the figures published reveal an impressive growth. Thus in 1954 0·4 per cent of all full-time general school places were allotted to handicapped children; by 1978 the proportion was up to 1·2 per cent (the absolute rise being from 129,000 to about half a million). If we exclude the possibility of a massive increase in infantile infirmity, we must conclude either that provision for it was grossly inadequate in the earlier years or that much broader definitions were used subsequently.

Crime in the Soviet Union (as elsewhere) is committed predominantly by young people with a low standard of education, so it is not surprising that special arrangements should be made for training them when incarcerated. Unfortunately, most aspects of crime and detention are under a rigorous censorship ban, and national magnitudes cannot be discerned. The educational facilities for delinquents fall into two clear-cut categories: 'special' closed institutions for 11- to 15-year-olds, and classes of various kinds at adult labour colonies (often described as 'camps' in Western literature).

The 'special schools' and 'special *PTU*', established in 1964, were based on the old 'children's educational colonies'. There are separate institutions for boys and girls, and direction into them is by court order or through the 'commissions for youth affairs' attached to local soviets. Although the programmes of study are basically identical with those of open schools, a great deal of emphasis is laid on production practice and physical labour. Parental visits are allowed only with the permission of the directors, but the pupils may send and receive letters, and good conduct may bring permission to spend holidays at home. The commissions for youth affairs are supposed to help newly released inmates to find work or a place in a regular educational institution. Delinquents' parents are, interestingly enough, expected to pay something towards their maintenance expenses.[3]

The classes at regular labour colonies must, of course, function in a very specific manner. The pupils tend to be over-age (the upper age-limit for pursuing general education in these circumstances is 40) and are in any case required to spend most of their day in socially useful toil. Nevertheless, school attendance is said to be obligatory for persons with less than eight classes of schooling behind them, and some may be encouraged to proceed to ten. In addition, trade training is organised for beginners and those who wish to improve existing qualifications. It is normally of twelve to fourteen months' duration and is split into two parts. The first comprises theory and simple practice, while the second is more advanced and involves production work. In order to accommodate newcomers fairly quickly, groups are supposed to be formed at least once every two months (Tkachevski, p. 100).

Such at least are the designated paths. How many people tread them, and to what effect, can only be a matter of conjecture.

SPECIALIST TRAINING FOR PARTY AND STATE OFFICIALS

The Communist Party establishments for training party and state officials in ideology and administrative skills form a distinct administrative entity. At the top of the hierarchy is the Academy of Social Sciences attached to the Central Committee of the CPSU; next come various 'higher party' and 'party' schools, in Moscow and the provinces, while a network of seminars and courses run by local party offices forms the base of the system. We will work our way downwards.

The Academy of Social Sciences is the Party's highest educational and research establishment and the centre-point of all formal ideological training in the land. It was set up in 1946 to train 'theoretical workers', that is, for the central, republican, *oblast* and district offices of the CPSU; teachers of ideological subjects at higher educational and research institutes; and senior staff for learned journals and the propaganda media. It admits officials experienced in party and propaganda work who already have a complete higher education and who aspire to the *aspirantura*. They must be proposed by party committees from the *oblast* level up.

The subjects researched at the Academy span the social sciences and the humanities, including even pure art. The individual faculties may grant their own Candidate of Sciences degrees, subject to confirmation by the Academy's learned council; there are also arrangements for granting doctorates. It seems that in the mid-1950s about seventy applicants were accepted annually, the figure rising to about 100 by the mid-1970s (Table 6.2).[4] The Academy is thus, in its way, a select and prestigious institution.

Not surprisingly, it has been rather susceptible to political currents at the summit. The narrowness and superficiality of its work was sharply criticised in a Central Committee decree of 3 September 1954, and it was ordered, amongst other things, to lengthen its course of study from three to four years (*Voprosy ideologicheskoi raboty KPSS*, 1961, p. 69). In May 1959 when Khrushchev was particularly concerned about ideological matters, it came under fire for not promoting enough topical research and for being insufficiently demanding in its choice of *aspiranty*. The course was again shortened to three years, and the upper age-limit for entry was dropped from 40 to 35, suggesting concern about the age of applicants. In 1964 the

Table 6.2 *Professional Party Schools and Courses: Graduations (absolute figures)*

Type	1957	1965	1976
Academy of Social Sciences	(70)	(127)	107
Higher Party School (Central Committee)	(318)	(329)	296
Higher party schools (regional)	(6,000)	(1,200)	1,863
Correspondence Higher Party School	(600)	(2,000)	3,566

( ) Average over a number of years, according to source.
Sources: 1957, 1965 derived from Mickiewicz, p. 168, and *KPSS – naglyadnoe posobie*, 1973, p. 139; 1976: *SPR*, 1978, p. 397.

Academy acquired its own Institute of Atheism, which meant greater involvement in anti-religious matters.

The reinvigoration of ideological work envisaged by the massive decree of 14 August 1967 did not, as far as one can tell, bring any major change of structure or function.

In April 1978, however, during another campaign to improve the propaganda network, the Academy was reorganised to form a 'qualitatively' new institution on the triple basis of the old Academy, the Higher Party School and the Correspondence Higher Party School (both of which we shall consider below). The new conglomerate had eighteen faculties as against eight previously, and acquired greater administrative control over party schools in the provinces. Its aims, as stated, were virtually identical with those which had been proclaimed before; but the reorganisation was supposed to promote 'a more exact distinction between the functions of the Academy and those of the regional higher party schools', and the Academy was now 'charged with organising the training of cadres on a higher level'. There seems to have been a new emphasis on recruiting officials above the position of first secretary of town party committee (*BSE*, Vol. 1, 1970, p. 323; *PZh*, no. 7, 1978, p. 3).

The disappearance of the old Higher Party School as a separate entity marked, in a way, the end of an epoch. The Moscow Higher Party School had been founded in 1939, and offered a full-time two-year course for would-be party officials. It was reorganised in June 1956 so as to offer extra ideological training to technical and other specialists who already had a degree (Loeffler, p. 116). It enjoyed a higher standing than the party schools in the provinces, and served as a methodological centre for them. Students of the Moscow HPS graduated not only with a diploma in higher party-political education but also with a candidate's minimum certificate which facilitated entry into the *aspirantura*. After 1956 it began to train communists from the 'socialist countries', and enthusiasts from capitalist lands were certainly admitted. Its part-time facilities, of which more in a moment, were expanded as a result of Khrushchev's interest in this type of study, and the splitting of party organisations into industrial and territorial sectors (between 1962 and 1964) entailed some reorganisation. But afterwards, until its incorporation in the Academy, it was apparently left alone. Graduations were fairly steady, at around 300 a year.

In the early 1970s the Moscow HPS had eleven faculties, covering (apart from basic ideological subjects) international affairs, law, journalism, literature, Russian and foreign languages. A shake-up of the curriculum, demanded in a mild decree of September 1972, resulted in the introduction of courses in economic management, social psychology, the use of pedagogy in party work and Comecon practices (*BSE*, Vol. 5, 1971, p. 382; Vol. 19, 1975, p. 246; *SPR*, 1973, p. 241).

Applicants were recommended by one of the middle-range party committees (republican, *oblast* or *krai*) from among party, state and *Komsomol* functionaries and journalists who had been in the CPSU for at least three years. Workers and collective farmers who had shown administrative promise could also be selected. As HPS students they either continued to receive their former salaries or were given generous maintenance grants, with allowances for dependants. After graduation they were directed to responsible positions in party and state offices at the *oblast* and republican levels; a few of them eventually achieved membership of the Central Committee (*Iz opyta*, p. 272; Kirstein, p. 220).

Regional party schools were established in republican and provincial centres in 1946. By the early 1950s there were over seventy of them, offering a full-time course of three years for people who already had a degree, and one of four years for those with only general education. Like the Moscow HPS they trained administrative officials and professional propagandists in the various forms of mass enlightenment. Overall, graduations then seem to have averaged about 5,000–6,000 a year.

In June 1956 Khrushchev closed thirteen of them, regraded twenty-nine as 'inter-republican and inter-*oblast* party schools' with a four-year course for people without a degree, and allowed the remainder to continue as two-year institutions for degree-holders (*SPR*, 1957, p. 411). Soon afterwards these schools also came to be designated as 'higher', and their graduates were given a diploma officially rated as equivalent to that of a 'grade 2' *VUZ*.

The 'higher' schools were inevitably affected by Khrushchev's splitting of the party organisation in November 1962; by the following year amalgamations and closures had reduced their number to twelve (Kirstein, p. 215). From then until the late 1970s, however, they enjoyed a period of organisational quiescence, and produced on average 1,600 graduates a year. By 1978 there were fifteen schools in all. After the July restructuring of the Academy they were criticised for being behindhand in their treatment of the theory and practice of communism: their curriculum was revised and several were given their own part-time departments (*PZh*, no. 10, 1978, p. 45).

The June 1956 decree established a *Correspondence Higher Party School*, based on the existing HPS in Moscow and clearly intended to make up the shortfall in numbers from the regional schools. A correspondence course had been available in the Moscow Higher Party School since 1944, but it had not, in numerical terms, been very important (*Iz opyta*, p. 271). The correspondence HPS became a more important source of trained officials than the regional schools, and was retained by the Brezhnev leadership (Table 6.2). It is perhaps surprising that aggregate graduations from the party schools (and indeed the Academy itself) should have remained so stable over a period of rapid educational and party growth. The most obvious explanation is that the range of jobs that the graduates were supposed to fill did not expand accordingly.

The advanced courses at the Academy and higher party schools were supplemented in the 1950s and 1960s by a country-wide system of classes and seminars of an uneven *ad hoc* nature, based on local party offices or the HPSs themselves. Such undertakings could last from a few weeks to a year, depending on local conditions and needs. They were designed primarily for officials and propagandists who needed extra training or had to be kept up-to-date on official attitudes and responses. When funds permitted or places were available, rank and file party members could also be inscribed. As far as I am aware, no systematic figures for enrolments were ever published.

The Brezhnev leadership showed a particular interest in study at this level. In December 1966 and October 1967 three- and four-week courses, evidently of a 'refresher' kind, were introduced for responsible party and state officials below *oblast* level, and by the mid-1970s about 45,000 people were completing them annually. In August 1976 part of the system was refashioned into republican and *oblast* courses for 'Raising the Qualifications of Leading Party and Soviet Cadres', backed by a new Institute of the same name attached to the Higher Party School in Moscow (*SPR*, 1977, p. 354). Attendance at these courses was declared to be obligatory for all such personnel once in the five-year intervals between party congresses.

Finally, mention must be made of the 'soviet-party schools', which were established in the early 1920s to provide agricultural personnel (including collective farm chairmen) with middle-grade political training. The courses lasted two to three years, depending on the educational attainment of the participants. The network was, however, reduced in the 1950s as the educational levels rose; and by the mid-1970s sixteen establishments were still in existence, with just under 4,000 auditors (*BSE*, Vol. 24 (1), 1976, p. 38).

MASS PARTY-POLITICAL ENLIGHTENMENT

The CPSU has always required a 'correct' ideological stance on the part of its mass membership. Part-time training designed to promote this was arranged, after 1938, in a three-tiered system of study circles, from elementary to advanced, at workplaces, clubs or party centres. It was termed 'enlightenment' to distinguish it from the higher level of 'training' just considered. Overall control of it was vested in the Central Committee – the Department of Propaganda and Agitation before May 1966 and the Department of Propaganda afterwards – while day-to-day administration was invariably a major concern of local party offices. In August 1956 the system was turned into a network of political schools (*politshkoly*) for beginners, with circles and seminars for the more advanced.

The second major reorganisation, conducted in 1965, involved a return to a distinct three-part scheme which was still valid in the late 1970s. The *politshkola* was retained as the lower, or primary unit, its basic task being to provide participants with the 'necessary minimum' of political knowledge and prepare them, in the course of instruction, for the study of the history and theory of the Communist Party.[5] The whole course of 126 hours was designed to be taught in seminar fashion, with some written work, over a two- or three-year period. It concluded with simple tests of the participants' knowledge, and those who passed were considered to have acquired 'elementary political education'. The coverage of this type of school tended to fall as general educational levels rose, but by the mid-1970s it still ran at 2½ million (Table 6.3).

Table 6.3   *Party-Political Enlightenment Courses*
            (participants; millions)

Type of Course	1955	1965	1976
Higher	NA	3·7	10·3
Middle	NA	2·7	7·9
Lower	NA	4·7	2·5
TOTAL	6·2	11·1	20·7

NA – not available.
Source: SPR, 1978, p. 398.

The middle stage of the system was based, in the early 1950s, on a network of 'circles' for the study of the history of the CPSU, dialectical and historical materialism, political economy and other selected topics (*BSE*, Vol. 32, 1955, p. 167). The circles met between two and four times a month, during a teaching year of about eight months. In her study of them E. Mickiewicz came to the conclusion that despite their more advanced nature they did not offer particularly systematic teaching or retain a stable membership (pp. 85 ff.). The 1965 reorganisation mainly involved, at this level, the replacement of the circles by 'fundamentals of Marxism–Leninism' schools. These demanded, it seems, more serious application; in any case, by the late

1970s their range of studies had been extended to include scientific communism, economics and administration, and problems of party structure (*BSE*, Vol. 19, 1975, p. 241). The figures in Table 6.3 give an idea of attendance rates.

The highest level of mass party enlightenment comprises, in the official phrase, a 'differentiated system of evening universities of Marxism–Leninism, district and town schools of party activists, theoretical seminars and other collective and individual forms of training' (Petrovichev, p. 312). Study is promoted by lectures, theoretical seminars and the participants' own papers, since a great deal of emphasis is placed on independent work. Participation rates, as may be seen, rose from 3·7 million in 1965 to 10·3 million in 1976.

The main type of institution, and the one to which we shall restrict comment here, is the evening university of Marxism–Leninism. These 'universities' were first established in 1938; between 1956 and 1975 their numbers rose from 288 to 352, while the student body, if the term is appropriate, increased from 149,000 to 334,000, about two-thirds of whom were party members. In the mid-1950s the courses took three years to complete, but by the mid-1970s a two-year course, leading to a 'diploma', had been instituted for better-prepared students (*BSE*, Vol. 32, 1955, p. 167; Vol. 27, 1977, p. 21). Admission seems to be completely in the hands of local party committees, which act on the recommendation of primary party organisations. The students are said to be mainly party, soviet and cultural officials who already have higher education.

Universities of Marxism–Leninism have three faculties – general studies; administrative and economic studies (for party activists in full-time employment); and propaganda (for party propagandists). The programmes include (apart from Marxism–Leninism, party history and policy) the principles of production administration, party and state structure, literature and art, the principles of Soviet law, social psychology, Soviet foreign policy and international relations. Teaching materials are supposed, when possible, to be practical in orientation, and may be varied to fit current needs. Problems can arise as a result. 'Two extremes are very often encountered,' wrote a commentator recently. 'Some propagandists see the "link with life" as necessitating concentration on the participants' production problems. But these classes . . . are not a production conference or a workers' meeting. It would, however, also be a mistake to get lost in theorising' (Afanasieva *et al.*, p. 247).

The figures available for participation at the various levels of party enlightenment, though incomplete, show some breathtaking swings. When Khrushchev started to reorganise and invigorate the system in the mid-1950s there were about 6 million students. The total is said to have risen to a staggering 36 million by 1964 (though this may have included some 5 or 6 million persons engaged in non-party courses).

The 1965 reorganisation, however, caused enrolment to plummet to 11 or 12 million. The drop can be explained either by mass closures (a whole new set of teaching materials from which Khrushchev's image had been purged not being immediately available) or by a much more rigorous assessment of numbers. The data series then started reveals another expansion to nearly 21 million by 1976–7 (Petrovichev, p. 319).

The question of how far participation is voluntary is an elusive one. Party members are expected to be enthusiastic about all approved activities, and political education is certainly among them. But the response in any particular organisation depends in no small measure on the pressure which the secretary is able to exert. The following quotations from a party instruction manual show what can happen.

Sometimes party bureaux and committees desire, at any cost, to register all old-age pensioners [who are party members] into a political school or seminar, and oblige them to attend classes regularly, although it may be difficult for them to do so on account of their health . . .

One of the basic principles of organising Marxist–Leninist instruction is that of *voluntariness*. But this is sometimes incorrectly understood by party members. They say, 'I'll only study if I want to' . . . The party statute obliges every communist to concern himself with raising his ideological and theoretical level . . .

The party organisation must strictly observe the principle of voluntariness in the party member's choice of subject and type of study, so that these suit his general educational level, theoretical training and interests. This does not prevent the secretary of a party bureau from recommending the most suitable form of study to a comrade after a chat . . . Perhaps the party bureau will be obliged to insist on this recommendation in cases where, for example, certain communists who, to judge from their backgrounds, are fully capable of studying in a 'fundamentals of Marxism–Leninism' school, register for a primary political school so as to have less work. (Afanasieva *et al.*, pp. 243 ff.)

Finally, a word must be said about the people who have to shoulder these massive teaching operations. Traditionally, the work has fallen upon an army of professional propagandists, aided by ordinary party members who are specialists in a relevant field and have had some training in propaganda work. Since the task is unpaid for non-professionals it is not always very popular. By 1975 the number of people listed as 'propagandists' was 2·2 million, though several million more were pulled in for occasional lecturing and campaign work.[6]

OTHER PUBLIC COURSES AND LECTURES

The party system of political enlightenment is but the hub of a very large and ill-defined universe. The *Komsomol* and trades unions have their own

networks, and since 1956 great emphasis has been placed on a wide
variety of classes in economic studies (Table 6.4). There are, in
addition, two major organisations concerned only with public information and propaganda, the first being the 'People's Universities (of
Culture)' and the second the *Znanie* (or Knowledge)' Society. All of
these bodies, regardless of their subordination, may integrate and share
activities. It will be sufficient for purposes of illustration to consider the
last two.

Table 6.4   *Mass Indoctrination Systems*
(all figures in millions, unless otherwise stated)

Organisation, type of course/lecture	1950	1960	1970	1975
Party (auditors)	NA	12·9	15·3	19·6
Komsomol (auditors)	NA	4·5	6·2	6·5
Economics (auditors)*	NA	5·0	13·8	36·1
Trades union				
lectures	3·8	5·8	11·2	13·7
auditors	239·0	395·0	676·0	805·0
People's universities†				
institutions	—	(6,300)	(15,800)	(28,800)
auditors	—	1·5	3·2	6·9
Znanie Society				
lectures	0·9	9·9	18·2	23·0
auditors	89·0	631·0	951·0	1,190·0

NA – not available.
* Including those on party and *Komsomol* courses.
† Absolute figures, in brackets, to nearest 100, for 1961, 1969, 1973.
Sources: SPR, 1976, p. 469; 1978, p. 397; *NONK*, 1977, pp. 344, 393; *Sputnik
komsomolskogo aktivista*, 1961, p. 196.

The concept of a 'people's university' appealed greatly to the
Bolsheviks as a means by which workers and peasants could promote
their intellectual development. Such universities were in fact mentioned in the 1919 party programme, but never became numerically
important. The idea was resuscitated during Khrushchev's campaign to
expand 'popular' as opposed to 'state' institutions in the late 1950s; and
by 1960 there were said to be over 6,000 'people's universities of
culture', with 1½ million participants. Their task, according to a party
decree published some time before August 1960, was 'to raise the
communist consciousness of the broad masses of the population,
advance their ideological and aesthetic education, and propagate the
most recent achievements of science, technology and working experience' (*SPR*, 1961, p. 548). The universities were officially regarded as a
spontaneous growth, but there is little doubt that they were actively

promoted by local party offices. The *Znanie* Society was charged with setting up a curriculum council to serve them.

The methods of instruction included talks, excursions and meetings with leading personalities in the field of interest. Meetings were held, naturally, outside working hours, and backed by radio or television programmes. Admission was strictly unlimited; indeed, the efforts of teachers to introduce tests and examinations were on occasion condemned. Two early examples of such establishments were the University of Technical Progress for Railwaymen, organised by the All-Union Railway Research Institute in Moscow, with 300 students, and the People's University of Culture at the famous I. A. Likhachev Automobile Works, consisting of nine faculties, of which four worked in direct contact with the factory's workshops (*Kultura, nauka, iskusstvo SSSR, slovar-spravochnik*, p. 40).

The Brezhnev leadership continued to favour the movement, and a party decree of 8 October 1968 envisaged further considerable growth. Under the terms of this measure more universities were established at educational and research establishments; new sets of curricula were introduced; radio, television and cinematographic assistance was improved. The curriculum council was upgraded and given overall responsibility for the co-ordination of their work. The principle of voluntary teaching by outside specialists was retained, but hourly payment was introduced and moral rewards for such activities, including the issue of certificates of honour, were stepped up (*Voprosy ideologicheskoi raboty KPSS*, p. 215). By 1976 there were no less than 38,000 institutions with 10 million auditors.

Though they could clearly play no serious part in the nation's educational processes, the people's universities received due mention in the 1973 USSR Fundamental Law on Education. It may well be that they were of some benefit to the masses; but to describe them as universities was surely most misleading.

The *Znanie* Society was founded in 1947 as 'The Society for the Spread of Political and Scientific Knowledge': it was given its present less forbidding title in 1963. Despite its formal autonomy it has always functioned as a propaganda arm of the Central Committee, running a network of museums, planetaria, a publishing house and public lecture service. This last is probably its most important activity and one which has, over the years, achieved incredible proportions (Table 6.4). If the data (which exclude radio and television broadcasts) are to be believed, in 1975 every adult throughout the land attended, on average, seven meetings, while the number of people at each was about fifty.

The *Znanie* figures, particularly for attendance, are no doubt exaggerated, as the lectures, with few exceptions, have little popular appeal. (A public discourse on economic progress that I attended in the Moscow Gorki Park in 1978, for example, attracted no more than five people, two of them female park-keepers who had obviously come to rest their feet.) But it would be unfair to dismiss them out of hand. *Znanie* lectures are widely publicised and sometimes given by well-known figures. The number of talks, sermons and exhortations absorbed by the public in Western lands is by no means negligible. Furthermore, the *Znanie* figures may include some lectures given in the regular enlightenment systems, so that they are public and voluntary only in a specific sense.

The growth in the work of the people's universities and *Znanie* Society raises some interesting questions. Does increasing exposure to such cultural and political persuasion really affect people's views, and if so, how? Given the scarcity of reliable information on this matter, it is wellnigh impossible to say. I would, however, point out that a rising level of education may to some extent increase the public thirst for knowledge, while the censorship restrictions on unauthorised material undoubtedly heighten curiosity. The open lecture system is a typically Soviet way of filling a painful gap.

PROFESSIONAL MILITARY EDUCATION

In the late 1970s the Soviet Union was thought to have about 3½ million men under arms, of whom perhaps a third were professionals. The problem of military training is therefore one of considerable moment. As we have seen, the groundwork is laid in ordinary educational establishments, from the general school through the *VUZ*. It remains for us to consider the specialist training provided for those who wish to make a career in the armed forces. Unfortunately, although the Soviet authorities take great pride in their military and para-military training establishments and are anxious to make them known to all possible applicants, an obsessive concern with security inhibits the publication of information on enrolments or function.

Most, if not all, of the specialist military establishments are run by the Ministry of Defence, possibly with help from the Ministry of Higher and Secondary Special Education. There are four main types. The oldest and most senior are the academies, of which no less than eighteen were listed in a 1971 volume of the *Great Soviet Encyclopaedia*. In general the academies provide further training for experienced officers with secondary special or higher education, the average age of applicants being between 28 and 32. The second and evidently most numerous type of establishment is the higher military college or *uchilishche*: most of these were established in the 1950s and 1960s, were based on military *SSUZy*, and are in fact a close equivalent of the civil *VUZ*. In their 1972 handbook for applicants I. A. Kamkov and V. M. Konoplyanik referred, by way of example, to forty-three such colleges, categorised as follows (pp. 18–47):

General and tank commander *uchilishcha*   13
Artillery and engineering *uchilishcha*   5
Anti-aircraft *uchilishcha*   5
Naval *uchilishcha*   6
Aviation *uchilishcha*   7
Military-political *uchilishcha*   7

The third type is the military faculty attached to a civil *VUZ*, sometimes used for medical, financial and physical training. Curiously enough, the Moscow State Conservatory has special arrangements for training military orchestral conductors. Fourthly, there are the three-year military *SSUZy* of which Kamkov and Konoplyanik give only nine examples. These institutions, which seem to have been somewhat superseded as a result of the rising educational levels, train junior lieutenants and serve as feeders for the higher military establishments (*VVUZy*).

It is difficult to estimate the overall number of students (traditionally called *kursanty*), but obviously it must be large. Half a million or so serving officers must be kept up to date on new military technology, and retiring officers must be replaced. It is significant, in this context, that the above-mentioned handbook had a print run of no less than 80,000 copies, while of the 1,215 Lenin stipends shared out among Soviet students in 1977, the Ministry of Defence *VUZy* got 275. In addition, the 'closed' *VUZy* of the Committee of State Security and the Ministries of Foreign and Internal Affairs (see page 110) must also train some military and para-military personnel.

VVUZ courses normally last four years for serving officers and five years for new recruits or other ranks. The courses appear to be organised much as in civil institutions, but with a strong martial admixture. A distinction is made between *kursanty* who are training for 'command' and those who are training for 'technical' posts, but all are regarded as being on active service and subject to military discipline. The usual instruction burden is thirty to thirty-six hours a week, but vacations are short and 'production practice' is done in suitable military units. *Kursanty* seem to be under great pressure to get good results in their examinations; extra rights and honours are granted to those who achieve excellent marks. Graduates get a full state diploma indicating the military specialities mastered (Kamkov and Konoplyanik, p. 16).

Part-time study has an important place in the military sector, though it, too, has assumed a rather specific form. It is restricted, naturally enough, to service personnel, including civil *VUZ* graduates who find they cannot use their degree in a military context. Serving officers are occasionally registered for part-time study in civil *VUZy* if they cannot be satisfactorily placed in a military establishment. The upper age limit here is 35–40, depending on the course; the length of study is five, as opposed to four years full-time; and part-time *kursanty* are entitled to a reduction of duties so as to take examinations and attend classes. This form of study can offer advantages over full-time courses at certain points in a person's career.

The military equivalent of the *aspirantura* is called the *ad'yunktura*. This is a three- or four-year course (depending on whether it is done full- or part-time) for officers who wish to specialise in teaching or research. Admission is again by examination and competition, and the upper age limit is 40. The *ad'yunktura* involves passing a candidate's minimum, writing a dissertation and undergoing some teacher-training. Officers who have acquired a candidate's minimum by other means may be allowed to complete the remaining requirements in a year. The authorities take pride in the apparently large number of senior officers – Doctors and Candidates of Sciences – who are on the teaching staffs of military establishments.

A word needs to be added on the more elementary types of professional military training. There are two varieties of general school where children may seriously prepare themselves for such a career: the single Nakhimov *uchilishche* for naval, and eight Suvorov *uchilishcha* for military personnel. Founded in 1943–5 for the sons of servicemen killed in the war, these institutions accept children from ordinary eight-year schools on a competitive basis, and give them a complete general education with a military component. This places them, as we have seen, in a favourable position for admission to more advanced military establishments. Finally, it must be borne in mind that training troops is arguably *the* major function of any army in peacetime, and that Soviet rank and file servicemen receive a considerable amount of practical instruction while they are in their units (*BSE*, Vol. 5, 1971, pp. 223, 239; *SES*, pp. 877, 1,294).

THE NON-STATE SECTOR

The nationalisation of the school system after the Revolution entailed the take-over or closure of most independent educational institutions. A few centres for training clergy of various denominations were, however, allowed to continue, and individual private coaching was tolerated, perhaps because it was impossible to suppress. An onerous tax was imposed on would-be tutors. We shall now consider what has been happening in these areas more recently.

Although the Soviet Union is thought to have anything between 40 and 70 million religious believers, provision for their spiritual needs is meagre in the extreme.[7] All spiritual movements, with the exception of Judaism – the Orthodox, Catholic and Protestant churches, Islam and Buddhism – are administered by religious boards which are answerable to the State Council for Religious Affairs attached to the Council of Ministers. Each community has had its own history of repression.

Let us take the problem of religious instruction for the laity first. The church (meaning all religious foundations) was separated from the state and the school by the famous decree of 20 January 1918 (Old Style), and religious teaching was forbidden in the classroom. Thereafter citizens could only give or receive such instruction privately. The April 1929 Law on Religious Associations was even more restrictive: the clergy was now limited to practising at registered places of worship (private homes being now excluded); no religious meetings, circles, playgroups or libraries could be organised for children, young people or women; and the teaching of religious faith could take place only as part of officially approved theological courses (Matthews, 1973, pp. 33, 64, 65, articles 17, 18, 19). These provisions are now enshrined in a 1975 version of the law, and the strictness with which they have been implemented has varied. Even so, such religious instruction as is now given to children can legally come only from their family or friends.

The training of clergy has likewise been severely curtailed. For a period during the 1930s and 1940s all establishments involved in it were, in fact, closed; only after the wartime *rapprochement* between Stalin and the church was there some relaxation.

Most of the information to hand appertains to the Russian Orthodox Church. When Khrushchev came to power there were apparently eight Orthodox seminaries and two academies, but his anti-religious campaigns led to the closure of no less than five of the seminaries. During the Brezhnev period, according to one careful observer, pressures on theological training eased and the remaining institutions (the theological academies in Moscow and Leningrad, and the Moscow, Leningrad and Odessa seminaries) were allowed to operate peacefully and even expand.[8]

In the academic year 1973–4 the seminaries together contained 422 full-time resident students (of whom 90 per cent were to be ordained on completion of the four-year course) plus 600 correspondence students who were mostly ordinates already. The annual contingents of new priests must therefore have been in the region of 200 – a modest figure indeed for so large a national congregation. The eligible age for admission to the seminaries was 18–30, and applications were said to outnumber places by four to one. A few of the applicants came with complete or incomplete higher education. Instruction and upkeep were paid for by the church authorities. A major snag for seminarists who had not done their military service beforehand was call-up during their course of study; unlike ordinary *VUZ* students they did not qualify for deferment or exemption. However, they were held to have a high sense of calling, and few failed to return after the break.

Two further types of study are offered at academy level. In 1973–4 there were about 145 priests on a postgraduate course and another twenty-seven in an *aspirantura* leading to the degree of Candidate of Theology (which is not recognised by the state). Since these were both three-year courses and since twenty-eight of the participants were foreigners anyway, the number produced would have been less than fifty a year. These priests were mostly preparing themselves for a teaching career or employment in posts abroad.

The seminaries and academies had a total teaching and research staff of about 100, most of whom were ordained. They included prominent Orthodox scholars and some bishops. The courses offered were said to be thorough but very conservative, concentrating on such basics as the Bible, theology, liturgy, homiletics, church history and church Slavonic. Classical and some modern languages were also taught. The students were not, apparently, given any training in the Christian response to Marxism.

The Orthodox educational establishments, small though they may be, are by far the most important centres of Christian training in the USSR. In the late 1970s the Roman Catholics maintained two seminaries (one in Kaunas with 72 students, and another in Riga); the Lutherans had a small seminary in Estonia and a correspondence course in Latvia, while the Baptists had only a correspondence course with, reportedly, 200 students. A single Jewish *yeshiva*, which met in the Moscow synagogue, was reported in 1976 to have only six students. References are occasionally made to a few Buddhist monasteries in Mongolian areas, which may take novices.

Of all religious communities, however, the Muslims seem to have been treated most shabbily, if numbers are of any account. For many years the only training centre in existence for twenty-five or more million believers was the modest Mir Arab school in Bukhara. In 1970, 'owing to the growing demand for religious personnel', the Imam Al-Bokhari higher religious school was opened in Tashkent; in 1979 it was upgraded and renamed the Tashkent Islamic Institute. Its task was to instruct students in 'religious and secular studies, train and prepare highly qualified personnel for all the [Muslim] religious boards, cathedrals and mosques'. The curriculum included, on the traditional side, Muslim law, interpretation of the Koran, the hadith, theology, hadith terminology, the history of Islam, and a good deal of literary Arabic; the secular component was mostly Oriental philosophy, political economy, Russian, English, Persian, the history and geography of Arab countries, poetry, the USSR constitution and the history of international relations (*Muslims of the Soviet East*, no. 4, 1979, p. 14). In the 1970s the Soviet authorities showed an increased awareness of the propaganda value of their Islamic establishments but have not, as far as I am aware, revealed the number of students taught. Given the extreme sensitivity of the Muslim world to the suppression of the Faith, this is in no way surprising.

Private tuition is seldom discussed in official or, for that matter, scholarly sources, and most of what we know about it comes from people who were personally involved. Private teachers find their pupils by advertising in the personal columns of local newspapers (the *Evening Moscow* weekly advertising supplement may carry thirty or forty such offers), through urban information agencies (Nosenko and Shilov, p. 232) or, more usually, with the help of friends and acquaintances.

Soviet tax legislation is still just about the only reliable index we have of the official attitudes towards private tuition. According to information available, the rate payable on income from private teaching in the mid-1970s ranged from 2·5 per cent of the first rouble to a maximum of 69 per cent on earnings of 583 roubles a month or more. This compared with a maximum of 13 per cent for sums over 100 roubles earned through state employment. The present tax legislation dates from 1943, and the fact that so high a rate has been retained surely betokens unyielding official hostility. Private tuition has certainly, on occasions, been attacked in the press. The taxation tends to deter private teachers from declaring their earnings and to turn their work into an illegal activity. In the late 1970s the going fee was about 5 roubles an hour for pre-university teaching and 10 for more advanced work, as compared with the state average wage of about 3 roubles an hour.

The relatively high cost of tuition means that it is mainly used by the more opulent families, particularly those anxious to get their children into a good *VUZ*. The only scholarly analysis of the practice that I have seen was made at Gorki University in the late 1960s (Matthews, *Soviet Studies*, no. 1, January 1975, p. 88). This showed that about 20 per cent of the first-year students had received private tuition, the great majority of them coming from better-educated families of the white-collar group. The private sector may thus have been quite considerable in absolute terms, though, again, the *VUZ* preparatory courses established in 1967 may have adversely affected it.

Most of the advertisements in the *Evening Moscow* weekly advertising supplement were for mathematics and physics, with languages (English, French, German and Spanish) coming next, which suggests preparation for prestige *VUZy* and language schools. Music lessons and typing have also, to judge from the same source, been popular subjects for tuition, and indeed lend themselves to it. As noted above, music classes organised after hours at state schools have always had to be paid for; 36 roubles a year was the sum mentioned to me as the cost of a child's tuition in Moscow in 1978.

Despite a large bureaucracy, training for office work was neglected in the USSR, even after the death of Stalin. Shorthand and typing were not, it seems, widely taught anywhere, and most typists were trained on the job. A public part-time typing course was available in the 1970s in Moscow, though I have no details on its size (*Moskva – kratkaya adressno-spravochnaya kniga*, 1971, p. 212; 1977, p. 237). In any case there was scope for private teachers to co-operate unofficially in training typists for local offices. Recently there seems to have been more official interest in the provision of secretarial skills, exemplified by the introduction of typing as a practical option in the general school curriculum.

The expansion of state facilities in various areas may thus have reduced the need for private tuition, but there is no doubt that the services of competent individuals will continue to satisfy an important social need.

NOTES

1 For details see Manevich *et al.*, pp. 286, 289; Dvornikov *et al.*, p. 87; Klochkov, p. 83.
2 Manevich *et al.*, p. 284; see also *SPR*, 1976, p. 313; Sonin, 1954, p. 78; Bulgakov, p. 263.
3 *Entsiklopedicheski slovar pravovykh znanii*, 1965, p. 440; Tkachevski, pp. 87 ff.
4 E. Mickiewicz gives a figure of 2,920 graduations for 1946–66 (*Handbook of Soviet Social Science Data*, p. 168). Any attempt to collect and systematise figures on party and other ideological courses soon turns into a nightmare, owing to gaps and glaring inconsistencies. I hope I have avoided major error in this table, but several entries are, unavoidably, no more than approximations based on long-term averages.
5 The 1973 programme, for instance, included:
    (1) the biography of Lenin (30 hours),
    (2) fundamental political knowledge – that is, Soviet Marxist theory (32 hours),
    (3) fundamental economic knowledge – that is, production organisation – for workers, or
    (4) fundamental economic knowledge for collective farmers and state farm workers (both 64 hours).
    Programma nachalnoi politicheskoi shkoly, 1973. See also Mickiewicz, 1967, p. 64; *Spravochnik propagandista*, 1968, p. 120.
6 The sources from which these points have been taken are Simon, p. 336; Mickiewicz, 1967, p. 43; 1973, p. 11; Petrovichev, p. 316; *SPR*, 1977, p. 465.
7 A suggested breakdown, in millions, probably erring on the side of caution, would be: Orthodox – 30, Catholic – 4, Muslim – 25, others (mainly Protestants, Orthodox Jews and Buddhists) – 3.
8 Most of the points in this and the following three paragraphs were taken from Raymond Oppenheim's informative article, 'Russian Orthodox theological education in the Soviet Union', in *Religion in Communist Lands*, vol. 2, no. 3, 1974.

Conclusion
Soviet Education:
Successes and Failures

The Soviet system of education underwent many modifications between the death of Stalin and the beginning of 1979, which is the period
covered by this study. In these concluding pages it remains for us to
summarise the most salient of them, and suggest possible development
in the future.

Education has for a long time been one of the most positive facets of
Soviet reality, and one which has grown strongly. By the mid-1970s
general schooling, in one form or another, had become the norm for the
great majority of children aged 17–18. Since a plateau has been
reached, the next changes in this sector may well involve a lowering of
the age at which the general school starts, an improvement in the
network of facilities, further modification of school programmes to suit
current needs, and a closer relationship with the vocational sector. Any
extension of full-time general schooling to higher age-groups seems
pointless, and anyway proved impracticable under Khrushchev.

Vocational training, in both low- and middle-grade establishments,
has continued to expand steadily, accompanied by a slow reduction in
training on the job. But it is doubtful whether the latter will ever cease
to be important, despite its manifest drawbacks. A growing conver-
gence can be detected between the *PTU* and the *SSUZy*, and perhaps a
marriage of the two types will eventually take place; but the diversity of
skills involved at present militates against it. Developments in this
sector depend more directly on macro-economic forces, particularly the
capitalisation of industry and the need for unskilled labour, which has
remained very great by advanced Western standards.

Higher education continued to expand at an annual rate which was
both steady and, it appears, suited to the needs of the economy. In
terms of full-time opportunity, the growth under Brezhnev has just
about kept pace with that of age contingents: so here too a plateau
situation obtains. It seems that at present the equivalent of an eighth of
the relevant age-group can find full-time places. This proportion may
improve during the 1980s, as the numbers of children of the 'war dent'
parents fall away. The arrestation of the growth of research degrees
means an absolute cut-back in opportunity at this level, but this must
surely be temporary.

It is arguable that just as education is among the regime's principal successes in the social sphere, so the growth of opportunity is the most impressive aspect of education. When we turn to other aspects, the changes have been less impressive, or even retrograde.

The growth of the various networks was eventually accompanied by a marked strengthening of their administrative base. This need not in itself be a bad thing, but the long-term trend has been towards increasing the intrusive power of state bodies and strengthening party control, at the expense of institutional autonomy. Views may differ on the desirable balance of interests, but I would suggest that in the Soviet context more centralisation is generally bad.

This movement has been accompanied by two others. First there has been a massive wave of legal codification, covering activities inside and around all types of educational establishment. It almost seems as though the authorities wished to circumscribe every possible gesture in the education drama. Secondly, one can perceive a drive to imbue the work of the whole system with a kind of democratism which, in the light of the existing centralisation, could not be very meaningful. A glance back at happenings in Soviet education in the 1920s, let alone the practice of pluralistic systems, will throw into relief the extremely low degree of teacher or pupil influence on the running of Soviet institutions of learning. At the same time the emphasis on discipline, fixed curricula and formal examinations has remained fairly central. Paternalism of the Soviet variety, however, is not without its advantages: state control and standardisation may, in difficult circumstances, serve to protect standards of work or conduct. It also maintains the principles of free education and financial support.

As for teaching materials, there has been a great deal of modernisation. The technological advances made in the economy have inevitably required changes in the vocational and professional content of courses. In this, however, the USSR is only following a path familiar to all industrialised nations. The Soviet system of education has not, I believe, generated any striking innovations which are not in great measure attributable to the importation of 'capitalist' equipment or techniques. The genius of the Soviet peoples could have expressed itself just as well through many other kinds of system. Suggestions that socialist education, of the Soviet variety, has much that is worthy of quick imitation by outsiders should, in view of what has happened, be treated with great circumspection.

When we turn to the humanities we find that the demands of Marxist–Leninist ideology have kept their absolute pre-eminence. The moderate relaxation of official dogma in the decade after Stalin's death was followed by policies of increasing rigidity. The materials available to pupil and student have remained, therefore, exceptionally narrow and sectarian. Hardly a trace of non-Marxist thought, or shift from the long-standing anti-Western orientations, are to be discerned.

The linked questions of 'streaming' by ability and affording pupils some choice in curricular matters continued to be viewed with suspicion at all levels. Although some progress was for a time made in lessening the rigidity of the curricular framework, it did not go very far. The curriculum was always regarded as something wholly within the competence of the education ministries and, by definition, of the central party apparatus. Few Western observers would deny that the increased importance given to military training in the majority of educational establishments has, from a liberal point of view, been thoroughly unhealthy.

The placement of trainees, not forgetting general school leavers, is still thought of as an extended function of the educational system. Here we observe both the sturdy maintenance of practices tried in the 1930s or earlier and the introduction of new ones designed to supplement individual choice by administrative order. Such evidence as is available (for the Soviet authorities are extremely secretive about matters of employment) suggests that intervention of this kind is not always effective. It requires complex machinery and a battery of regulations; and the offices involved are often incapable of reconciling the disparate interests of employers and work-seekers. The most successful operation, I suspect, is the placement of *PTU* trainees, but this is explained by the existence of voluntary choice at the point of entry. Perhaps placement procedures can be improved by computerisation or other means, but given the practical difficulties so far encountered it seems unlikely.

An educational system, according to current views, is supposed to do more than pass on an appropriate body of knowledge or provide a national economy with suitably trained labour. It is also called upon to inculcate an acceptable set of moral and ethical values. Soviet educationalists in fact set great store by this, and claim that their efforts are directed towards producing a new, communist man. How successful have they been in this respect?

Not very, I would argue, cynical though this may sound. To begin with, the Soviet educational system has failed to secure uniformly satisfactory attitudes towards 'socialism'. True, many Soviet citizens think positively about this particular condition, but they do so, I think, not so much from practical conviction as from ignorance of the nature of modern capitalism, which is a subject of denigration in the media. The idea of equality, which lies at the heart of the socialist creed, is still far from being popularly accepted. This can be illustrated by the sociological investigations of young people's attitudes to the 'prestige' of different trades and professions. Despite decades of socialist education (and periods of egalitarianism in the wage system) jobs are still highly differentiated in the popular mind. The ordering of them, moreover, is remarkably similar to that encountered in capitalist lands. The response of students – the most knowledgeable and mature recipients – towards the socialist educational system is by no means always positive.

Conversely, there is the matter of 'capitalist' attitudes among the public at large. It would be utterly naïve to think that the Soviet school has excised all the shadows of the past. As a result of the material shortages and queues which plague their lives, most Soviet citizens are intensely market-oriented. They have a good grasp of unofficial (black market) prices, not to mention the real value of the goods they possess and services they can offer others. If they come to live in the West they have no difficulty whatever in adapting to this degrading aspect of reality. Such reservations as they may have about private enterprise need not blind them to the advantages it provides.

Of no less significance is the evidence of social malaise in the USSR. Few official data of any real worth are published on delinquency, but there is every indication that it remains an exceedingly serious problem. Alcoholism is an area in which some external investigation is now becoming possible, and there is no doubt about the gravity of the situation. The educational system cannot be blamed, in any simplistic fashion, for widespread public attitudes or for social behaviour, as the family and social circumstance are no less relevant. But the continuing existence of these problems confirms that communist man is not ubiquitous within the Soviet boundaries.

One may be sceptical about the moral transformation of the masses, yet agree that education has had a very positive impact on Soviet social structure. Educational levels have risen vastly over the years, and this must have contributed to social homogeneity here as elsewhere. Possession of a degree or some other vocational qualification will in time become the rule rather than the exception in the Soviet Union. It is tempting to interpret this as wholly admirable, but I think that caution is again essential. Higher levels of educational attainment in capitalist lands have lessened, but by no means removed, class distinctions; socialist varieties of élitism may be protected regardless of educational advance; and the Soviet educational system, particularly in its general and higher sectors, has shown a tendency to adapt to the existing socio-political hierarchy rather than change it.

The authorities make a great deal, for propaganda purposes, of the widespread thirst for learning, and list it among the benefits of a socialist order. I am not at all sure that this thirst is stronger in the USSR than elsewhere; but if it is, the most plausible explanations are not especially laudable.

Since very little private economic activity is recognised outside the despised collective farm, all employed persons have to be state employees; and responsible positions in all state organisations have, by regulation, to be filled by degree-holders. There are no respected and autonomous professions which offer their own qualification. Ambitious youngsters cannot start their own business or freely emigrate to countries where degrees are less important. A period of rigorous and virtually unpaid service in the armed forces is compulsory for all men who have not undergone military training as part of a *VUZ* course, a fact which may sharpen the educational aspirations of many. Finally, poverty is still readily recognised as such in the Soviet Union, and professional training is one of the surest ways of avoiding it. In these circumstances a widespread desire for schooling is in no way surprising.

What possibility is there of mass education generating a fundamental *political* change in the Soviet Union and bringing it closer to the kind of pluralistic society so dear to liberal ideologies? Many observers have toyed with this idea. In the mid-1950s, for example, when Russia's educational expansion was much discussed and destalinisation was in the air, I heard a prominent Marxist historian forecast the transformation of the Soviet system as a direct result of more – much more – schooling. The younger generation would, he held, become more demanding intellectually, and fracture the sterile Stalinist ideas which stultified Soviet reality. It is, alas, not easy to imagine anything of the sort happening at present. The Soviet educational system has been matured and moulded to support the regime in every way possible. The political docility of the overwhelming majority of its participants is hardly open to question. Censorship excludes non-Marxist or anti-Soviet ideas; schools propound only Marxism and a cult of permanent optimism about Soviet achievement.

The Soviet educational system is designed to be all-embracing and complete in itself. It offers no real possibility for study outside the Soviet bloc: one would not regard the few hundred exchange visits with the West as significant in this respect. It bans critical appraisal of government policies in the classroom: the mere idea that any teacher or pupil could criticise the Soviet constitution, extol important aspects of life in capitalist societies or propose an educational tour to see them, is unthinkable. Moreover, it seems to have become progressively more remote under Brezhnev. The contribution of the educational system to *political* change has been so subtle as to be almost untraceable. This system has trained officials to be technically more skilled, without making them more sceptical of official dogma; it has given pride of place to professional competence rather than to the search for social truths. One can find little encouragement in the fact that although, by the late 1970s, some 11 million *VUZ* graduates were employed in the economy, no more than a few score were prepared to stand up and press for political change in public. The contrast with some of the satellite countries of East Europe is stark indeed.

Finally, there is the question of whether the Soviet educational system is likely to undergo any change of nature or direction in the foreseeable future. This is like asking whether it will rain in Scotland. The answer is: certainly. So large and complex an organisation is bound to undergo continuous modification and development. It is more pertinent to ask: will there be any really *fundamental* change? Here one can direct the reader's attention to the Scottish climate, which has maintained a damp and dismal permanence for longer than anyone cares to remember.

A look back over past decades is not encouraging. Stalin never deserted the basic centralistic principles of state education which Lenin had expounded. Rather, he squeezed them into a narrow disciplinarian mould. Khrushchev, for all his experimentation, remained true to them, and so did Brezhnev. If conservatism is a hallmark of Soviet power, one can see no reason for it to be abandoned in the sphere of education. Having said this, however, one must add an important rider. Centralised control means that the leadership can, within limits and over a certain time, do as it likes. Brezhnev, or his successor, may decide on another shake-up. But if that happens, it will surely, like Khrushchev's, be within the framework of what is concordant with Soviet political traditions.

Some observers may object that such a forecast is too rigid and that 'pressure groups' in or outside the educational sector may promote changes of their own. The teacher may change in the classroom. I would be the last to deny that such groups exist or that they have, on occasion, influenced the course of events. But it is easy to overrate their size and effectiveness, or to misinterpret contradictions in official policies (due to hesitation in the top leadership) as a consequence of their intervention. Clearly, there must be some interplay inside the system, and between different layers of it. The leaders in the Politbureau and Central Committee are neither deaf nor blind to what transpires beneath them, and they have their own disagreements. Nevertheless I believe that Soviet educational policy will, in all probability, continue to be one mostly of dictation from on high.

Happily, the creativity of the Soviet peoples is beyond doubt and allows us at least to hope for better things in the future. Perhaps the Soviet educational system is indeed generating some hidden potential for change, both of itself and of the political organs which control it. If it can eventually help to improve them, and produce a more open society, with a stronger humanitarian colouring, then the efforts of those who have worked and studied in it will be in every sense justified.

Appendix A *Total Enrolments in Soviet Educational Institutions (selected years; millions, unless otherwise indicated)*

	1950	1955	1960	1965	1970	1975	1978
Kindergartens and nursery/kinder-gartens	1·2	1·7	3·1	6·2	8·1	10·5	12·2
General school:							
full-time	33·3	28·2	33·4	43·4	45·4	42·6	39·9
part-time	1·4	1·9	2·8	4·8	3·7	5·0	4·8
Vocational schools (*PTU*)	0·5	0·8	0·9	1·5	2·4	3·1	3·4
Secondary special educational institutions (*SSUZy*):							
full-time	1·1	1·5	1·1	1·8	2·6	2·8	2·9
part-time	0·2	0·5	1·0	1·8	1·8	1·7	1·8
Higher educational institutions:							
full-time	0·8	1·1	1·2	1·6	2·2	2·6	2·9
part-time	0·4	0·7	1·2	2·3	2·3	2·2	2·2
postgraduate research (thousands)	(12)	(17)	(20)	(53)	(57)	(56)	(NA)

Sources: NONK, 1977, pp. 26, 113, 119, 145, 154, 214, 310; Bulgakov, pp. 72, 94; *Trud v SSSR*, p. 303; *Nar. khoz.*, 1978, pp. 378, 417, 468, 472.

Appendix B *The State Education System*

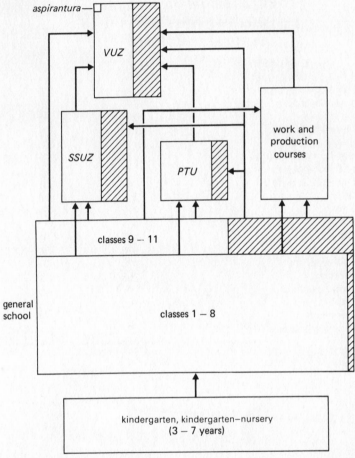

The areas of the various sectors approximate to enrolments in 1978. Shaded areas on the right show part-time study. Arrows indicate the principal, but not all possible, directions of flow.

Appendix C Comparative Educational Costs, circa 1972 (per pupil; roubles)

Type of institution	General direct costs	General cost to the state economy
General schools (all classes)	134	184
Lengthened day schools	186	255
Schools with boarding facility	270	370
Boarding schools	768	1,052
Special boarding schools	1,019	1,396
School–orphanages	1,171	1,604
Schools of Working Youth	112	225
Schools of Rural Youth	80	161
Correspondence schools	65	151
PTU: urban	609	840
rural	872	929
special	459	633
Technical uchilishcha	508	701
FZO schools	620	850
VUZy: full-time	920	1,071
evening	268	471
correspondence	107	345
SSUZy: full-time	502	575
evening	137	259
correspondence	55	245

Source: Korchagin, p. 96.

Glossary of Soviet Administrative and Other Terms

Terms explained in the body of the text are listed in the Index.

administration

Common translation of the Russian term *upravelenie*. Apart from describing the function, this term may mean (1) a major section in a ministry or (2) a kind of junior ministry, less important than a 'state committee' but with some organisational identity. In senses (1) and (2) it may be prefixed by the word 'main', depending on its status. Sometimes translated 'directorate'.

all-union

Referring to central bodies located in Moscow whose authority extends directly to all areas of the Soviet Union.

autonomous republic

See 'republic'.

Brezhnev, L. (1906–)

Member of the Politbureau (Presidium) of the CPSU, 1957– ; First Secretary of the CPSU, 14 October 1964 – 8 April 1966; thereafter General Secretary.

bronya

A Russian term indicating a 'reservation' or 'quota', much used for deficit goods or services.

censorship

Known officially as *Glavlit*, the Main Administration for the Preservation of Military and State Secrets in the Press; the Soviet system goes far beyond most Western security practice.

Central Committee (of the CPSU)

Formally the supreme elective body of the CPSU between Congresses. Backed by a permanent apparatus of departments which have supervisory powers over virtually all state activities.

circular letter

A common type of instruction sent to a limited number of officials and employees.

Civil War

Post-revolutionary struggle, mainly between 'Red' and 'White' forces, with some foreign intervention, 1918–21. Affected large areas of the country.

collective

A group of people linked by daily work or other shared social activity.

collective farm

Also known by the Russian acronym *kolkhoz*. An association of agricultural producers working on a co-operative rather than a nationalised basis, but in fact under strong state control.

collegium

Group of senior officials in a ministry or other body, directly subordinate to the head.

Committee of State Security (KGB)
An organisation of ministerial stature with secret police, espionage and defence functions.

communist
A member of the CPSU; also a believer in Marxist–Leninist ideology.

Congress (CPSU)
Demonstrative meeting of leading and active members of the CPSU, held once every five years. Its resolutions are landmarks for purposes of state administration.

Council of Ministers
Principal executive body at the USSR and republican levels. Its authority exceeds that of individual ministries as a signatory of decrees.

CPSU
Communist Party of the Soviet Union, the sole political party in the USSR; mass membership in 1977, 16·2 million. See also 'Central Committee', '*VKP(b)*'.

dialectical and historical materialism
The dual philosophical basis of the teachings of Marx, Engels and Lenin, as interpreted by subsequent Soviet leaders.

Directorate
See 'administration'.

Economic Council
See '*Sovnarkhoz*'.

edinonachalie
The principle of state control through one man, usually a director, as distinct from management from below by common decision.

employee
A translation of the Russian term *sluzhashchi*, or non-manual worker; includes all predominantly white-collar personnel, from highly skilled specialists to unskilled service staff.

Executive committee
A formally elective body in a local soviet, served by its own permanent apparatus.

Gosplan
The State Planning Committee of the USSR Council of Ministers, responsible for all forward and current economic planning, including that of the educational system.

GTO
The Russian initials for 'ready for labour and defence (of the USSR)'. An all-union physical training and sports organisation with civil defence functions.

KGB
See 'Committee of State Security'.

Khrushchev, N. S. (1894–1971)
Member of the Politbureau (Presidium), 1938–14 October 1964, when he was dismissed. First Secretary of the CPSU from September 1953; Chairman of the USSR Council of Ministers, March 1958–October 1964.

Komsomol
A Russian acronym for the All-Union Leninist Communist League of Youth; operates as a youth arm of the CPSU. In 1977 the mass membership was 35 million (14- to 28-year-olds).

kontrol
A Soviet term which appears to mean primarily 'supervision', but may also imply administrative control and verification.

krai
A large, sparsely populated administrative unit. In 1978 there were six, all in Asiatic Russia. Sometimes translated 'territory'. Administratively equivalent to *oblast*.

mechanisors
Agricultural personnel trained to drive and maintain lorries, agricultural machinery and similar vehicles.

ministry
Executive body operating at all-union, union–republican or republican levels. Hence the existence of different 'ministries' of higher and secondary special education ('*MinVUZ*'), and of enlightenment. Some Soviet ministries resemble those in pluralistic societies, but Soviet production ministries are more like boards of nationalised industries in the UK.

Nakhimov, P. S. (1802–55)
Famous Russian admiral.

NEP
The New Economic Policy which was inaugurated in the spring of 1921 and involved a partial retreat from the extremes of War Communism. Abandoned with the introduction of the five-year plans, c. 1928.

Nomenklatura (Nomenclature)
A listing of the most responsible state posts, together with a register of candidates for them. The Soviet nomenclature is country-wide and under the ultimate control of the CPSU apparatus.

oblast
The most common administrative unit immediately below union–republican level. There were 121 in the USSR in 1978, in eight of the union republics. The *oblasts* themselves contain *raiony* (districts), towns, settlements and villages.

Old Style (of dates)
Refers to the Julian Calendar, which lagged thirteen days behind the West European (Gregorian) Calendar in the twentieth century. The old reckoning was abolished in the RSFSR on 14 February (1 February, OS) 1918.

Orgnabor (Organised Recruitment)
A nation-wide network of offices for recruiting labour, primarily manual, for work in distant or difficult areas.

Party
See CPSU.

peasant
Member of a collective farm; usually unskilled, involved in field work or animal husbandry, and having a distinct status in Soviet law.

People's Commissariat
The Bolshevik equivalent of a ministry. The term was discarded in 1946.
Polozhenie
General set of rules or statutes.
profession
Translation of the Russian term *professia*; covers any type of skill, from simple manual to advanced specialist.
PTU **(professionalno-tekhnicheskoe uchilishche)**
Vocational or technical school.

regional economic council
See *Sovnarkhoz*.
republic
One of the fifteen 'union' republics which together comprise the Union of Soviet Socialist Republics; one of the twenty minor 'autonomous' republics established to preserve a vestige of administrative autonomy for certain national minorities.
rouble
Russian and Soviet unit of currency. Difficult to evaluate in terms of pounds or dollars. Rates I have quoted elsewhere for 1971 were (against the pound sterling) – official Soviet rate: 2 roubles 16 kopeks to the pound; Soviet free market (illegal): 12–15 roubles to the pound; London free market (illegal): 8–10 roubles to the pound. The rouble was revalued at 1 new for 10 old in January 1961.
RSFSR
Russian Soviet Federative Socialist Republic, the largest of the union republics in the Soviet Union.

soviet
The Russian word for 'council'. Formally elective bodies found at all levels of the system of state administration, from the Supreme Soviet of the USSR down to the village.
Soviet Sociological Association
An all-union state-run organisation for individual sociologists and research groups, founded in 1958.
Sovnarkhoz
Regional administrative councils with primarily economic functions, established in 1957 to replace and decentralise major production ministries. Originally they had approximately the same territorial coverage as an *oblast*, but were gradually enlarged and 'centralised' themselves. Abolished when the ministries were restored in 1965.
SSUZ (srednee spetsialnoe uchebnoe zavedenie) **(pl. – *SSUZy*)**
Middle (or secondary) special educational institution. My own acronym, not to be found in Soviet sources.
Stalin (Dzhugashvili), I. V. (1879 – March 1953)
Member of the Politbureau (Presidium) of the Party, 1919–53; General Secretary, 1922–53. From 5 March, the official date of Stalin's death, until the 14th, G. M. Malenkov led the CPSU. His release from this post was followed by six months of 'collective leadership'. Then Khrushchev assumed the role of First Secretary.

state committee
An executive body, generally of lesser status than a ministry at the same level, but superior to an administration.

Supreme Soviet
See *'soviet'*.

Suvorov, A. V. (1730–1800)
Famous Russian count and general; also military strategist.

tekhnikum
A secondary special educational institution offering primarily training in technical subjects.

Trotskyism
The 'left' communist doctrines associated with the early Soviet leader.

***uchilishche* (pl. – *uchilishcha*)**
Usually (1) a low-grade vocational or (2) middle-grade school or junior college. There is no adequate equivalent in English.

union republic
See 'republic'.

ustav
Set of regulations, usually covering one institution or establishment.

VKP(b)
All-Russian Communist Party, Bolsheviks' title of the CPSU from 1925 to 1952.

***VUZ (vysshee uchebnoe zavedenie)* (pl. – *VUZy*)**
Any higher educational institution recognised as such by the state.

War Communism
A set of extreme left-wing policies, backed by the use of 'red terror' against opponents of the regime, particularly in the months following the revolution.

Young Pioneers
All-union socio-political organisation for children in pre-*Komsomol* age-groups. The membership stood at 25 million in 1977.

Bibliography

As mentioned in the Preface, this bibliography contains works and periodicals mentioned in the text, together with a few others I have consulted for background reading or purposes of verification. I have mentioned that I attach some importance to accounts of personal experience as a supplement to the legal and statistical material on which most of my analysis is based. Reports of such experience lasting from two to nearly forty years were obtained from twenty-four former Soviet citizens who worked in full-time institutions. Their workplaces were as follows: general schools (urban) – 6, special schools – 6, village schools – 2, *PTU* – 2, *tekhnikumy* – 1, *VUZy* – 4. In addition I interviewed three people with considerable experience of part-time teaching and discussed specific points with other teachers, parents and students. The aims of this, more specifically, were to find out how certain rules and regulations were applied in practice, to elucidate popular responses and attitudes not otherwise discernible, and to clear up important points which were not covered at all in the published sources.

Abakumov, A. A., *et al.* (eds), *Narodnoe obrazovanie v SSSR, obshcheobrazovatelnaya shkola; Sbornik dokumentov 1917–1973* (Moscow: 1974).

Afanasieva, A. I., *et al.*, *Spravochnik sekretarya pervichnoi partiinoi organizatsii* (Moscow: 1977).

Aleksandrov, N. G., *Trudovye pravootnoshenia* (Moscow: 1948).

Aleksandrov, N. G., *et al.* (eds), *Zakonodatelstvo o trude, Kommentarii* (Moscow: 1954) (Izdanie numerovannoe).

Altschuler, M. N. (ed.), *Posobie po nachisleniu i vzimaniu platy za soderzhanie detei v detskikh doshkolniykh uchrezhdeniakh* (Minsk: 1972).

Astrakhan, E., *et al.*, *Rol sovetskogo trudovogo prava v planovom obespechenii narodnogo khozyaistva kadrami* (Moscow: 1955).

Balabanov, S. S., *Sotsiologicheskoe issledovanie dvizhenia studencheskikh kontingentov v protsesse obuchenia avtoreferat* (Moscow: 1978).

Balov, N. N. (ed.), *Vechernyaya shkola. Spravochnik po voprosam ochnogo i zaochnogo obuchenia* (Moscow: 1973).

Batyshev, S. Ya., *Formirovanie kvalifitsirovannykh rabochikh kadrov v SSSR* (Moscow: 1974).

Batyshev, S. Ya., and Shaporinski, S. A., *Osnovy professionalnoi pedagogiki* (Moscow: 1977).

Belyaeva, N. A., 'Otnoshenie uchitelya k svoei professii', in Turchenko, V. N., *et al.*, pp. 372, 375.

Berezin, B. J., *Samouchitel mashinopisi*, 2nd edn. (Moscow: 1965).

Blinchevski, F. L., and Zelenko, G. I., *Professionalno-tekhnicheskoe obrazovanie rabochikh v SSSR* (Moscow: 1957).

BMV See *Byulleten ministerstva vysshego i srednego spetsialnogo obrazovania.*

Boldyrev, N. I. (ed.), *Direktivy VKP(b) i postanovlenia sovetskogo pravitelstva o narodnom obrazovanii, sbornik dokumentov za 1917–1947* (Moscow–Leningrad: 1947).

Boldyrev, N. I. (ed.), *Sbornik rukovodyashchikh materialov o shkole* (Moscow: 1952), kniga III.

Bolshaya sovetskaya entsiklopedia, 2nd edn., 50 vols (Moscow: 1949–57); 3rd edn., 30 vols (Moscow: 1969–78).

Bolshov, M. M., and Podoprigov, A. I., *Sbornik zakonodatelnykh aktov po okhrane truda v kolkhozakh* (Moscow: 1971).

Bowen, J., *Soviet Education: Anton Makarenko and the Years of Experiment* (Madison, Wisconsin: University of Wisconsin Press, 1962).

BSE See *Bolshaya sovetskaya entsiklopedia.*

Bulgakov, A. A., *Professionalno-tekhnicheskoe obrazovanie v SSSR na sovremennom etape* (Moscow: 1977).

Butenko, A. M., *Voprosy vosproizvodstva rabochei sily mekhanizatorskikh kadrov massovykh kvalifikatsii MTS v 1953–1957 gg. na primere voronezhskoi oblasti*, *avtoreferat* (Voronezh: 1958).

Byulleten ministerstva vysshego i srednego spetsialnogo obrazovania (Moscow: 1933–), monthly.

Chekharin, I. M., *Postoyannye komissii mestnykh sovetov* (Moscow: 1975).

Chernenko, K. Yu., and Smirtyukov, M. S. (eds), *Zabota partii i pravitelstva o blage naroda, sbornik dokumentov (1964–1973)* (Moscow: 1974).

Chkhikvadze, V. M., *et al.* (eds), *Entsiklopedicheski slovar pravovykh znanii* (Moscow: 1965).

Chutkerashkili, E. V., *Razvitie vysshego obrazovania v SSSR* (Moscow: 1961).

Counts, G. S., *The Challenge of Soviet Education* (New York: McGraw-Hill, 1957).

Dainovski, A. B., *Ekonomika vysshego obrazovania* (Moscow: 1976).

Danev, A. M. (ed.), *Narodnoe obrazovanie, osnovnye postanovlenia, prikazy i instruktsii* (Moscow: 1948).

Davidyuk, G. P., *et al.*, *Student i ego deyatelnost* (Minsk: 1978).

Deineko, M. M. (ed.), *O kommunisticheskom vospitanii i ukreplenii svyazi s zhiznyu, sbornik dokumentov* (Moscow: 1964).

De Witt, N., *Education and Professional Employment in the USSR* (Washington: US Govt., 1961).

Direktivy KPSS i sovetskogo pravitelstva po khozyaistvennym voprosam, 1917–1957 See Malin, V. N., and Korobov, A. B.

Direktivy VKP(b) See Boldyrev, N. I., 1947.

Dobson, R. B., 'Mobility and stratification in the Soviet Union', in *Annual Review of Sociology*, 3 (1977), pp. 297–329.

Dobson, R. B., 'Social status and inequality of access to higher education in the USSR', in Karabel, J., and Halsey, A. H. (eds), *Power and Ideology in Education* (OUP: 1977), p. 254.

Dodge, N. T., *Women in the Soviet Economy* (Baltimore, Md: Johns Hopkins Press, 1966).

Dunstan, J., *Paths to Excellence and the Soviet School* (Windsor, Berks: National Foundation for Educational Research (NFER), 1978).

Dvornikov, I., *et al.*, *Trudovoe zakonodatelstvo, spravochnaya kniga* (Moscow: 1967).

Elyutin, V. P. (ed.), *Vysshaya shkola SSSR za 50 let* (Moscow: 1957).

Entsiklopedicheski slovar pravovykh znanii See Chkhikvadze, V. M., *et al.*

Fainsod, M., *How Russia Is Ruled* (Cambridge, Mass.: 1963).

Feshbach, M., and Rapawy, S., *Soviet Economy in a New Perspective* (Washington: US Govt., 14 October 1976).
Field, M. G. (ed.), *Social Consequences of Modernisation in Communist Societies* Baltimore, Md, Johns Hopkins Press: 1976).
Fillipov, F. R., *Vseobshchee srednee obrazovanie* (Moscow: 1976a).
Fillipov, F. R. (ed.), *Obrazovanie i sotsialnaya struktura, sbornik nauchnykh trudov* (Moscow: 1976b).
Fitzpatrick, S., *Education and Social Mobility in the Soviet Union, 1921-1934* (CUP: 1979).
Florinsky, M. T., *Russia – a History and an Interpretation*, Vol. 2 (New York: Macmillan, 1947).

Georgadze, M. P., Vasiliev, V. I., and Gureev, P. P. (eds), *Verkhovny Sovet SSSR* (Moscow: 1975).
Glowka, D., *Schulreform und Gesellschaft in der Sowjetunion, 1958-1968* (Stuttgart: Klett, 1972).
Grant, N., *Soviet Education* (Harmondsworth: Penguin, 1979).

Hodnett, G., and Ogareff, V., *Leaders of the Soviet Republics, 1955-1972* (Canberra: Australian National University, 1973).

Ibragimov, I. A., *Voprosy nauchnoi organizatsii raboty VUZa* (Baku: 1971).
Ikonnikova, S. N., *Molodezh, sotsiologicheski i sotsialno-psikhologicheski analiz* (Leningrad: 1974).
Ivanov, Yu. Yu. (ed.), *Spravochnik rabotnika narodnogo obrazovania* (Moscow: 1973).
Ivanov, Yu., 'Dostizhenia i zadachi sovetskoi shkoly', in *Vospitanie Shkolnikov*, no. 2 (1976), transl. in *Soviet Education* (Nov. 1976), pp. 29 ff.
Iz opyta ideologicheskoi raboty partii (Moscow: 1973).

Jacoby, S., *Inside Soviet Schools* (New York: Schocken, 1975).
Jones, T. A., 'Higher education and social stratification', Ph.D. thesis, Princeton, NJ, 1978.

Kairov, I. A. (ed.), *Narodnoe obrazovanie v SSSR* (Moscow: 1957).
Kalinychev, F. I. (ed.), *Ob ukreplenii svyazi shkoly s zhiznyu i o dalneishem razvitii sistemy narodnogo obrazovania v SSSR* (Moscow: 1961).
Kamkov, I. A., and Konoplyanik, V. M., *Voennye akademii i uchilishcha, dlya tekh, kto khochet v nikh uchitsya* (Moscow: 1972).
Karpov, L. I., and Severtsev, V. A., *Vysshaya shkola, osnovnye postanovlenia prikazy i instruktsii* (Moscow: 1975).
Kasimovski, E. V. (ed.), *Trudovye resursy – formirovanie i ispolzovanie* (Moscow: 1975).
Kell, L. N., and Michik, Yu. M., *Organizatsia priema v VUZy i tekhnikumy* (Leningrad: 1970).
Khairullin, F. G., 'Istochniki formirovania i sotsialnaya struktura studenchestva', *in Trudy ufimskogo aviatsionnogo instituta im. Ordzhonikidze*, vyp. XXXVII (1971), p. 122.
Khaldeev, M. I., and Krivoshein, G. I., *Gorkom, raikom partii, opyt, formy i metody raboty* (Moscow: 1977).
Khrushchev, N. S., *O kommunisticheskom vospitanii* (Moscow: 1964).

Kirstein, T., 'Das Sowjetische Parteischulsystem', in B. Meissner *et al.* (eds), *Einparteisystem und bürokratische Herrschaft in der Sowjetunion* (Cologne: 1977).

Klochkov, I. D., *Sovershenstvovanie podgotovki kvalifitsirovannykh rabochikh* (Moscow: 1975).

Kogan, L. N., *Molodezh, ee interesy, stremlenia, idealy* (Moscow: 1967).

Kolesnikov, L. F., *et al.*, 'Opyt izuchenia byudzheta vremeni uchitelya', in Turchenko, V. N., *et al.*, p. 293.

Kologreev, G. V., 'Razvitie nauchnykh issledovanii v vuzakh po khozyaistvennym dogovoram i ikh vlianie na podgotovki nauchnykh kadrov', in Zhamin, V. A. (ed.).

Kommentarii k zakonodatelstvu o trude, Mishutkin, A. N., *et al.* (eds) (Moscow: 1965); Terebilov, V. I., *et al.* (eds) (Moscow: 1975).

Kommunist, no. 14 (1974); no. 9 (1978).

Korchagin, V. P., *Trudovye resursy v usloviakh nauchno-tekhnicheskoi revolyutsii* (Moscow: 1974).

Korol, A. G., *Soviet Education for Science and Technology* (Cambridge, Mass.: MIT, 1957).

Korotov, V. M. (ed.), *Spravochnik klassnogo rukovoditelya* (Moscow: 1979).

Korshunov, Yu. N., *Sovetskoe zakonodatelstvo o trude* (Moscow: 1976).

Kostanyan, S. L. (ed.), *Ekonomika narodnogo obrazovania* (Moscow: 1979).

Kostanyan, S. L., 'Problemy ekonomiki i planirovania obrazovania', in *Sbornik trudov laboratorii MGPI imeni Lenina* (Moscow: 1973).

Kotlyar, A. E., 'Trud molodezhi', in Kasimovski, E. V., p. 169.

Kozyrev, Yu. N., *Vysshee obrazovanie v zhiznennykh planakh molodezhi* (Moscow: 1975).

Kozyrev, Yu. N., Filippov, F. R., and Nikiforov, R. I. (eds), *Sotsiologicheskie issledovania professionalnoi orientatsii molodezhi* (Moscow: 1975).

Kozyrev, Yu. N., Orekhova, I. M., and Orlova, L. P., 'Vybor professii: prognozy i realnost' in Kozyrev, Yu. N., *et al.*, p. 42.

KPSS – Naglyadnoe posobie (Moscow: 1973).

KPSS o kulture, prosveshchenii i nauke, Sbornik dokumentov (Moscow: 1963).

Kreindler, I., 'The changing status of Russian in the Soviet Union', Research Paper no. 37, Hebrew University of Jerusalem, 1979.

Krotov, V. M., *et al.* (eds), *Spravochnik klassnogo rukovoditelya* (Moscow: 1979).

Kugel, S. A., and Nikandrov, O. M., *Molodye inzhenery* (Moscow: 1971).

Kultura, nauka, iskusstvo SSSR, slovar-spravochnik (Moscow: 1965).

Kulturnoe stroitelstvo RSFSR, Statisticheski sbornik (Moscow: 1958).

Kulturnoe stroitelstvo SSSR. Statisticheski sbornik (Moscow: 1956).

Kurov, M. N., 'Komsomol – aktivny pomoshchnik partii v podgotovke i vospitanii kvalifitsirovannykh kadrov rabochego klassa v sisteme Gosudarstvennykh Trudovykh Rezervov SSSR, 1946–1950', unpublished Candidate dissertation, Leningrad, 1955.

Kuzin, N. P., and Kolmakova, M. N., *Sovetskaya shkola na sovremennom etape* (Moscow: 1977).

Kuznetsov, V. V., Rygalin, A. G., and Tverdov, A. A., *Spravochnik po zakonodatelstvu dlya predsedatelya kolkhoza* (Moscow: 1962).

Kyaembre, A., *et al.* (eds), *Problemy vysshei shkoly*; I, *Povyshenie effektivnosti uchebnogo protsessa v vysshei shkole* (Tartu State University, 1977).

Lane, D., and O'Dell, F., *The Soviet Industrial Worker* (London: Martin Robertson, 1978).

Lebin, B. D., *Podbor, podgotovka i attestatsia nauchnykh kadrov v SSSR* (Moscow–Leningrad: 1966).

Lemelev, S. M., 'Rasshirennoe vosproizvodstvo rabochei sily v promyshlennosti SSSR', unpublished Candidate dissertation, Moscow, 1955.

Lewis, E. G., 'Bilingual education and social change in the Soviet Union', in Spolsky, B., and Cooper, R. L., *Case Studies in Bilingual Education* (Rowley, Mass.: Newbury House, 1978), p. 203.

Lisovski, V. T., and Dmitriev, A. V., *Lichnost studenta* (Leningrad: 1974).

Loeffler, R. G., 'The education of Soviet party executives: the impact on their careers and on CPSU', Ph.D. thesis, Cornell University, USA, January 1975.

Malin, V. N., and Korobov, A. B. (eds), *Direktivy KPSS i sovetskogo pravitelstva po khozyaistvennym voprosam, 1917–1957*, Vols 1–4 (Moscow: 1957–8).

Manevich, E. L., *et al.* (eds), *Osnovnye problemy ratsionalnogo ispolzovania trudovykh resursov v SSSR* (Moscow: 1971).

Matthews, M., *Class and Society in Soviet Russia* (Harmondsworth: Allen Lane, Penguin, 1972).

Matthews, M., 'Educational growth and the social structure in the USSR', in Field, M. G. (ed.), p. 121.

Matthews, M., *Privilege in the Soviet Union* (London: Allen & Unwin, 1978).

Matthews, M., *Soviet Government – a selection of official documents on Soviet internal policies* (London: Cape, 1973).

Matthews, M., 'Soviet students – some sociological perspectives', in *Soviet Studies*, no. 1 (January 1975), p. 86.

Matthews, M., 'Top incomes in the USSR', in *Survey*, vol. 21, no. 3(96) (1975), p. 1.

Matthews, M., 'Youth employment in the USSR', unpublished D.Phil. thesis, Oxford, 1961.

Medynski, E. N., *Narodnoe obrazovanie v SSSR* (Moscow: 1947).

Medynski, E. N., *Prosveshchenie v SSSR* (Moscow: 1955).

Mickiewicz, E., *Soviet Political Schools* (New Haven, Conn.: Yale University Press, 1967).

Mickiewicz, E., *Handbook of Soviet Social Science Data* (New York: Free Press, 1973).

Minkina, K. N., Sizova, M. G., and Terentiev, A. A., 'Sotsialnaya kharakteristika studentov pervokursnikov universiteta', in *Sotsiologia i vysshaya shkola*, II, *Uchenye zapiski Gorkovskogo universiteta*, vyp. 100 (Gorki: 1970).

Mishutkin, A. N.   See *Kommentarii k zakonodatelstvu o trude*.

Morozov, M. A. (ed.), *Spravochnik propagandista* (Moscow: 1968).

Morozov, N. M., 'Svobodnoe vremya i vsestoronee razvitie lichnosti budushchego inzhenera', in *Uchenye zapiski Moskovskogo Oblastnogo Pedagogicheskogo instituta*, tom 210, vyp. 1 (Moscow: 1968), p. 144.

Moskva – Kratkaya adressno-spravochnaya kniga (Moscow: 1958 and subsequent editions).

Moskovich, V. M., *Zakonodatelstvo o trude* (1954).

Movshovich, M. I., and Khodzhaev, A. M., *Vysshaya shkola – osnovnye postanovlenia, prikazy i instruktsii*, 2nd edn. (Moscow: 1948).

Mriga, V. V., *et al.* (eds), *Yuridicheski spravochnik dlya naselenia* (Kiev: 1974).
Muslims of the Soviet East (Tashkent: 1968, 1979), quarterly.

Nar. knoz. See *Narodnoe khozyaistvo SSSR*, relevant years.
Narodnoe khozyaistvo SSSR. Statisticheski sbornik (Moscow: 1956 and subsequent editions).
Narodnoe khozyaistvo SSSR za 60 let (Moscow: 1977).
Narodnoe obrazovanie (Moscow: 1947), monthly, various numbers.
Narodnoe obrazovanie, nauka, i kultura v SSSR. Statisticheski sbornik (Moscow: 1971, 1977).
Nazimov, I. N., *Proforientatsia i profotbor v sotsialisticheskom obshchestve* (Moscow: 1972).
Neave, G., *Patterns of Equality* (London: NFER Publishing Co., 1976).
Noah, H. J., *Financing Soviet Schools* (New York: Columbia University, 1966).
NOb See *Narodnoe obrazovanie*.
NONK See *Narodnoe obrazovanie, nauka, i kultura v SSSR. Statisticheski sbornik*.
Nosenko, A. V., and Shilov, I. A. (eds), *Spravochnik khozyaistvennoi sluzhby byta*, Vol. 2 (Moscow: 1974).
Novikov, M. A., and Grechanik, G. A. (eds), *Spravochnoe posobie po obucheniyu rabochikh kadrov na proizvodstve* (Moscow: 1970).

Oppenheim, R., 'Russian Orthodox theological education in the Soviet Union', in *Religion in Communist Lands*, vol. 2, no. 3 (1974), p. 4.
Orlovski, Yu. P., 'Pravovoe regulirovanie podgotovki i povyshenie kvalifikatsii rabochikh kadrov v SSSR', unpublished Candidate dissertation, Moscow, 1955.
Osipov, G. V., and Shchepanski, Ya. (J. Szczepański), *Sotsialnye problemy truda i proizvodstva* (Moscow: 1969).

Panachin, F. G., *Upravlenie prosveshcheniem v SSSR* (Moscow: 1977).
Partiinaya zhizn (Moscow: 1954–), fortnightly, various numbers.
Pechat SSSR v 1978 godu. Statisticheski sbornik (Moscow: 1979).
Petrovichev, N. A., *Partiinoe stroitelstvo* (Moscow: 1978).
PMP RSFSR (Prikazy ministerstva prosveshchenia RSFSR) See *Sbornik prikazov i instruktsii ministerstva prosveshchenia RSFSR*.
Professionalno-tekhnicheskoe obrazovanie (Moscow: 1953–), monthly.
Proftekhobrazovanie See *Professionalno-tekhnicheskoe obrazovanie*.
Programma nachalnoi politicheskoi shkoly (Series: *Sistema partiinoi ucheby*) (Moscow: 1973).
Prokofiev, M. A., *et al.* (eds), *Narodnoe obrazovanie v SSSR, 1917–1967* (Moscow: 1967).
PZh See *Partiinaya zhizn*.

Rachkov, E. P., 'Podgotovka gosudarstvennykh trudovykh rezervov v gody Velikoi Otechestvennoi Voiny', unpublished Candidate dissertation (Moscow, 1955).
Religion in Communist Lands (London: 1973 and 1974), quarterly.

220   Education in the Soviet Union

Reshenia partii i pravitelstva po khozyaistvennym voprosam. Sbornik dokumentov, 1917– , vols 1, 4, 5 (Moscow: 1967–).

Rigby, T. H., Communist Party Membership in the USSR 1917–1967 (Princeton, N.J.: 1968).

Riordan, J., Sport in Soviet Society (CUP: 1977).

Rozofarov, M. S. (ed.), Trudovye rezervy. Sbornik ofitsialnykh materialov (Moscow: 1950).

Rubin, V., and Kolesnikov, Yu., Student glazami sotsiologa (Rostov-na-Donu: 1968).

Samilova, E. S., Naselenie i obrazovanie (Moscow: 1978).

Samilova, E. S., 'Sotsialnye aspekty formirovania kontingentov sovetskikh studentov v period stroitelstva kommunizma (1961–1971)', unpublished Candidate dissertation, Moscow, 1972.

Samsonov, N. F., Partkom Vuza (Moscow: 1973).

Sbornik prikazov i instruktsii ministerstva prosveshchenia RSFSR (Moscow), 36 issues a year, various numbers.

Sbornik zakonodatelnykh aktov o trude (Moscow: 1956 and subsequent editions).

SDSh See Shustov, A. I.

Sergeev, S. S., Tubina, A. P., and Tsipin, B. L., 'O nekotorykh itogakh izuchenia byudzhetov vremeni uchitelei goroda Sverdlovska', in Turchenko, V. N., et al., p. 324.

SES See Sovetski entsiklopedicheski slovar.

XXI S'ezd KPSS. Stenograficheski otchet (Moscow: 1959).

XXIII S'ezd KPSS. Stenograficheski otchet, 2 vols (Moscow: 1966).

XXV S'ezd KPSS. Stenograficheski otchet, 3 vols (Moscow: 1976).

XIII S'ezd VLKSM – stenograficheski otchet (Moscow: 1959).

Shapovalenko, S. G., Politekhnicheskoe obuchenie v sovetskoi shkole na sovremennom etape (Moscow: 1958).

Shishkina, L. I., 'Nekotorye dannye ob orientirovannosti shkolnikov Orla na trudoustroistvo i obrazovanie', in Kozyrev, Filippov and Nikiforov, p. 78.

Shkaratan, O. I., Problemy sotsialnoi struktury rabochego klassa SSSR, Istorikosotsiologicheskoe issledovanie (Moscow: 1970).

Shumilin, I. N., Soviet Higher Education, Institute for the Study of the USSR, series I, no. 67 (Munich: 1962).

Shustov, A. I. (ed.), Spravochnik direktora shkoly, sbornik rukovodyashchikh i instruktivnykh materialov (Moscow: 1971).

SI See Sotsiologicheskie issledovania.

Silver, B., 'The status of national minority languages in Soviet education: an assessment of recent changes', in Soviet Studies, no. 1 (1974), p. 28.

Simon, G., 'Parteischulung und Massenagitation in der Sowjetunion', in Ost Europa, no. 5 (1974).

Skatkin, M. N., Trud v sisteme politekhnicheskogo obrazovania (Moscow: 1956).

Skorodumov, V., Struktura rukovodstva sovetskoi shkoly, Institute for the Study of the USSR, series II, no. 32 (Munich: 1955).

Sokolov, S. I., 'Gosudarstvennye Trudovye Rezervy kak istochnik popolnenia rabochego klassa SSSR', unpublished Candidate dissertation, Moscow, 1955.

Sonin, M. Ya., Podgotovka Kvalifitsirovannykh rabochikh na proizvodstve (Moscow: 1954).

Sonin, M., Aktualnye problemy ispolzovania rabochei sily v SSSR (Moscow: 1965).

Sonin, M., and Zhiltsov, E., 'Povyshat uroven podgotovki molodezhi k trudu', in *Kommunist*, no. 14 (September 1974), p. 37; no. 9 (1978), p. 26.

Sotsialisticheskii trud, no. 8 (1957); no. 8 (1973); no. 12 (1974); no. 12 (1975).

Sotsiologicheskie issledovania (Moscow: 1974), quarterly, various numbers.

Sotsiologia i vysshaya shkola, II, *Uchenye zapiski Gorkovskogo Universiteta*, vyp. 100 (Gorki: 1970).

Sovetskaya pedagogika (Moscow: 1937–), monthly.

Sovetski entsiklopedicheski slovar, Prokhorov, A. M., et al. (eds) (Moscow: 1979).

Soviet Education See Grant, N.

SPR See *Spravochnik partiinogo rabotnika*.

Spravochnaya kniga o profsoyuzakh (Moscow: 1968).

Spravochnik dlya postupayushchikh v vysshie uchebnye zavedenia SSSR (Moscow: 1945 and subsequent years).

Spravochnik dlya rabotnikov selskikh i poselkovykh sovetov (Moscow: 1970).

Spravochnik partiinogo rabotnika (Moscow: 1957 and subsequent editions).

Spravochnik propagandista (1968).

Spravochnik rabotnika narodnogo obrazovania (Moscow: 1973).

Sputnik komsomolskogo aktivista (Moscow: 1961).

Srednee spetsialnoe obrazovanie (Moscow: 1954–), monthly.

Stepnov, D. M., et al., *Organizatsionno-partiinaya rabota; problemy i opyt* (Moscow: 1974).

SZAT See *Sbornik zakonodatelnykh aktov o trude*.

Tarasov, A. N., and Trutneva, M. P. (eds), *Spravochnik po vechernei (smennoi) srednei obshcheobrazovatelnoi shkole RSFSR* (Moscow: 1963).

Terebilov, V. I. See *Kommentarii k zakonodatelstvu o trude*.

Tiktin(a), D., 'A Rural Secondary School in the Ukraine (1948–1962)', Soviet Institution Series, Paper no. 10, Hebrew University of Jerusalem. Text in Russian.

Titma, M. Kh., *Vybor professii kak sotsialnaya problema* (Moscow: 1975).

Tkachevski, Yu. M., *Sovetskoe ispravitelno-trudovoe pravo* (Moscow: 1971).

Tomiak, J. J., *The Soviet Union* (Newton Abbot: David & Charles, 1972).

Trud v SSSR. Statisticheski sbornik (Moscow: 1968).

Tsarkov, A. S., and Korolev, N. S., 'Opyt raboty leningradskoi gorodskoi komissii po kontrolyu za priemom uchashchikhsya v SSUZy', in Kell, L. N., and Minchik, Yu. M., p. 30.

Turchenko, V. N., et al. (eds), *Sotsiologicheskie i ekonomicheskie problemy obrazovania* (Novosibirsk: 1969).

Ushakov, G. I., and Shuruev, A. S., *Planirovanie i finansirovanie podgotovki spetsialistov* (Moscow: 1980).

Vasiliev, V. I. (ed.), *Sovetskoe stroitelstvo* (Moscow: 1967).

Vasilyeva, E. K., *Semya i ee funktsii* (Demografo-statisticheski analiz) (Moscow: 1965).

Veselov, A. N., *Professionalno-tekhnicheskoe obrazovanie v SSSR* (Moscow: 1961).

Vestnik vysshei shkoly (Moscow: 1940–), monthly, various numbers.

Vidavski, A. M., Geikhman, V. L., and Rubtsov, A. B. (eds), *Spravochnik po pravovym voprosam vysshei shkoly* (Moscow: 1969).

222   *Education in the Soviet Union*

Voilenko, E. I. (ed.), *Vysshaya shkola. Sbornik osnovnykh postanovlenii, prikazov i instruktsii*, Vols 1, 2 (Moscow: 1978).

Voprosy ideologicheskoi raboty, Sbornik vazhneishikh reshenii KPSS (1954–1961) (Moscow: 1961).

Voprosy ideologicheskoi raboty KPSS, Sbornik dokumentov, 1965–73 (Moscow: 1973).

Vospitanie shkolnikov (Moscow: 1966–), bimonthly, various numbers.

Vsesoyuzny slet studentov, 19–20 oktyabrya 1971, dokumenty i materialy (Moscow: 1972).

VVSh See *Vestnik vysshei shkoly.*

Vysshee obrazovanie v SSSR. Statisticheski sbornik (Moscow: 1961).

Zarikhta, T. R., 'Sotsialno-ekonomicheskie aspekty trudoustroistva molodezhi', in Maykov, A. Z. (ed.), *Problemy ratsionalnogo ispolzovania trudovykh resursov* (Moscow: 1973), pp. 338, 343.

Zhaleiko, B. A., *Pochetnye zvania SSSR i soyuznykh respublik* (Moscow: 1975).

Zhamin, V. A. (ed.), *Ekonomika vysshego obrazovania, materialy vsesoyuznogo nauchnogo kongressa* (Kazan: 1973).

Zhiltsov, E. N., and Lyalyaev, V. G., *Planirovanie razvitia vysshego obrazovania* (Moscow: 1977).

Zinoviev, S. I., *Uchebny protsess v sovetskoi shkole* (Moscow: 1975).

Zyuzin, D. I., *Osnovnye printsipy formirovania kontingentov uchashchikhsya srednikh spetsialnykh uchebnykh zavedenii, avtoreferat* (Moscow: 1974).

Zyuzin, D. I., Baranova, T. S., and Orlova, L. P., 'Sotsialnye predposylki razlichii doshkolnoi podgotovki uchashchikhsya', in Filippov, F. R. (ed.), 1976b, p. 102.

Index